HIDDEN ARMY

Cover Design: Gary Smailes @ BubbleCow

Review

"Every page is worth reading. I highly recommend it to anyone who wants to truly get a sense of how it was in Vietnam for the almost 90 percent of us who served as support troops." -- David Willson, The VVA Veteran's Books in Brief

ALSO BY LAWRENCE ROCK

The Tooth and the Tail

HIDDEN ARMY

SUPPORT TROOPS TYPES IN VIETNAM: AN ORAL HISTORY

EDITED BY LAWRENCE ROCK

SGT   USMC (1964 – 1967)

Published through Create Space by Lawrence Rock

April 2013

May 2013

June 2013

August 2013

November 2013

ISBN

13 978 1484841860

10   1484841867

This book is dedicated

To those who served

CONTENTS

Introduction

The Tooth and the Tail, completed in August, 2012, ran to over 113,000 words. Despite the size of that book I realized that there was still more to say and perhaps a better way to say it. I had interviewed 150 men and women for the support troop project and used just 62 in *Tooth*. So there were stories untold. *The Tooth and the Tail* was organized to tell, chronologically, a more detailed story of the tours of those who served in a support capacity, perhaps concentrating more on who they were than what they did. *Hidden Army*, while following the same oral history mode, will focus more on the types of support provided while using most of the 150 participants. Out of necessity most of the sixty-two participants from *The Tooth and the Tail* also appear in *Hidden Army* to ensure coverage of the support function so there is some repetition of stories in both books for some of the participants.

Hidden Army examines the types of support (medical, communications, logistics, etc.) in Vietnam with an attempt to portray what the specific issues were for each group and how they dealt with them. The selection of support categories was made by me based on the job descriptions of my 150 participants. In some cases a veteran might qualify for two categories; a navy doctor on a ship could be naval or medical support. I tried to make sensible decisions on things like that.

One of my concerns when I began the support troop project early in 2010 is that the veterans would have little to say; that their jobs, while averaging eighty hours per week, would be uninteresting. Thankfully this was not the case. Due to the nature of the Vietnam War most of the support troops found themselves exposed to occasional danger. A Veteran's Administration study some years back found that over seventy percent of veterans were shot at directly or indirectly during their tours, and over half saw someone killed or wounded. The consensus is that the support troop stories are interesting.

Preface

Reviewing *The Tooth and the Tail* for VVA Veteran's Books in Brief, David Willson wrote that if our support troops "were hidden, they were in plain sight." And so we were. While support personnel comprised ninety percent of our force in Vietnam, we labored in obscurity.

An army is composed of divisions and regiments and battalions of infantrymen, along with tanks and artillery. Bombers and fighters and cruisers and battleships complete the tip of the spear. The men and women behind the spear's tip are the focus of this book – America's Support Troops.

The combat troops made the headlines, for better or for worse, while the seemingly transparent support troops supplied them, fed them, transported them, and clothed them, and built the South Vietnamese infrastructure as well. The image of a combat troop holding a lighter to the thatched roof of a hut lingers, but the orphanages, hospitals, schools and roads constructed by American support personnel will endure; they are what the people of the southern half of Vietnam remember.

In 1965 Vietnam was a primitive country lacking infrastructure and resources. The war would require record levels of achievement on the part of our military. Despite the challenge a decision was made to move forward without calling up the reserves. This decision put many of the support troop functions in a very difficult position. As is customary for the United States we were not ready for the Vietnam War but, as is also customary, our military overcame the initial problems and deficiencies and got the job done.

Some war stories remain untold long after the shooting has stopped, perhaps because they are too painful to revisit. But in every war many combat veterans return from the battlefield to share their tales. Hundreds of books have been written on the Vietnam War by and about the combat troops. These books extol the bravery of grunts, tunnel rats, tankers, fighter and chopper pilots, snipers and other combat troops. And these men fully deserve our admiration for the tough job they did in Vietnam. They were heroes.

There was another group of men who served but whose stories remain untold. These men served in the capacity known as support troops, and for them eighty-hour work weeks, 110-degree heat or monsoon rains were the daily routine and occasional enemy fire an occupational hazard. Support troops were the unsung but not unworthy supporting actors of our Vietnam War.

Support troops are defined as men who, while they may find themselves in combat situations, have a primary responsibility to support the combat troops. Most support personnel were so classified during testing while in basic training, or even before they enlisted if they were guaranteed a job description as part of the terms of their enlistment.

Support troops are common to all wars. But there was nothing common about support troops in the Vietnam War, which placed a greater burden on our support troops than previous wars, and needed more of them to do the job. The 10:1 ratio of support to combat troops was higher than any of our previous wars. Vietnam was our first war in which there were no secure rear areas.[i] There would be no "in the rear with the gear" jobs; every base and road was subject to enemy fire. What was common to Vietnam and all our wars is that we expected to win.

CHAPTER ONE

BLUE WATER NAVY – THE EARLY YEARS

Months before the Marines walked ashore at Danang (March, 1965) the U.S. Navy was engaged in activities in the Gulf of Tonkin. The CIA was also active; they sponsored a series of South Vietnamese commando raids (code named Desoto)[ii] on the North Vietnamese coast designed to collect information on radar sites and other installations. These raids were always classified and clandestine, only marginally successful, and carried the risk of escalation. The Gulf of Tonkin Incident (August 2, 1964) – in which the Navy destroyer USS Maddox won a duel with North Vietnamese torpedo boats -- was the predictable next step and from which there was no turning back. The U.S. Navy was already on the stage when the curtain opened on the Vietnam War.

Our Navy proved to be more "hidden" than the rest of the support troops. Out on the water, away from reporters and cameras, the activities of our sailors often went unnoticed and unreported. Unlike the other services a Navy tour usually lasted six months at which point they returned to their home ports. After six months in port they often did another six-month tour in the Vietnam area.

DESTROYERS

Our destroyers, many of them of World War II vintage, had two major jobs during the Vietnam War. They provided an escort screen for the carriers, including search and rescue (SAR) of downed pilots, and they supplied gunfire support to ground units within reach of their 5" guns – up to seven miles inland.

The USS Joseph Strauss DDG-16 was named for Admiral Joseph Strauss (1861 – 1948), who was responsible for laying the great North Sea barrage of 57,000 contact mines from Norway to Scotland during World War I. When the war ended in 1918, Strauss found himself in charge of removing the very mines he had laid -- a four-month operation. The Strauss was commissioned in April, 1963.

USS Joseph Strauss
Courtesy: James Hansen

Though a large ship the Strauss was a highly maneuverable guided-missile destroyer with anti-submarine and anti-air warfare capabilities, including the TARTAR guided missile weapons, ASROC (anti-submarine rockets), anti-submarine torpedoes and two 5-inch 54 caliber dual-purpose gun mounts.

Radar Man Chief **O. W. Bartholomew,** *USS Joseph Strauss DDG-16*

Petty Officer 2nd Class **Rick Dolinar,** *USS Berkeley DDG-15*

TM3 **Ted Harris,** *Torpedo Man, USS C. Turner Joy DD-951/USS Joseph Strauss DDG-16*

Seaman 3rd Class **Bill Pratt,** *Radar Man, USS Joseph Strauss DDG-16*

*Radar Man 3rd Class **Bill Milligan**, USS Joseph Strauss DDG-16*

Arrival/Duties

Ted Harris: When the Gulf of Tonkin incident occurred, the *Joseph Strauss* was in Yokosuka, Japan. We were immediately summoned to the Gulf of Tonkin. We cruised by Hong Kong, picking up the carrier *USS Constellation* -- already launching planes for the Gulf of Tonkin -- and we arrived there on August 4, 1964. The whole Seventh Fleet was there; I've never seen so many ships! The second incident, which allegedly occurred between the *Maddox, C. Turner Joy* and some Vietnamese patrol boats happened that day and led to the Gulf of Tonkin Resolution, which resulted in our combat role in Vietnam. We stayed in the Gulf until September, and then we returned to Japan with the *USS Ticonderoga,* another of our carriers.

We returned briefly to the Gulf of Tonkin in November of 1964, for about a month, and then we again returned to Japan. Several of us had orders to leave the *Strauss* to return to the states, which we did by boarding a troop transport, the *USNS General Daniel I. Sultan.* We shared that ship with lots of Korean soldiers and American military dependents. We landed at Oakland Army Annex on New Year's Eve, 1964. We boarded buses for the San Francisco Airport and that is the first time I saw protesters.

I took some leave and then did some SP (shore patrol) duty in Los Angeles before boarding the *C. Turner Joy*, which was in dry dock repairing the bullet holes from their excitement in the Gulf of Tonkin. We did our trial runs and then set sail for the Pacific in June of 1965. That tour ended in February of 1966 despite the predictions of a well-known psychic, who foretold that we would sink at sea!

I guess it was my mechanical aptitude that got me into ordnance in the Navy. On the *Strauss* I was in charge of ASROC, anti-submarine weaponry. This is an 8-tube rocket launcher system and I did the maintenance. The *C. Turner Joy* didn't have ASROC so I worked on torpedo tubes, depth charges and concussion grenades, which we used to deter sappers when in port. I had three people working for me.   The *C. Turner Joy* gave a lot of naval gunfire support to in-country infantry units in South Vietnam.

O. W. Bartholomew: I enlisted in the Navy in June of 1949, and served on a cruiser during the Korean War. I was in the service for twenty years.

The *Joseph Strauss* did radar searches for enemy planes and ships and rescue of our downed pilots in the Gulf of Tonkin, shore bombardment of coastal gun sites and radar control of friendly planes and helicopters. I was a chief petty officer, radar man chief.

Bill Pratt: I had hopes of getting into meteorology and I had the test scores I needed, but there were no openings and I ended up in radar. I had hoped for an icebreaker out of Boston, and I got a destroyer out of Long Beach! We left Long Beach in the summer of 1964, headed for Yokosuka, Japan, with a plan to "show the flag" of our new ship in the Far East. We were expecting a 3-year tour. After just a couple of weeks in Yokosuka, the "incidents" with the *Maddox* and the *C. Turner Joy* changed that plan and we steamed for the Gulf of Tonkin. We would spend a month or two at sea and then steam into Yokosuka, or Subic Bay for a rest and replenishment, then back to Vietnam. We returned to Pearl Harbor in the summer of 1966.

We worked five hours on, five hours off on the radar consoles in the CIC (Combat Information Center). There were normally ten or twelve people in the CIC, but it was crowded during GQ (General Quarters); maybe twenty or thirty guys. It was a madhouse then.

Bill Milligan: The *Strauss* departed for Vietnam from Norfolk; I joined the ship when they pulled into Long Beach, CA. We were departing for a 3-year WESTPAC tour; the ship was brand-new and an admiral was coming aboard, and we were going to go and show the flag in various ports. It was a PR thing. But the incident in the Gulf of Tonkin interrupted the best laid plans of mice and men.

Rick Dolinar: I was sent to FT (Fire Technology) School at Great Lakes for eighteen weeks following basic training and was assigned to the *Berkeley*, a guided missile destroyer. We left Long Beach, California in August of 1965. Although the trip over was uneventful it was pretty exciting for me since it was my first time on a ship. We were on station off the North Vietnamese coast about three weeks later. On that tour we would be at sea for about two months, getting replenished every few days from transport ships, then into port (Hong Kong or Subic Bay) for a week or so, then back out for another two months.

My job description was Fire Control Technician. Fire as in gunfire. Our fire control radar had input into an analog computer, and our job was to operate and maintain the gunfire control systems, to synchronize radar, the analog computer and the guns, basically calculating how much to lead the target in order to hit it. As an E-3 I also had to stand regular watches when off duty. My watch was usually in the after steering compartment.

We were assigned to SAR (search and rescue) duty; we were also an early warning for enemy planes that may have taken off from North Vietnam. We also kept an eye on junks and sampans coming out of North Vietnamese waters. They would send pseudo-fisherman out in small boats, armed with a couple of nets and tons of sophisticated radio equipment. We knew what they were doing. It was our job to screen them and we did destroy a few of them if they didn't heed our warnings. We also did a lot of shore bombardment work, mostly into North Vietnam, but for our last month or so we were mainly in the DMZ area.

The day was four on, eight off, but some days, depending on your shift and when after duty watches fell, you might be working 12 hours. There was also underway replenishment that required taking on provisions. This was usually done after dark since it put both ships in a very vulnerable position, tethered together with cables and fuel lines. Both ships would usually be moving along at about eight knots. Underway replenishment usually took a couple of hours. This was done every three days or so.

Adventures

Ted Harris: On the *Turner Joy* we picked up small arms fire when we were down around the coast at Vung Tau. We were out to sea far enough that they had trouble reaching us. I never received any fire when I was on the Strauss but a guy did get wounded by an artillery round later on; he was sitting in the head (toilet) when the round landed; a totally unexpected Purple Heart I'm sure.

The *C. Turner Joy* was the first U.S. ship into the Gulf of Thailand, on September 23, 1965, due to the increased importance of the Ho Chi Minh Trail. We also did a lot of cruising around Vung Tau and the mouth of the Saigon River. We were in the Delta a lot but we couldn't go up into the shallow canals. The PBR's would capture some VC and they'd put them on our ship, in handcuffs, until we could drop them off somewhere. There might be ten or fifteen of these guys at one time. We provided gunfire support for operations up into the canals and along the coast.

Viet Cong Prisoners aboard the *C. Turner Joy*
Courtesy: Ted Harris

On October 25, 1965, we provided naval gunfire support to allied troops near Chu Lai. We destroyed several enemy positions and repulsed a VC attack during a 24-hour battle. During this action our gun mount 53 blew up. This killed three guys and wounded three guys. We steamed to Danang to offload the casualties and went to the Philippines for a captain's inquiry into what happened. Then we did a temporary repair to the gun mount. The reason for the explosion may have traced to our captain accepting a fire mission before our guns had a chance to cool off from the previous mission and a round cooked off in the barrel. One man's wife wrote to us for years wondering what happened to her husband. This man had four boys.

We found ourselves up near the top of North Vietnam, near China, one time; near Hainan Island. This was around the time the Chinese shot down one of our aircraft that came too close to them. The only ships the Chinese had at the time were diesel-engine submarines. Very early one morning sonar picked up a submarine contact. Most of us went to our battle stations in our skivvies and shower shoes! I don't know what we were doing up there but we definitely irritated the Chinese.

Off the coast of Danang, we could watch the firefights on Marble Mountain at night. One time our duty was to sit behind the carrier *Constellation* as they were launching planes. We were changing stations with another destroyer and our captain forgot what he was doing and we almost ran into the stern of the carrier. We really had to hit the brakes hard to avoid that collision.

One of our bosses had learned in school that you need to fasten the attachments on the torpedo mounts with screws due to the vibrations at sea. We tried to explain that in the real world, while that procedure did stop sea water from getting in, it made it difficult to get inside the tube to do your checks. We finally convinced the guy that we were right and we used to lubricate the screws with Vaseline.

The *C. Turner Joy* was there at the beginning and there at the end. She fired the final round of naval gunfire on January 28, 1973, seconds before the ceasefire went into effect.

O.W. Bartholomew: The *Joseph Strauss* was fired upon by North Vietnamese coastal defense sites – twenty-one sites. All of these sites were silenced by our After Mount guns. In one case we were shelling from about 10,000 yards off shore when enemy shells began to land near us. Over a hundred rounds landed in our vicinity and we pulled back to 13,000, then 17,000 yards. They were still bracketing us and we got no respite until we retreated to 23,000 yards.

The *Strauss* was involved in a dozen gun battles with shore batteries during 1967. The *Strauss* had one mission where we were firing on an enemy log bridge; we had Sky raiders spotting and correcting our fire. Another time we provided NGFS (naval gunfire support) for a Marine company south of Danang. This action did not work out well for our side; things got quiet from the Marines on the ground and I don't think there were many survivors of that fight.

Bill Milligan: On June 17, 1965, we were off the North Vietnamese coast, in international waters, on an air search and rescue detail, doing picket duty for the carrier *Midway*. One of our pilots had ejected in the Gulf of Tonkin and two of our A1H Sky raiders were flying a protective ring around the pilot while a helicopter raced to pick him up. Bill Pratt and I were manning the radar console and we picked up unidentified aircraft moving toward the Sky raiders, and we sounded the alarm. I don't think they believed us at first, but then they turned the *Midway* into the wind and launched jet planes. Meanwhile our Sky raiders jettisoned their excess armament and dropped down to skim the waves. Our Phantoms arrived quickly and claimed two Mig kills that day, but they also thought a third Mig was hit by debris from the first Mig hit. This was later confirmed as the third kill of the day. Once the planes dropped down just above the waves we lost the radar contact with them.

Bill Pratt: Bill Milligan and I were both working the radar consoles the day the Migs were shot down (June 17, 1965). We were providing backup for each other. It was very hard to see anything on radar because there were so many planes in that area. We were talking to the air controller, who was standing right beside us; he was talking to the planes based on what we were telling him. We had previous occasions when our planes were going after Migs but this was the first time there was an actual fight; the first time our planes had shot down enemy planes since the Korean War.

Bill Milligan: Three days later, two A1H Sky raiders (propeller planes from the WW II era), also from the Midway, were jumped by Migs probably looking for revenge. One of the Sky raider pilots realized he had a Mig on his tail and he hit the brakes, causing the Mig to overfly him. As the Mig went by the Sky raider pilot, a Lt. Johnson, fired at him and shot him down.

Bill Pratt: One of our radar operators, Tony LaPino, was in a General Quarters situation, and he was marking all these surface contacts on a 30" screen in front of him, and the guy behind him wearing the headphones gets seasick and throws up all over Tony's board. Tony got a pat on the back afterwards because he just grabbed a rag, wiped the board clean, and went on marking his contacts.

We were operating in the vicinity of Haiphong Harbor, near the islands of Hon Me and Hon Du, and we spotted a bunch of PT boats on our radar. Our planes requested permission to take them out. Permission was denied. For some reason, at least at that time, this was an off limits thing.

I always thought the worst part of the whole deal was the lack of sleep. We worked a lot of hours and it was too noisy to sleep; consequently, we were too tired to be fully alert. Sometimes, when you had the time to sleep, you couldn't get into your berth because they were cleaning the area or something. You'd end up finding a dark corner somewhere and curling up on the floor. I don't know why they felt it was more important to buff the floors than to let guys get some sleep. There was an OI office that wasn't used much, and it was dark, so we'd go in there and curl up on the floor like a bunch of dogs. The *Strauss* was a new ship and they wanted it to look perfect all the time.

Bill Milligan: I loved it all, although the long hours could be difficult some times. We worked with the pilots via radar, we did shore bombardments, and night time replenishments; there are only so many hours in the day.

I was proud all the time but, in a way, I was always waiting for the other shoe to fall since we didn't really know where we stood in a political sense. What were we supposed to do? Were we at war or weren't we? The war situation was still developing. But in the CIC we were all cleared for Top Secret, so we knew what was going on. There was a shroud of ambiguity over our situation. If you shoot down a Mig, you could be in a lot of trouble. On the other hand, the U.S. seemed to want to build their commitment to the war. I had just come off the *Maddox,* the destroyer that was fired upon by their PT boats, which resulted in the Gulf of Tonkin Resolution, and to be denied permission to fire at PT boats appearing on our radar was really frustrating.

Rick Dolinar: On the *Berkeley* we berthed once at Danang, but we never went ashore. On the SAR picket line we would see the North Vietnamese "fishermen" as they pulled their junks and sampans up close to our ship. Our captain just loved to go through them and tear up their nets because he knew what they were doing. He would basically play Chicken with them. We had .50 caliber machine guns ready, and in cases where the North Vietnamese showed any kind of weaponry the captain would cut their ship in half.

There were two islands maybe ten or fifteen miles outside of the North Vietnamese port of Haiphong, Hon Me and Hon Met. You could see North Vietnam from these islands. We were on our SAR picket station and we were advised that an F-4 was shot down between North Vietnam and these two islands. The pilot had bailed out between the islands and the mainland and two ships, including the *Berkeley*, were told to go in and get him. We immediately picked up fire from both islands and from a gun battery on the mainland. Our return fire was said to be the first rounds fired into North Vietnam. The other ship actually rescued the pilot but we did take fire and had some shrapnel hit our ship. It was a pretty exciting day. I was the range finder operator at general quarters. Our radar would usually give us the exact range to the target, but when the target was located on land the radar would only give us the range to the beach; how far inland the battery was emplaced was not known. I got the range on that gun emplacement and subsequent reconnaissance told us it was totally destroyed. My eighteen weeks at FT school did not go to waste!

My station during refueling was Midships Signalman. Refueling was going on fore and aft, but amidships, you would transfer people back and forth between ships on a bosun's chair, or medicine, mail or movies, or food would be coming aboard via the midshipman's high line. I was the signal guy, with the flashlights, to get this done. It was like the guy at the airport with the flashlight wands moving the plane around. The high line was a very large steel cable. There was a flinching device on the cable that would adjust as the ships came closer or moved further apart. Well the clutch on the flinching device froze, the ships moved apart, and the cable snapped. If I hadn't hit the deck I probably would have been cut in half. The cable hit our ASROC locker so hard it dented it; it required service before it could be used again. It was a very touchy, scary situation. There were a lot of people on the deck when it snapped but luckily no one was hurt. We were taught that if you ever heard a snap you should hit the deck and we all did.

Refueling operations are not to be taken lightly. We were taking on fuel once from the *Sacramento*, a large oiler, and we rolled to within two feet of each other. It was actually our captain's fault and it cost him his command. We had an Emergency Breakaway where both ships should turn away from each other. Anyway, we came real close. I know I could have reached off the deck of the *Berkeley* and touched the *Sacramento*; it was that close!

CARRIERS

*Boson Mate **Gary Skibo**, USS Coral Sea CVA-43/USS Oriskany CVA-34*

*Boson Mate **Cliff James**, USS Constellation CVA-64*

Arrival/Duties

Gary Skibo: I joined up right after high school. Since I was seventeen I had to get my dad's permission and he outlawed the Marines and the Army. He had been in the Army in WW II. So I ended up in the Navy. Less than a year later I was on the *USS Coral Sea* and we arrived during May of 1966. We became one of four carriers off the Vietnamese coast at what was known as Dixie and Yankee Stations.

When I returned from my first tour on the *Coral Sea*, I went into the Oakland Naval Hospital for six weeks. If you are off your ship for more than thirty days, you can request a transfer to another ship. I requested a ship going to the east coast but they put me on the *USS Oriskany*, a World War II Essex-class carrier heading for Vietnam, in June of 1967.

My duties included bringing bombs, fuel and other cargo aboard from supply ships. We took on these supplies about once a day. Another duty I had was standing watch on the bow and communicating with the bridge. I worked sixteen to twenty hours a day. A number of times I worked two straight days without any time off.

Cliff James: My first Vietnam tour was in 1966 on the *USS Constellation CVA-64*. I was assigned to the weatherman division, which provided pilots with information such as wind velocity for their carrier landings. We had about twenty guys in the bridge doing this work and plotting the data for the pilots. Everyone in this division had been to school for these duties. Everyone except me! I was not qualified for this and it could have resulted in a life-threatening situation for someone. They finally realized their mistake and took me out of this job late in the tour.

Adventures

Gary Skibo: We would get lots of sampans and junks alongside our carrier but no one ever fired at us. We did have to fire at the junk boats occasionally.

On my first tour on the *USS Coral Sea* we went through a typhoon and they asked for volunteers to tie stuff down. I was one of the nuts that went out there trying to tie down life rafts and other stuff. We lost a few rafts and later they sent Skyhawks up to sink them so the enemy couldn't use them. We also lost one of our screws (propellers). The *Coral Sea* had four screws and somehow one of them was broken off. On that first cruise we had fourteen pilots shot down, ten KIA's and four MIA's.

Also on the *Coral Sea*, one time they sounded the collision alarm, so everybody was to clear the deck. One guy wasn't going to make it and I tackled him. He could have been cut in half by a cable that snapped.

On my second tour, on the *USS Oriskany*, I saw the carrier *USS* Forrestal blow up. This happened on October 29, 1967. I was down in the hanger bay looking at it when it blew. A rocket from one of the jets on the flight line went off and it killed something like 120 sailors. We sounded general quarters and went nearby to pull guys out of the water. One African-

American guy had burns over 95% of his body. The *Oriskany* had lost forty-four guys during a magnesium flare fire a year or so before I joined her. On this tour the *Oriskany* had seventeen pilots KIA and twelve MIA.

Lt. John McCain was shot down flying off the Oriskany for his twenty-third combat mission on October 26, 1967.

The *Oriskany* was sunk as an artificial reef off the coast of Florida in May, 2006; the largest vessel ever sunk to make a reef. It sits about 100 feet below water and is known as the "Great Carrier Reef."

Cliff James: We had one occasion where some suicide PT boats tried to make a run against our carrier. Our planes sunk them before they ever got close.

I was in charge of the high line when we transferred the comedienne Martha Raye from our carrier to a submarine. She sat there bravely in the boson's chair, and showed more courage than many men might on that trip across the water.

OTHER SHIPS

*Petty Officer Third Class **Gary Simons,** Quartermaster/Signalman, USS Fortify, MSO-446*

*Fireman **Bill Pitts,** USS Mogoffin APA-199*

Arrival/Duties

Gary Simons: Our ship, the minesweeper *USS Fortify,* arrived in the Danang area early in 1963. My duties involved navigation, working on the bridge plotting our course on the charts. Our ship was acting in the role of "advisor," helping South Vietnamese boats interdict sampans running weapons down to South Vietnam. Our ship was a MSO (Mine Sweeper Ocean), post WW II with a wooden hull, about 175 feet long, and a crew of 65. For armament we had one 40mm gun and two .50 caliber machine guns. By definition, MSO's went "before the fleet."

Bill Pitts: I flew into Subic Bay, in the Philippines to catch up with my ship, the *USS Mogoffin*, a troop transport. We steamed into Danang with a load of bombs and some Korean troops in December, 1965. I was unloading bombs in Danang on Christmas Day with my recruiter's words "You'll never see Vietnam" floating through my head. For my first couple of months aboard the *Mogoffin* I cleaned the head. Then I did some pre-school indoctrination in the shop, working under supervision. I also stood generator watch, making sure the power factors were okay and the load wasn't going out of whack.

Adventures

Bill Pitts: We had a (drunken) cook fall off a gangplank while we were docked. There was no safety netting. He hit his head on something on the way down. The tide was in and the water was high. He died. The *Mogoffin* was going back to the states for a senate investigation because one of our seamen wrote to his congressman that our XO brought Filipino women aboard ship.

As we sailed to Danang it was frustrating to watch the South Korean troops eating right out of our garbage cans. They were given regular meals from the mess deck but they didn't mind eating from the garbage cans on top of that.

Gary Simons: We were over there in a strange capacity; we were there to kind of train the South Vietnamese. As a ship I think we did our mission very well. A small ship like ours was somewhat like a submarine; everyone had to learn other people's jobs. The fact that we did this brought us closer together as a crew.

A minesweeper is a small ship that rides the waves like a cork, as opposed to a carrier or some other big ship that just cuts through the waves. We had a typhoon once and the ship did a 66 degree roll from a wave, which means you are pretty much walking on the walls. But we rolled back the other way about 48 degrees, which corrected the problem.

The minesweeper hull is made of wood which overlaps in three directions. In big storms sometimes the wood would separate enough that you could see outside; you would worry that you had a hole in the ship. If it was a problem I guess the pumps in the bilge were up to the occasion and pumped the water back out. But new guys looking at those beams separating were somewhat taken aback.

I had some diving skills and one time our propeller got snagged in some bamboo fishing pots, similar to lobster cages, in the water. They figured we'd have to make for Subic Bay for repairs, but me and another guy who had some diving skills went down and removed the bamboo.

On the way over to Vietnam, myself and two or three others were going up to the bridge and we smelled smoke. A sailor is required to report smoke on a ship and we did. They discovered a fire in the magazine and sounded general quarters. As the battle against the fire began we had a sailor, an avowed atheist, who was found up near the bow crying out "My God, my God, save us." Or at least that is what we accused him of. Anyway, the fire was brought under control very quickly; it was an electrical fire and they isolated the panel and fixed it.

It was hard for us to get replacement parts. Another frustration was we were always undermanned. And that hurt every department on the ship. It necessitated a lot of port/starboard watches and a man is simply not as alert when he is overworked as when rested. I guess we were low on the totem pole when it came to getting people. I'm sure the carriers and cruisers were getting people before we did. It's marvelous that no one ended up getting hurt because of that condition.

I had an opportunity to go ashore in Hue one time. We came ashore in the whaleboat for some of our officers to get an intelligence briefing. I took this occasion to buy a nice porcelain tea set for my wife in a department store. This was a two-story building, and at one end they had a banner hanging down that said "HO CHI MINH – FATHER OF OUR COUNTRY" I asked about this and a lady said that Ho Chi Minh was indeed the Father of their Country. This may have differed from the understanding that some of our political leaders had of the situation at that time. The lady was adamant about this. I thought quite a bit about that afterwards.

*Shooting down Migs, shore bombardments -- that certainly **sounds** like war. But the closest our congress could come to a formal declaration of war was the Tonkin Gulf Resolution (August 7, 1964), which granted President Johnson sweeping powers to aid the South Vietnamese. The House of Representatives debated the issue for forty minutes before rendering unanimous approval for what would become up till then the longest war in our nation's history; there were but two dissenting votes in the Senate. [iii]*

Rick Dolinar

Ted Harris

CHAPTER TWO

SUPPLY/LOGISTICS SUPPORT

During WW II our chief naval officer, Admiral Ernest J. King, supposedly said "I don't know what the hell this logistics is that General George Marshall is always talking about, but I want some of it."

General Giap, commander of the Viet Minh (communist) forces that defeated the French at Dien Bien Phu, is reported to have said "Logistics is as important as tactics."[iv]

*On April 1, 1965, the 1st Logistical Command was activated in Saigon. Our nearest logistical base to Vietnam was on Okinawa, 1800 miles away. [v] Construction on the Ho Chi Minh Trail had been underway for six years by that time. [vi] We would be playing catch-up. When the war began it would be the first time in our modern history the U.S. Army had to establish a major logistical base with all ground under continuous enemy observation and hostile fire; with no terrain under friendly control.[vii] The supply personnel would be operating behind the scenes, as always, but NOT behind the lines. There **were** no front lines.*

A manual logistics control system (actually sixteen different systems)[viii] was used for two years until automation was achieved. We had to automate so we could manage.[ix] From a logistic standpoint the challenges we faced were enormous. Electricity demands were four times that of World War II,[x] ammunition expenditure rates, erroneously based on World War II results, were greatly exceeded, [xi]piers were lacking, warehouse personnel were largely untrained, and the pilferage and sabotage incidents were unsettling. Combat troop deployment developed faster than a logistics base could be developed.[xii]

Heavy use was made of civilian contractors including Vinnel Corp. (trucks, stevedores, beach and port clearance and vessel maintenance); Han-Jin provided trucks and stevedores around Qui Nhon.[xiii] The Vietnamese railway system operated from Saigon to the DMZ.[xiv] The use of containerization was a big help.[xv]

In 1965 most cargo arrived at the Port of Saigon[xvi] which was under the control of RVN Port Authority; we never knew what piers were available and the resulting confusion and congestion affected operations.[xvii] By December 1967 we had ten ports. Average pier wait time fell from 20 days (1965) to two days (1970).[xviii]

To handle an army in battle is much less difficult than to bring it on to the field in good condition. [xix] Not only were supply/logistics troops a Hidden Army, their obstacles and challenges went largely unspoken.

By 1967 a million tons of supplies were arriving, averaging one hundred pounds per day per each soldier.[xx] When we started to wind down our involvement, three times the effort was needed to process the equipment as was required to receive it.[xxi] To carry General Giap's thought a step further: Without logistics there is _no need_ for tactics.

For a combat troop to eat it, drink it, shoot it, throw it, wear it, walk on it, sleep on it or talk through it, somebody has to get it to him. The some bodies that get things to the combat troops are supply/logistics personnel. Unlike the sailors out on the water, they are not hidden. But during the buzz of activity surrounding the supply/logistics duties, they are sometimes transparent; the proper supplies and ammunition are **expected** to be there and in a timely manner.

SUPPLY DUMP/WAREHOUSE/FUEL FARMS/UNREPS

Petty Officer 3rd Class **Gordon Brown,** Radar Man, USS Vega AF-59, USN

Spc4 **Frank H. Voytek,** Quartermaster Supply, USA Support Group Vietnam, Saigon, USA

Spc4 **Jimmie Johnson,** Truck Driver/Wrecker Operator, 155th Transportation Company, 1st Logistics Command, II Corps, USA

Spc4 **Dennis Newara**, *Generator Oper./Repair, Long Lines Det., 1ˢᵗ Signal Brigade, Saigon, USA*

Spc4 **Joe Patterson**, *General Supply, 855ᵗʰ General Supply Unit, 1ˢᵗ Logistics Command, Danang, USA*

Spc4 **Garry Ramsey,** *Truck Driver/Supply Clerk, 524ᵗʰ Quartermaster/61ˢᵗ Transit Company, 1ˢᵗ Logistics Command, Cam Ranh Bay, USA*

Captain **Rick Spriggs**, *Battalion Supply Officer, 28ᵗʰ Infantry, 1ˢᵗ Infantry Division, Lai Khe, USA*

SSgt **Dave Warman**, *Supply, 1ˢᵗ Signal BrigDE, 1ˢᵀ Logistics Command, Nha Trang, USA*

Spc5 **Les Daulton**, *Truck Driver, 198ᵗʰ Infantry Brigade, Americal Division, Chu Lai, USA*

Spc5 **Dan Vinson,** *33ʳᵈ Ordnance Company, 194ᵗʰ Ordnance Battalion, Cam Ranh Bay, USA*

1stLt **Kirk Lea,** *Property Disposal Yard, USA Support Command, Cam Ranh Bay. USA*

Sgt **Don Wilson,** *Aviation Supply, 31ˢᵗ Marine Amphibious Force, USS Tripoli LPH-10, USMC*

Cpl **Larry Rock,** *Embarkation Clerk/Driver, H&MS-11, 1ˢᵗ Marine Aircraft Wing, Danang, USMC*

Arrival/Duties

Frank H. Voytek: In April, 1963, I flew Pan Am into Tan Son Nhut and the heat nearly floored me as I deplaned. We were located along the Saigon River in some old French and Vietnamese warehouses. My job was to requisition supplies from the Navy since the Army was not in a position to supply the effort at this point.

I started out in the office in the morning and the sergeant would tell us what he thought needed to be done that day. I might end up going into the warehouse later that day to drive forklifts and things like that, or spend all day in the office. One way or the other I worked from morning till night. I guess I did the work of two, working up requisitions in the morning, then pulling supplies from the warehouse in the afternoon based on the requisitions I just filled out. We would have worked more I think, but there was no electricity available. Part of the problem was due to the European (French) influence the power system wouldn't accommodate our equipment very well. We had to buy adapters to get things to run. I also stood guard duty from time to time.

I came into contact with Vietnamese people more than Americans. They drove our trucks and they worked in our warehouses. They were our cab drivers and waitresses. We had three Vietnamese guys who worked in our office. The older guy was known as Papasan. The youngest was known as Babysan. They were all good folks; we got along fine. They tried to teach me Vietnamese; I tried to teach them English. I can't say whether working with us was their daytime job and they were VC at night, I don't know.

Quartermaster Warehouse Yard – Saigon 1964
Courtesy: Frank H. Voytek

Gordon Brown: After high school I was living with relatives and working in Kansas City. I was not ready for college so I figured I'd join the Marines. At the recruiting office I went into the Marine office first, and I thought I recognized the recruiter. He was an E-8 with about thirty years in the

Corps. We realized we knew each other; he was a distant relative. He told me I should go to the Navy; he recognized that I was detail-oriented and thoughtful. He said "You wouldn't be good for the Marine Corps and they wouldn't be good for you." He said the Marines wanted guys that just did what they were told; they didn't analyze the order. He introduced me to his fellow recruiter, a Navy Chief Petty Officer.

My first trip to Vietnamese waters was on the USS *Vega*, in November of 1963. I spent much of the next three years over there on the *Vega*, but I went to a minesweeper, the USS *Engage*, in October of 1966. The *Vega* was a refrigerated supply ship, the Navy's fastest supply ship. We once delivered 117 tons of provisions to the carrier *Ranger* in 27 minutes; that's a rate of 245 tons an hour. The *Vega* was built in 1954, in Pascagoula, MS, and was 502 feet long. The *Vega* could make 20 knots, on one propeller, and she had a provision capacity of 4,650 tons. Our crew was 350 officers and men, and we mounted 2 dual 3" 50's.

My primary duty was radar man, working in the Combat Information Center. I did maintenance on the radar units as required. I had a Secret security clearance so I also updated the security grids (map locations) the CO used to determine where our ship was to go for the next unrep.

The average unrep (underway replenishment) takes two to three hours. We tie lines and hoses to the ship being replenished, and deck crews on both ships work fast and professionally to get the job done. Naturally this is more difficult in rough seas. Unreps are not to be taken lightly. All sailors are taught if they hear a snap, that means one of the cables between the ships has popped and they should quickly hit the deck. That never happened to us while I was aboard the *Vega,* but the *Hancock* (a carrier) had one snap while I was over there, and there were casualties. During my time on the *Vega* we were involved in Operation Market Time and Operation Yankee Station. In addition to supplies, we sometimes also transferred fuel to the other ship, but never ammunition. If we were just cruising, there would be maybe just two of us in the CIC. If we were in operation there might be six or seven of us. But if we were just cruising we watched the air and surface radars and we monitored the radio for any mention of us. After I had some time aboard the *Vega* I was the second-in-command of our radar group. Since the *Vega* was not attached to a battle group or anything, we were more of a free agent out on the water.

Larry Rock: I arrived by ship in August of 1965. I spent my first few days helping to construct wooden frames for our ten-man tents. Then I had mess duty, which meant walking outside our wire and down the road a bit to the 1st MAW compound around 0500 each morning.

The Embarkation job involved the loading and unloading of ships and planes for combat operations. Well, we were **already** in combat, so what do we do? The embarkation personnel (me and a captain) were folded into the Supply (S-4) group. I spent my entire tour as a supply clerk and driver; any embarkation duties needed were apparently handled at the 1st Wing level. In addition to the daily workload I spent three or four months on the Defense Platoon where we were assigned a bunker in case the siren sounded. There were about six enlisted guys in the S-4 office, and four or five officers. The officers were pilots with supply as a backup job. I remember one captain, on the day he made major, coming in for a cup of coffee before going off to bomb North Vietnam.

While on mess duty I noticed the mess chief, a corporal, donning his green utilities. He told me he was a gunner on the Huey choppers in his spare time. I asked him if I could go and he said yes. 'I'll ride with you the first time to learn the ropes", I replied. He said I had to fly the first time on my own. I told him I had never been in a chopper and had never seen the M-60 machine gun; I could be a safety risk for the rest of the crew. He said I had to fly my first flight without any training. I declined.

All units had a greater need for generators than the Table of Equipment envisioned. I spent a lot of my time typing up One Time in Excess of Allowance requisitions. Late in my tour MSgt Hart decided I should be more involved in the important duties. I was told I would be ordering the bombs for the next day's flights and also doing a report on unexploded ordnance. I cannot remember doing these things beyond the night (as noted in a letter home) that a sergeant and I were still working at 0100 trying to complete a report.

Rick Spriggs: I joined the Army as an enlisted man in December of 1957. My first job was as a mortar man with the 82nd Airborne Division, and then I became a supply clerk. Due to the angst over the newly-completed Berlin Wall I was transferred to the 8th Infantry Division in Germany. While working as a supply clerk I was selected to be one of the Security Police in the same area where my father had driven General Patton over the newly-erected bridge into Wiesbaden, Germany near the end of World War II.

My unit arrived by ship at Vung Tau in October, 1965. We climbed down cargo nets into smaller boats and waded ashore. We were then trucked up to Lai Khe, about thirty or forty kilometers north of Saigon. We were right in the bend of what they call the "fishhook" area of Vietnam.

I spent about seven months as A Company commander in the 28th. I tried to spend all my tour there but they had some regulations that officers only spend six months with a line unit so I transferred to a staff job. Because of my Korea background in Intelligence I was made S-2 (Intelligence) within the 2nd Battalion, 28th Infantry. When the S-4 officer was killed in the re-supply mission to Bau Bang I was put in his place since I also had previous S-4 duty.

As the battalion S-4 (Supply/Logistics) officer, I was in charge of all supply, transportation and maintenance functions. I also had Graves Registration responsibilities. Overall, I had about thirty guys reporting to me. We did not have a supply warehouse like we would have in the States. We had large tents for all functions – supply, motor pool, ammo, etc. We worked full days and then at night if there was something going on. In particular, the Graves Registration duty was necessary when casualties were brought in.

Dan Vinson: I worked the first summer out of high school on a pipeline back in Poplar Bluff, Missouri. I did boot camp at Fort Leonard Wood during winter, where I froze my ass off. Then they assigned me to Heavy Trucks. I flew into Cam Ranh Bay in 1967 and got orders to the 82nd Combat Engineers but I never went there. I ended up going to the 33rd Ordnance Company right there at Cam Ranh Bay.

When I showed up at the 33rd Ordnance Company they asked me if I could run a crane. I said "where's this crane at?" They told me it was right there at Cam Ranh Bay. I said "Sure, I can run it." They took me out to a 25-ton American, and a Staff Sergeant points to one and says "that one there is yours." I said "If you got a minute, show me how to start it." He says "What? You don't know how to run it?" I told him I'd figure it out. I said if he'd give me about ten minutes, I'd be fine.

After I figured out how to run the crane I spent all day loading artillery rounds. The ammo would come in to the pier at Cam Ranh Bay and be trucked to us at the ammo dump, where we would store it or load it onto convoys going to the field. Occasionally I loaded 55-gallon drums of fuel. I also ran a bulldozer once in a while. And of course there was guard duty at night, usually three or four times a month. I worked at the ammo dump a minimum of twelve hours a day; usually fourteen hours a day. I only had about five days off during my entire tour.

Kirk Lea: I had an armor recon rating, which would translate into helicopter door gunner in Vietnam, so I opted for OCS. I arrived at Cam Ranh Bay in May, 1967. We ran the administration end of a property disposal yard in which we determined what was to be sent back to Manila for repairs and what was to be scrapped. There were about ten of us in the office including a major, two lieutenants, a sergeant major and others. We had hundreds of vehicles come through the yard. The damaged equipment was dragged in to us by the responsible units.

Joe Patterson: In June, 1968, we were supposed to fly into Cam Ranh Bay, but it was being shelled as we approached so we diverted to Saigon. We spent three days there and then flew in a C-130 to Danang. Our facility was located south of China Beach, before you got to Marble Mountain. There was some kind of an air strip right outside our compound and I know the South Koreans were there.

I worked in a warehouse and operated a forklift on the night shift. I asked for the night shift because if you worked days the shelling at night prevented you from sleeping. Sometimes the shelling at night kept you in a bunker for half of your night's work. I also packed boxes out for shipment to the line troops. I pulled occasional guard duty and occasional shit burning detail. Our supplies came in from ships berthed at the Danang deep water pier and were trucked to us at our warehouse, and we in turn repacked it for shipment to the units.

I would work all night; sometimes we'd go to the beach in the morning and sometimes we'd sleep right away. After the war I was a police officer for 35 years, and the night shift was my favorite time to work. My work schedule in Vietnam was either 10/7 or 10/6, but I don't remember having a day off.

Garry Ramsey: I was drafted at age 19. I arrived at Tan Son Nhut by commercial airliner on December 13, 1968. After orientation we flew a C130 to Cam Ranh Bay.

I spent several months with the 524th Quartermaster when I first got to Vietnam. That was part of the 1st Logistics Command. I worked at the tank (fuel) farm. We would bring fuel in from ships with a big hose and transfer it to tankers at our fuel farm. I would climb up on the truck and monitor the pressure gauges. I also did some guard duty on the perimeter. We had over twenty fuel bladders there holding about a million gallons

Dave Warman: I arrived at Bien Hoa in April of 1969 by plane. I was then choppered to Nha Trang, on the coast. That chopper ride scared the living hell out of me!

I ran the Supply Shop for the Battalion, which included five companies. We handled weapons, bedding, clothing, equipment; everything. We worked from dawn to dusk, but there was nothing else to do but work anyway. I also pulled CQ about once a month. CQ is charge of quarters.

We had house girls cleaning the hooch and raking the gravel but none of the Vietnamese worked in the Supply Depot. I just didn't trust them. They were big at pilferage. You had to shake them down every night.

If you saw a Vietnamese out raking gravel and he was counting off his paces, you knew he was measuring distances for a mortar attack. I'd turn those guys in. Get them out of here. One night I had CQ duty and I shook the Vietnamese down as they left the mess hall. I asked to have the colonel's interpreter come over to help me. She was reluctant to tell the people but I told her I'd strip search them if I had to. We found a .45 and lots of silverware and other stuff.

Don Wilson: A few months after I left Recon and Vietnam I went to Memphis for three months of aviation supply training. Then I returned to Vietnam as part of the 31st Marine Amphibious Force in February of 1972. Our squadron rotated every six months with another squadron so I did two six-month tours in this capacity. My first time was on the *USS Tripoli LPH-10* and the second tour was on the USS *Okinawa LPH-3*.

The plan was to organize a helicopter squadron around a Marine BLT (Battalion Landing Team) and station them on an LPH (Landing Platform Helicopter). We had some Cobra helicopter gunships (CH-53's) and some medium transport helicopters (CH-46's), and a few light helicopters for this mission. We were all up and down the coast of South Vietnam.

I worked about four hours a day doing my supply job, ordering spare parts and replacement parts for helicopters, and then I spent the rest of the day flying on helicopters inside South Vietnam, dropping off mostly South Vietnamese recon patrols at various landing zones. I flew on every type of helicopter; when somebody needed a rest they called me. Virtually all of my work was done during the day. I regularly flew to Danang for supplies. Supply guys there worked a 9 to 5 schedule. Nothing was done without the proper paperwork

Our choppers hauled more Vietnamese troops than we did Americans. I thought the Vietnamese Marine Corps was very efficient. I had the feeling that the commanders of the regular ARVN had to watch their troops very carefully. We were shot at a lot when we inserted the patrols into the LZ's. Once in a while we had somebody that wouldn't get off the chopper; most of the time we shoved him off. We were shot down once and the co-pilot broke his leg in the crash. This happened in a dangerous location but there were four helicopters with us and they picked us up very quickly.

The ARVN had a habit of leaving heavy equipment behind them when we dropped them off at the LZ's. Once they were off the chopper I'd notice claymore mines, LAW's (Light Anti-Tank Weapons) and things like that. They'd leave half their ammo on the chopper.

Kirk Lea: We frequently jeeped over to Nha Trang. This required passing through a number of little villages. On one of these trips someone had killed a ten foot cobra; they had it stretched across the road.

Adventures

Frank H. Voytek: I had a lot of frustrations over there. There was one incident where a ten year-old Vietnamese girl ratted on a French guy who was stealing our supplies at night and selling them to the VC. Our captain placed this guy under surveillance. The French guy found out about it and beat the girl nearly to death. I wanted to get my hands on this guy and kill him but he took off and we never saw him again. It took that girl a long time to heal.

Around the time of Diem's assassination (1963) I saw several Buddhist monks burn themselves to death. They would sit in the middle of a Saigon street, and other Buddhists would gather around so you couldn't get to the guy who set himself on fire. The burning person would sit there cross-legged and pour gasoline on himself but he wouldn't yell or anything. Finally when he was dead, he would just fall over. The joke going around then was "What uses a gallon of gas but doesn't go anywhere? A burning Buddha."

Saigon 1963
Courtesy Frank H. Voytek

I was fighting a losing battle supplying the troops through the system that was in place when I got there in 1963. Green Berets and other soldiers from the field would come down from the hills and yell at me for not getting them what they needed but we didn't have the system in place to do anything more than we did. Despite the limitations I was very proud of our work getting supplies from the Navy and out to the Army. The guys I worked with were wonderful. They showed me the ropes. I still communicate with one of them. When I was ready to come home I was the old guy showing new guys how to do it. Just before I left in April of 1964 we moved into our new, modernized supply office, which I had helped build. I spent my last week helping to set up the new facility and then I was gone.

New Supply facilities – Saigon 1964
Courtesy Frank H. Voytek

Gordon Brown: The *Vega* got too close to shore on one occasion, and enemy shore batteries started firing at us, but the range was too great for them; we could see the rounds hitting the water but they didn't come close.

During early 1966 we replenished our first two nuclear-powered ships, the *Bainbridge* DLGN-25 and the *Enterprise* CVAN-65. In April of 1969 the *Vega* joined Task Force 71, anchored by the *Enterprise*, in the Sea of Japan after some North Korean Migs shot down one of our surveillance planes.

During one unrep, a destroyer lost power and dented the starboard side of the *Vega.* This was kept hush-hush. I was on the flying bridge at the time, with some free time, and I was taking pictures. I sent the pictures in to the Exchange to have them developed and I got a new roll of film back, but the pictures were confiscated!

On 8Sep65, the *Vega* was the scene of an unusual change-in-command ceremony. At 0128 hours in the morning, by the light of filtered red flashlights on the port wing of the bridge, Captain P.A. McCluskey relieved

Captain R.E. Hill as commanding officer. We were also doing replenishment at the time, with the *USS Constellation*!

Being a smaller ship, the *Vega* didn't seem to get the consideration when it came to replacement parts. We had a radar repeater that never worked. This was in the days when we were still using tubes. Two weeks before we shipped out, one of my shipmates went to Radio Shack and bought two of the tube we needed. We were not supposed to be using anything in our equipment that wasn't issued by the Navy, so we made up a number and put it on the tube. It worked fine!

Late in 1966, the minesweeper *Engage* was in need of a radar man, so I was transferred over to her. I didn't want to leave my ship, but you do what you have to do. The *Vega* earned ten battle stars for her service in Vietnam. She was decommissioned on 29 April, 1977.

Larry Rock: On my first alert we assembled at the MP shack. Once we were formed we ran from bunker to bunker and the sergeant peeled two guys off at each location. The sergeant assigned me to guard the back door of an M-60 bunker manned by two grunts. I figured I was the only guy in the defense platoon who had never seen an M-60 but I knew better than to argue. Luckily there was no attack. It took ten minutes to man all the bunkers; this procedure was later changed.

Someone mandated a day off for people; flights from Danang to Chu Lai would give guys a "day off" where you could eat lunch in the Chu Lai mess hall and watch planes take off. I was one of the first to be sent on this bizarre trip. I assumed it was done to give pilots their required flight hours. One of my friends took a later flight and our Major Andrews was the pilot. It was raining on their return landing; my friend Jenkins was sitting in the co-pilot's seat and he watched the major wrap his arms around the wheel trying to win a battle with the plane on the slick runway. When they stopped, the major turned to Jenkins and said "That was **not** a good landing." A few weeks later, again with Major Andrews at the controls, the plane took off from Danang in good weather, and came straight down. About twenty-five Marines died.

Dan Vinson: There were a few mortar rounds lobbed at us when I was at Nha Trang, during Tet.

I was frustrated when the ROK Marines would come into the ammo dump and their paperwork -- their requisitions for ammo -- was all fouled up. For example, their request would be for two 175mm rounds. What are you going to do with two rounds? So I'd just load them up. I'd give them whatever they wanted. Somewhere down the line the inventory wasn't going to add up, it is going to be a couple of million dollars short of ammo, but what can you do?

When the ships unloaded their cargo of ammo in the harbor the crane on the ships would place their pallets of shells on the smaller boats (Larks) sitting alongside. If they didn't place the ammo near the middle of the lark it would tip over at some point. I saw that happen several times.

I was sent up to Nha Trang to work the crane up there for the 606th Ordnance Company, also in our Ordnance Battalion. This was about sixty or seventy miles north of Cam Ranh Bay, along the coast. I was probably there about three weeks doing the same stuff I did at Cam Ranh Bay.

Joe Patterson: We had a great big bunker, probably took 10,000 sandbags to build it. At night we would prop a white screen, made of plywood, and we would show movies against the bunker. One night a rocket came over the movie theatre and hit a building right over our tent area. It was written up in the *Stars and Stripes;* it said DaNang airbase was shelled and a rocket missed the drive-in movie theatre. But as everybody was scrambling to get to the bunker someone knocked over the movie projector. It was ruined and we didn't have movies for a couple of weeks. It was my job to show the movies, so everybody blamed me.

I went to Hawaii on my R&R and my parents joined me there. They sat next to a gentleman and his wife on the plane over and that couple joined us for dinner a couple of times. As it turned out, this man was the commanding general for the 1st Logistics Command. He gave me his card and told me if I ever needed anything to just get in touch with him. His name was Major General Joseph M. Heiser. So during my movie crisis when I wasn't getting anywhere, I wrote to him and told him my projector got wrecked. He wrote back and said he would take care of it and we would get a new movie projector. When he came to Danang to inspect everything he asked to see me, which totally blew away my lieutenant, my captain, and everyone else that was in charge of me. He called me out of formation and talked to me for about two minutes. The next day everybody wants to know what he said to me, so I told the captain "he just wanted to know if you were treating me okay." I didn't tell him why.

When on the shit detail you filled the 55-gallon drums with kerosene, and burned the stuff away. Once I put a drum that was too hot back in the outhouse, and the outhouse caught fire and burned down. It was the officer's outhouse! I got a little pin that shows I was a shit burner in Vietnam. But they never put me on that detail again! And we did have to build a new outhouse.

We would occasionally stick a *Playboy* magazine or a bottle of whiskey into a box going out to the front line units, and when we went to the PX there would always be marines standing outside. They weren't allowed to buy whiskey unless they were sergeants or above, so they would give us the money and we'd buy it for them.

Rick Spriggs: As the S-4, I flew a lot of re-supply mission to the outer areas. I flew so many I qualified for an air medal. On one occasion I called to tell them I was approaching their area. They cautioned us that they had a lot of sniper fire. Not long after this conversation our chopper was hit and the pilot started to auto-rotate us down. I didn't know how hard a landing we were going to make so I just bailed out. This turned out to be unnecessary since they landed safely.

Ann Margaret and Johnny Rivers visited our area. Johnny was the band leader, a diminutive guy wearing a shoulder holster. He was gung ho. I had a chance to talk with them and asked them if they wanted to accompany us on a food re-supply mission to the troops in the outer areas. They agreed to go and their military escort approved the plan. Their chopper flew in formation with us. The escort later got in a little bit of trouble for putting them in this situation. Anyway, we landed safely, I introduced her to my battalion commander, and she took pictures with the troops. I have a picture with her which I'd like to send to her.

As S-4 one of my jobs was to try to identify bodies as they were brought in. Our troops were out on one operation and they brought in thirty-five KIA's. Naturally I didn't know every person in the battalion, so we had some people from other units there to help with identification. On this particular night the first bag that I unzipped held the body of a sergeant that was in my A company before I started doing staff work.

What is unique about that sergeant is something that happened earlier. When I first started doing the S-4 job, I was sent back to the States escorting the body of the B Company commander, a friend who had been killed by friendly fire. I flew separately from the body to our Kansas City destination. My wife was living nearby at the time; she knew this man and his wife. I was given ten days free leave after the conclusion of the services. As I was waiting for my plane at Tan Son Nhut airport to begin the escort trip a sergeant called out to me. I knew this man from my days at A Company. He was also escorting a body home. He had been told that he was authorized no leave on this trip. I told him that was not true and told him to take ten days, and anyone who questioned that should see me. So I am forever grateful that this sergeant had his ten days leave before he was killed. This was one of the most broken-hearted times of my first tour in Vietnam.

We had most of the necessary items but it was harder to get the extras. We had a lot of down time with our equipment and we also had to do a lot of cannibalization on equipment to keep things working. Re-supply wasn't always timely, but we had the critical things we needed to do the job.

Dave Warman: My barracks got hit three times with mortar or rocket fire. Overall, I saw five mortar attacks, and one rocket attack. We used to show movies at night between our barracks and another building. We were watching this war movie, I don't remember what it was, and somebody finally yelled that all the shooting wasn't in the movie! We were taking incoming rounds. We headed for the bunkers.

Our Mess Sergeant had a pet monkey he kept in a cage. The sergeant got drunk one night and drove into the monkey's cage. The monkey lashed out at him and lacerated him; they had to take the sergeant to the infirmary.

I picked up a large splinter in my thumb one time, and I jumped in the jeep and drove over to the field hospital. Just as I was pulling into the emergency area, three choppers landed. The nurse told me to step to the side; they had some priority cases. One guy they brought in had been hit seventy times. This guy was actually saved! I was so busy watching them deal with casualties I didn't even feel her pull the splinter out of my thumb. There were constantly casualties coming in to that ER.

There was a huge demand for more power in Vietnam. At one point, the colonel asked my boss, a W/O3, if he could get him a generator. The colonel promised an in-country R&R to whoever could get him a generator over the next couple of weeks. I went back to my office and typed up a requisition for a generator for Long Lines North, which was Tuy Hoa. We were Long Lines South. Then I went to the depot at Cam Ranh Bay and handed the requisition to the E-7. He said they had five, and pulled two copies of my requisition, then sent me over to pick one up. I brought it back within three hours of the colonel's request, and dropped it right outside our barracks where the colonel would see it on his way to get a beer at the end of the day. The colonel walked up behind me as I was hoisting a beer, and asked me where I wanted to go. I told him I would rather just hang out at Nha Trang for a few days. He said okay, I had three days off. It took me three hours to get that task done!

When I first arrived at Nha Trang the E-4 that ran the place did not care. He was going home in ten days and he just didn't care. I quickly noticed that guys were walking around with holes in their dungarees and their boots. I asked everybody what was going on and they said the supply sergeant never got anything done for them. They needed everything. I called Cam Ranh Bay and told them our guys needed everything. I told them I didn't have any paperwork but if they could trust me, I needed everything. They told me they could do it so I went down there with a deuce-and-a-half. They forklifted a complete CONEX onto my truck; a complete issue. We put up a sign telling the other companies to come by that evening and we would direct-exchange boots and everything. They thought I was Santa Claus.

I was told that if I wanted things, I should send a request to all the companies that appeared in a *Playboy Magazine*. I wrote to these companies and told them we needed their help. A few weeks later, the sergeant at the APO called me over and he told me to bring a truck! We had stuff from everywhere! We had drinking glasses, playing cards, casino games, all kinds of stuff. I traded this stuff with everyone!

We had too much paperwork in Supply plus we couldn't get what we needed, except for the black market. Everybody did that, right up to the generals. Trading was the name of the game and they don't teach that at Supply School. I had three deuce-and-a-halves and the colonel was always getting on me for bad tires and flat tires and things. I made a deal with a guy to trade two cases of whisky for twelve tires and rims and inner tubes. He told me to be out at the end of the flight line at dusk with a white rag over the hood of my truck. I was there as instructed. Suddenly, a Chinook drops down out of the sky, and a voice is talking to me from the helicopter. "Are you SSgt Warman?" the voice asked. "Yes," I answered. "You got my booze?" the voice queried. I nodded, and the Chinook sat down and commenced offloading all the tires, rims, etc. I put my two cases of whisky on the Chinook, and it was gone.

I took my new tires, and my three hapless deuce-and-a-halves down to the motor pool. I never did see eye-to-eye with the motor pool E-7. I asked him to mount the tires for me and he refused. I went straight to the Sergeant Major and told him I wanted to talk to the old man on a personal matter. He sent me in to see the colonel. The colonel listened to my story and called the motor pool. He instructed them to mount the tires on my trucks, which they did. The E-7 had never cared for me, but I told him I wouldn't have done that if he had done the right thing.

The civilian head of the Cam Ranh Bay Fire Department told me his pet python (20' long!) had died. He wanted me to get him a new pet. So I made a swap of three cartons of cigarettes, one case of nuc naum sauce and a case of Hi Ho crackers to a Montagnard chieftain for a python! They didn't teach us that at Supply School, either.

I traded some frozen steaks for a jeep once. The jeep had only 8 miles on it; it was brand new. About this time, the colonel decreed that anyone possessing unauthorized vehicles would be going to LBJ (Long Binh Jail). So I parked my jeep outside of a nearby office; to get to my jeep each day I had to go out the back door of my office and walk around a few buildings.

Our sheets and blankets were always wet during the monsoon. I wrote to my sisters, and my sisters were good, they were always sending me things, and I wrote to them and requested a small heating blanket. Two weeks later, it arrived, and I put it on the bed and plugged it in, and set it on low. I figured I would really be snug that night. After work, I went to the club for a bit then back to my bunk. I pulled down the blanket and there were thousands of little chameleons there.

Our company commander had done his six month tour with the grunts, and he came to us for the last half of his tour. He was an asshole. I was called to see the First Sergeant one time, and I figured it was going to be about my dad. It was. He had passed. This was confirmed by the Red Cross official, who asked me if I wanted to go home. I told him I did if it was feasible. When I went in to see the company commander he asked me if I was there because of the news of my father and I told him that was right. He said "I guess you want to go home, right?" I told him I did. He asked me why. "Your dad's dead anyhow." I grabbed him by the neck, and it took several guys to get me off him. I was trying to kill him and he was ready to turn blue when they pried my hands off him. He was transferred to Saigon that night.

We had a regular mess hall. I guess the food was adequate, but it seemed like every time you were ready to eat they were spraying outside with DDT for mosquitoes.

Kirk Lea: There was a particular bend in the road on the way to Nha Trang which often housed a sniper. It seemed he purposefully missed us. Since there was a Korean unit nearby it is possible that he recognized that they would react if he actually shot somebody.

A lieutenant in Tuy Hoa had a trailer with air conditioning and a television. I went to see him when I was supporting a sweep in the area and he handed me a martini. We were sitting watching *COMBAT* on his television when we heard gunfire outside. We dove into the sand – laughing all the while – and we saw what the shooting was all about: Some VC's were trying to enter the camp from the South China Sea and our guys were gunning them down.

I had an opportunity to be a door gunner on a chopper once. A captain was flying and he just followed the railroad tracks. It was a very peaceful two-hour flight; no shooting.

We had a black sergeant whose specialty was "arranging things". He was the Property Disposal NCO. He had a pet gibbon who loved people – except Koreans. Some Korean had mistreated the animal at one time. The gibbon was three feet tall and very playful. He liked to sit on the sergeant's shoulders.

Don Wilson: After two years of working off the LPH's I started to do some things at Group Supply, on Okinawa. Early in 1975 one of the helicopter captains who was privy to the upcoming evacuation of Saigon asked me to come back to his unit. I joined this unit late in March, 1975, and we finished this mission in April.

The reason we used helicopters for the Evac rather than the much larger transport planes is that some of the deserting South Vietnamese bombed Tan Son Nhut airfield, putting it out of business. For some reason, when the Evac began we were about 3 ½ hours late getting started; somebody couldn't figure out the time zone changes or something. When we got started in the afternoon we flew straight through until the next morning. So our part of the final Evac lasted just under 24 hours. The Marine helicopters made 530 trips during this period; I personally did nine trips. Our trips all involved Tan Son Nhut and the American Embassy; other units may have been involved in other Saigon locations but we just did those two. Maybe four choppers went in at a time at Tan Son Nhut and two choppers could land at a time at the embassy, one on the roof and one in the courtyard.

One of the hardest parts of this job was trying to maintain order. Many of the Vietnamese had converted all their assets into gold; I had one Vietnamese who stood about 4' 9", but he weighed about 250 pounds with all the gold he was carrying. We had to throw a lot of people off the choppers. I carried a .45 and a .38 on this job.

We landed in the courtyard one time and I had brought a magnet with me because I had seen a lot of weapons in the swimming pool. We wouldn't allow anyone on the helicopter with a weapon so Americans and Vietnamese alike were discarding their handguns in the pool. I fished a couple of them out on this trip.

We had at least thirty people on each trip in my chopper. The CH-53's could take about 45 people. The pilots had some concerns about the weight on the choppers but the biggest fear was flying in there during the dark. My chopper was not fired upon during the Evac that I am aware of but some South Vietnamese did fire on a few other choppers. They fired on their own people. The South Vietnamese army had turned into rabble at this point. They took off their uniforms and ran around naked until they found some civilian clothes.

Those that were rescued were kept on the hangar deck of the LPH. Eventually we took them back to Okinawa, and ultimately back to the United States. I was back in the U.S. by May 12 and I got back there just in time to be assigned as a guard for the refugees when they arrived at Camp Pendleton. I met Vice President Ky there. I felt proud that the captain asked me to join him for the final trips into Saigon. He remembered me from my earlier tour.

My major frustration was during the Evac. President Ford stopped us from making the final trip that would have rescued the last remaining people. I have never seen so many grown men cry, including myself. The last trip plucked the American Ambassador off the roof – the ambassador was the second to last to leave – and we left eleven Marines there. We did go back and get those Marines; I was on that last flight. The NVA were knocking down the gate at the South Vietnamese President's house. It could have been a lot worse. We lost one CH-46 during the Evac. I don't know what happened to it.

During the Evac in 1975, I thought the guys were very professional. The pilots had all served in country before this event, and the junior enlisted men could see how important this was from the atmosphere around the carrier. We'd wasted almost fifteen years. And a bunch of American lives.

ON THE ROAD

Arrival/Duties

Jimmie Johnson: I enlisted after I received my draft notice. I trained as a heavy equipment operator at Ft. Leonard Wood and flew into Saigon in

July, 1966. Then we boarded an old LST – tents, equipment and all – for a two-day trip to Vung Ro. We established our compound in the small village of Phiu Heip.

For some reason, the Army, with all its' logic, made me a truck driver/wrecker operator. I would follow behind the convoys to move disabled trucks out of the way. This was a daytime job; we never ran at night. If you were caught out at night you would try to find someone's wire and spend the night. So you drove all day and took turns guarding our equipment at night, and then start the same thing all over again. Our average day was twelve to fourteen hours depending on the length of the trip and any guard duty. Everything we did was in II Corps, places like Pleiku, Quin Nhon, Cam Ranh Bay, Phan Rang, Phan Thiet, Dalat, etc.

Dave Warman: I also spent a lot of time on the roads, particularly from Nha Trang to Cam Ranh Bay. Cam Ranh Bay was a nice place. I rode in jeeps, ¾ ton trucks, deuce-and-a-halves. The road between Nha Trang and Cam Ranh Bay was nice; most of the rest was full of chuckholes. I also picked up small arms fire one time on the drive to Cam Ranh Bay.

Garry Ramsey: I spent the remainder of my tour (ten months) as a fuel truck driver with the 61st Transit Company. One of the first things they did was try to make sure everyone knew how to drive a tractor. A sergeant would get up on the truck with the guys and watch as they tried to back the truck between some 55-gallon drums. He gave most of them a hard time. When my turn came I told him if he hollered and banged the side of the door, I was going to knock the shit out of him. He laughed but he didn't bang the door. I had experience driving trucks before the military so I knew what I was doing. After the "training" I hauled fuel every day.

Dennis Newara: We were mortared the night I flew into Bien Hoa. When I went to the Tan Son Nhut Comm site in December, 1967 I noticed that they had generators there, which was what I was trained to work on, but they decided to use me as a truck driver. I drove convoys, I did frequent mail runs, and I performed light maintenance on the truck. For the most part I drove a deuce-and-a-half. I also flew on a C130 as a courier a few times, mainly to Vung Tau, which was the headquarters for the 1st Signal Brigade. I also built bunkers around our complex and other odd jobs. I think they considered truck drivers as guys they could call on for anything.

One of my duties was to truck guys back and forth from their barracks in the Cholon section of Saigon to their place of work at the Tan Son Nhut air base. I worked at least ten hours a day, seven days a week. My mail runs were a daily occurrence. Vehicle maintenance was more of a weekly thing.

Our work at the 524th Quartermaster began at 0500 at the motor pool. We could work as late as 10:30 at night but no later, since the trucks didn't move at night. As a fuel truck driver I was out on the open road. As our convoy passed the starving Vietnamese I would give them a lot of my C rations, it just hurt me so much to see their faces. An average trip would be to Phan Rang, about eighty miles. We usually spent the night at the compounds we serviced, including the Montagnard compound, and the Koreans. When we spent the night at a compound I usually slept under canvas in the tractor. I'd blow up an air mattress. At Cam Ranh Bay I slept in a barracks that held about twenty guys.

In November or December of 1968, I was driving a convoy down to Vung Tau on Highway 1. I had a shotgun and my driver had an M60. We picked up small arms fire. We kept moving and came out okay, but convoys were always tense. One of our ¾ ton trucks was hit by small arms fire in the radiator one time, and another time mortar fire destroyed one of our Comm sites in an old church.

The monsoon was a challenge, and I often drove through it with water up to my running boards. The ditches on the side of the road filled up with water, and the Vietnamese people would fish in the ditches! The people would catch fish, which we called "mudfish," and we wondered where the fish came from.

I was stunned by the severity of Tet68. Living in Cho Lon, we were unable to travel to Tan Son Nhut. At one point I volunteered to help the MP's try to restore order. We ended up on a roof along with some other volunteers. One time a shot came in and I hit the ground. This shell was ricocheting around the room.

Kirk Lea: We had no options for volunteering but when they needed somebody I was frequently sent on missions to Tuy Hoa.

Les Daulton: I flew to Cam Ranh Bay in March, 1971, and then a bumpy C-130 flight north. I spent my first four days helping retrieve a semi that had gone off the road. Then I went to Chu Lai. We drove supplies from Chu Lai to Quang Tri, Da Nang, Duk Pho, etc. In October 1971 we started to close down some of the outlying bases, turning them over to the ARVN and I pulled guard duty two or three times. Then in January of 1972 the Americans pulled out of Chu Lai and withdrew to Danang. The war was winding down so an everyday work routine was not in place. We would go days without driving anywhere. When we were loaded we might be gone for two days. It took a full day to go from Chu Lai to Danang (about sixty miles). We had to spend the night there; same thing from Chu Lai to Duk Pho – a full day getting there. The roads were, well, they weren't there. There really wasn't a road between Danang and Chu Lai. The road to Duk Pho was just a dirt road, a country road.

Adventures

Garry Ramsey: At a point out of Da Lat we were stopped and they were sweeping the road ahead of us. I climbed onto the top of my truck to get some C rations and I had my Polaroid camera; one of our choppers was coming in my direction so I took a couple of pictures and then a rocket hit the chopper. We went to the crash site to help. There were pieces of bodies that gave me nightmares for years. It never left my mind. Later we were driving past the Korean compound and we saw a bunch of VC heads on poles and other atrocities. I wondered afterwards if I really saw that. I was having nightmares about it and I wondered if it really happened; years later one of my friends assured me it did.

Many times on a convoy they wouldn't allow us to go back to the water trailer to refill our canteens. When it is 110 outside it is even hotter in the cab of a tractor. When the monsoon started the roads became seas of mud. Often a truck would slide off the road into a rice paddy. We had to have choppers pull the truck out of the paddy. I saw that happen at least three times.

Driving my fuel truck back from Da Lat the bridge we used had been blown. We did not know the bridge was out and we were going about 30 mph. The trucks ahead of me pulled off the road to the right and when I pulled off the trailer almost flipped on me. In that area there was a lot of high elephant grass growing near the road. I saw something big moving through the grass and coming right at me. I got my truck stopped and a big bull elephant ran right past me.

Dennis Newara: One of our convoy drivers was shot in the head. It was always a stressful trip. We were coming back from Da Lat one time and on the mountain side of the road there were six or seven black-pajamas clad guys wearing straw hats. I assume they were VC. Choppers came and cut them down.

Les Daulton: At Chu Lai I had to pull guard duty two or three times. We were manning this huge guard tower, about one hundred feet in the air. There were eight of us there for a 24-hour period. There was supposed to be one of us at each window looking out over the ocean. I had to pull the 24-hour duty by myself because the other seven guys were shooting up! Another time in a Quonset hut I pulled guard duty with a guy. First he took a tablet of Orange Sunshine. I asked him where he got that stuff. He told me he got it from the Air Force. He said "the pilots fly it in and bring it over here to sell to us." Then he had to snort heroin to come back down. I asked him why he would take a tablet to get high, and then take a snort to come back to where he started from. And then he's puking his guts out. Naturally I had to stand his shift that night too. I couldn't trust him.

In the morning we had a sergeant who was on the ball. He called us together and told us we had a problem. He had noticed some bare foot prints in the mud around the motor pool. So we had to pull the gas tanks off all the trucks and drain them out. And it's a good thing we did. Somebody had put grenades into some of the gas tanks with rubber bands wrapped around the spoons. As soon as the diesel fuel ate through that rubber band it would explode. They caught the kid; he was only fifteen years old.

They were really strict with us in the closing months. That one run we made to Duk Pho was the only time they let us lock and load. That time we had our rifles, helmets and bandoliers.

We had problems with the road between Danang and Chu Lai. There was a pass where we used to get held up all the time. I asked one of the drivers why we were stopped. He said they ran over something. "What?" I asked. He said we have to wait until we pay the bounty and then they let us go. What was happening is the Vietnamese would concentrate around this narrow pass and then one of them would throw one of their little kids out under the tires of a vehicle. They demanded we pay for the loss of life to their child. It was even worse if you hit one of their water buffalo!

Jimmie Johnson: Snipers would hide along the trail (I can't really call them roads) and shoot to hit the ammo we were carrying or anything to get the convoy to stop. If you stopped you were in the killing zone. The enemy sure wanted to stop the movement of ammo and supplies. Sometimes at the base camps we would be hit by mortar or rocket fire.

We pulled into a firebase one afternoon and a mortar attack started. I crawled under a truck for protection and in the middle of the barrage my truck sergeant grabbed me by the ankles and pulled me out from under the truck, yelling, "You stupid SOB. Don't you know that if one round hits the ammo in that truck you will never be found?"

I went to Hawaii for my R&R to marry my wife in October of 1971. When I returned to Chu Lai the base was empty. Prior to leaving guys told us to be sure to take care of our dogs before we leave for Danang because the Vietnamese eat them! Everybody had a pet dog; one guy had a pet monkey. Well I see these 55-gallon drums being used for stew pots and they're filled with dogs. One guy pulled a dog out of the drum and I was just . . . I couldn't believe it. The drums were full of dogs.

The reluctance to call up the reserves impacted the supply/logistics support troops. Valuable logistics skills were left behind. Despite the ominous beginnings, within three years the 14th Inventory Control Center was running a fully automated central inventory computerized operation out of Long Binh;[xxii] ironically, a place that didn't exist until the arrival of U.S. forces.

Among the lessons learned from Vietnam is the recognition that the reliance on civilians in the Continental U.S. warehouse facilities creates a shortage of trained military personnel during war, driver training programs should be increased and include driving under combat conditions, we should stockpile DeLong piers, use of petroleum pipelines is preferable to dangerous convoy reliance, and the mobile computers necessary to run the logistic operations should be developed.[xxiii]

SUPPLY/LOGISTICS PERSONNEL

Frank H. Voytek

Dennis Newara

Garry Ramsey

Larry Rock

Les Daulton

Danny Vinson

Don Wilson

CHAPTER THREE

ENGINEER SUPPORT

The challenge for engineers in Vietnam went beyond supporting the combat forces. In the last analysis they changed the face of the country.[xxiv] These changes were made despite erroneous assumptions, lack of resources at home and unforeseen conditions in South Vietnam. Back in early 1965 the amount of engineer effort that would be required in Vietnam was not appreciated,[xxv] partially due to political considerations. Nearly half of the Army's engineers and their equipment rested in the Army Reserves. Planners expected at least a partial call-up of the Reserves for a period of one or two years to meet the anticipated needs in South Vietnam. [xxvi] President Johnson's refusal to call up the reserves in a nationally televised speech (July 28, 1965) rendered all previous planning meaningless. This decision guaranteed shortages of trained men, equipment and materials.

The biggest challenges for engineers was the lack of natural resources in Vietnam, such as lumber and rock, a shortage of spare parts and the presence of sand, excessive heat and the monsoon. Security was almost a secondary worry to engineers who had so much on their plate. Every large combat unit had a force of engineers with them. In addition, there were eighteen autonomous engineer brigades, ten battalions and twelve separate companies.[xxvii]

ROCK CRUSHER OPERATORS

*Spc4 **Wayne Niccum**, A Company, 46th Engineer Battalion, USA*

*Spc5 **Robert Simmons**, A Company, 46th Engineer Battalion, USA*

Arrival/Duties

Wayne Niccum: I went over on the ship with the 46th Engineer Battalion in November of 1965. When we debarked from the ship we still didn't have ammunition. We stayed overnight at Vung Tau; they told us it was a secure area and to break out our pup tents. Several of us spotted some big cement culverts; instead of breaking out the tents we just slept in those. In the morning we trucked to Long Binh and set up our perimeter, dug foxholes and strung concertina wire. They told us not to shoot at anything since the 1st Infantry Division would be maintaining security for us outside our wire. That first night we had a black soldier in our unit who started blazing away with the M-60 machine gun. There was talk of court martialing him for firing without permission but he told them he didn't fire one time in Korea when he heard a noise, and the Chinese threw a grenade in on him. He wasn't going to let that happen again. That was the last we heard about that.

We spent a few days working on our perimeter before our equipment arrived. We dug holes and filled sandbags. Once the equipment arrived our first mission was to build the 93rd Evacuation Hospital, just down the road from us, and my job evolved from demolition work to running the rock crusher.

The 93rd Evacuation Hospital went from ground breaking to handling patients in forty-five days.[xxviii]

Wayne Niccum: I found that the rock in Vietnam was a lot harder than what I had seen before. Drill bits came in two foot lengths, and I know we drilled down two, four, and six feet, using a 55-pound air hammer. But before I did any rock crushing we had to get at the rock. When we hunted for rock we would take our air compressor out into the rice paddy's; when we found a rock we would run a test hole and drill down; if water came up we went looking for better rock. Later on we moved towards Bien Hoa where there were mountains.

It seemed like we always had a good stockpile of rock. We worked around the clock crushing it, and we seemed to be ahead of what was needed.

We worked six days a week and the seventh day was for maintenance on the equipment. The hard rock we were working with was hard on the equipment; every other week we would do some welding on the jaws of the rock crusher to help maintain this equipment. We would also weld beads on the corrugated roller every Sunday to build the corrugations back up. We also blew the dust off the crusher with an air compressor and looked for any other trouble.

The rock crusher worked around the clock. I worked both day and night shifts. It was a two-man operation; one guy on the primary unit, and one guy on the secondary unit. The primary unit was known as the jaw crusher; where the rock first came in, roughly 2' by 2', maybe a bit less, and got broken down. The secondary crusher broke it down further, maybe to about one inch. Whatever size rock you wanted was determined by the size of the screen you used.

Robert Simmons: I worked at the rock quarry. We did a lot of dynamiting in the beginning. We had to dig and drill for rocks at that time; later on we found some rock ledges that were easier to deal with. We did work into the evening some times. We crushed all the rock for the concrete that was used to build highways, the 93rd Evac Hospital, the ammo dump and lots of other things.

Blasting in the Rock Quarry
Courtesy: Harley Brinkley

Vietnamese

Wayne Niccum: I came into contact with the Vietnamese people every day. They had a holding pen where the Vietnamese would come to work; after their ID's were checked we used them at the quarry, specifically to sweep up any rock debris and rock chips. They worked at the Motor Pool and in the carpentry shop. Eventually the Vietnamese took over the carpentry shop, which freed our guys up for other duties. And of course they worked as house girls and on KP duty.

Robert Simmons: I saw Vietnamese when I went downtown. We also had some working with us at the quarry. The older guys worked hard but some of the younger men didn't want to exert themselves. Some of them used the empty canisters from our flares for a water pipe to smoke their tobacco, which was marijuana.

Adventures

Robert Simmons: We were hard at work on the crusher late one night, which is very noisy work as you might suppose, and the lieutenant yelled at us to get down because of a fire fight on the perimeter.

In those early days it was hard to get replacement parts for the crusher. We had to cannibalize our second crusher to keep the first one running. We had installed a new belt on the crusher, and Wayne was underneath tightening some bolts in the conveyor when another guy started the machine. Wayne was rolling up the belt; he couldn't go under the diesel motor but he was up there rolling around when I hit the emergency button. That stopped the belt.

Wayne Niccum: The third guy hit the belt not knowing that I was down in there. I screamed, and Bob ran around to the big red emergency button. In the short period of time it took Bob to reach the emergency button I was already up the conveyor and under the diesel motor. I couldn't go through there so it just started rolling me and the strapping on there was slapping at me. The short time it took Bob to get to the button and shut it off seemed like a lifetime to me.

Robert Simmons: Our equipment was inspected by a warrant officer because our stuff wasn't breaking down as much as other units. Our sergeant was really big on maintenance and it must have paid off. We used to shut down and grease all the conveyors every night but on Sunday we didn't work; that was maintenance day.

Wayne Niccum: After we got ourselves established and outfits started moving in around us there was a signal outfit over on the other hill. There was a water point in between us and there was another unit down that way too. One night somebody fired some rounds from the water point. Somebody from our bunkers returned fire. Well the signal outfit opened up with their .50 calibers. We were shooting our M-60's. Tracers were lighting up the sky and bullets are tearing up our tents. They finally got it stopped, but it was a three-sided war for a while.

Our procedure for warning people that we were about to blast was to yell "fire in the hole" three times. Since Vietnamese might be around, we also fired a carbine three times. We fired the carbine one time and a group of soldiers fell into a nearby ditch. Later on some Special Forces guys told us they had been tracking these guys, who were VC! They told us they must have been veteran VC soldiers; inexperienced guys would have fired back when we shot the carbine three times.

We used to do a lot of wheeling and dealing with the rock. That stuff was like gold over there. We could get anything we wanted with it. Everybody wanted up out of the mud.

I had guard duty one night and as the sun came up I was outside my bunker, which I wasn't supposed to be, soaking up some rays. There was a slab of cement near me and a bullet ricocheted off the cement. I don't know where it came from. I got down off the cement slab and laid there until they came to relieve me. Another night on guard we had an Italian boy who said he had been shot at and he refused to leave his bunker. No one else had heard any shooting. I talked to him and told him I was coming to relieve him. I told him not to shoot me. When I got to his bunker I told him I had just walked there and there was nothing going on. But he wouldn't leave the bunker. He stayed with me on my shift and then walked back with me later that morning.

During the monsoon we would get mud on the rock, and this would clog the crusher. So we brought in a pumper to wash off the rock. There wasn't enough water around during the monsoon, we had to add some more!

From 1969 to 1970 rock use doubled to 140,000 tons per week.[xxix]

HEAVY EQUIPMENT

*Spc5 **Tom Langley,** A Company, 46th Engineer Battalion, Long Binh, USA*

*Spc4 **Louis Kutac,** A Company, 46th Engineer Battalion, Long Binh, USA*

*Spc5 **William Wyrick,** A Co., 46th Engineer Bn., 503rd Combat Engineers, 1st Air Cavalry Division, USA*

*Spc5 **Frank England,** C Company, 46th Engineer Battalion, Long Binh, USA*

Arrival/Duties

Tom Langley: The 46th Engineer Battalion went over on the *USNS General Leroy Eltinge, T-AP 154*, along with other units. The ship broke down on the way over and we were towed into Guam. That added three or four days to the journey. We slept six high on the ship; it was at least 50% over-packed. Not a pleasant trip! We were scheduled to land at Cam Ranh Bay but we pulled into Vung Tau. We were only there a day and then we drove up and down Highway 1 almost to Saigon looking for a suitable base camp. We found a spot that was about five acres and clear and that was the birth of Long Binh.

Most of my work over there was operating a front end loader. I also ran a dozer and a paver (big cement mixer); mainly, I was loading rock into the crusher and rock and laterite (Vietnamese soil) onto dump trucks. Most of this work was done at Long Binh but I occasionally went TDY to various locations, one or two day trips to places where they needed a front end loader operator. We'd put the front end loader on a low boy and take it to the work location.

We always worked twelve hours a day, at least six days a week. Two of us got where we could load a 5-ton truck in twenty seconds!

Louis Kutac: I was primarily a front end loader operator working in the rock quarry. I did drive a dozer and a truck occasionally and also a jeep. I did some work in the evenings, under lights, double-shifting, until 0200. At that time I was operating a water truck, and we did some work watering down the dusty roads. With our fleet of dump trucks going down the roads, it didn't take long before it was so dusty you couldn't see.

William Wyrick: I was a Construction Engineer. I operated bulldozers, front end loaders and other equipment at least twelve hours a day. I worked on the roads and we built the ammunition dump at Long Binh. I worked on the 93rd Evac Hospital too. I carried an M1 carbine and a .45.

Frank England: I flew into Bien Hoa on May 10, 1970. At that time, C Company was at Fire Base Mace. We shared that base with the 199th Infantry Brigade. When the 199th rotated home the 1st AirCav moved in, and we moved to Camp Pratt; this was our own camp just a short distance from Fire Base Mace.

My job description was Wheeled Tractor Operator. I operated a scraper, or what is sometimes called a load hauler. The scraper is a six-wheeled vehicle with four wheel drive; it is ten feet wide and about thirty-five feet long. Once in a while we'd trade off with another guy and I would operate a dozer, just to get a break and gain some experience on other things. Even though the war was starting to wind down the construction effort was still underway. We were mainly working on roads. We were busy the whole time I was over there.

We built roads and expanded Fire Base Mace. The scraper's role was to haul the earth fill that went down before the asphalt. The pan on the scraper would hold ten to twelve yards of earth. I worked about ten hours a day. After we dumped the earth on the road the graders would come along and smooth it out, before the asphalt was poured.

The laterite was kind of hard clay. In the dry season it was dusty and hard to pick up. In the monsoon it was really, really slick. There was a piece of equipment known as an apron that sat in front of the scraper; you'd go along with the scraper on the ground and the force of you pulling against the ground would load the dirt itself.

William Wyrick: With the 1stAirCav we used dozers with twelve foot blades to carve LZ's out of the jungle. Sometimes we lined up two or three dozers side by side to carve out a clearing. We would have guards beside us because we couldn't hear any shooting above the noise we were making. We also had a machine gunner on the site with us. Our dozers were sling loaded into the LZ jungle by helicopter when we did our work. Some guys actually rode the dozers down. We had Rome Plows on the end of the dozer. We usually worked two or three days on an LZ before it was ready for the troops.

Vietnamese

Louis Kutac: After we were there a few months, they had some kind of government program where they were employing the Vietnamese people. I ended up in charge of about fifty of them, and they came down to the rock quarry. I would show them what to do; I was kind of like the foreman. They were hard workers, a real gentle, compassionate people. One time NBC News came down and interviewed us. I should have been on television but I never heard anything more about it. I don't know if it aired or not.

William Wyrick: There wasn't much socializing with the Vietnamese people in 1965 but that started to change by 1966. Rules had been relaxed. You could go into the village at Long Binh/Bien Hoa and when you did you didn't take any weapons. In 1967 you **couldn't** take a weapon into the village.

In 1969 and 1970, I was stationed north of An Loc and security was tight out on the Fire bases. There was no contact with Vietnamese people. They caught one of the houseboys at An Loc stepping off the distances from the water tower to the CO's hooch. I think that is when they discontinued use of domestic help. As the job foreman I would see to it that we gave any excess food to the Vietnamese kids.

Frank England: We had Vietnamese house girls but we saw Vietnamese mainly out on the road. We pulled a lot of their vehicles out of the mud. There was a lot of logging in our area and these guys would get stuck now and then. I guess the Vietnamese people were basically good but not trustworthy. I guess they were just trying to get by, like everyone else.

We had an ARVN compound next to us at Camp Mace. The whole time we were there they never caught one round of incoming fire. When they did go out on patrol, they'd go out in their skin-tight, starched fatigues and spit-shined boots. They'd go about a hundred yards into the jungle and kind of bivouac all day, then come back in the evening. They never broke a sweat. They just sat on their ass and let us do everything for them.

A bunch of Cambodian refugees arrived in the village of Soui Cat, ten or fifteen kilometers from us. They were moved into a swampy area near the village. The village was known to be sympathetic to the VC and nobody wanted to have anything to do with these people. One older Cambodian woman had five or six kids and they put her in a swampy area at the end of the camp. A few of us spent half a day hauling rock and fill and dirt to build up the place. When we were finished everyone wanted us to work on their place but it really meant a lot to her. She came out to give us a few trinkets in appreciation but she basically had nothing. Their base was hit one time with mortar fire and one of her little girls was hit during the attack. Some of our guys went and played Santa Claus with those kids.

Adventures

Tom Langley: When we picked Long Binh as our campsite in late September of 1965, there was nothing there. When we were finished it was a city. The 46th did a tremendous job there. And that was just in a year. It is unbelievable the stuff that was accomplished. When we arrived there was only Highway 1; when we left there were lots of side roads to various camps.

Our rifles were locked up except when we were working out on the road. The scariest night for me was the last night in Vietnam; I was in Saigon waiting for a flight out and heard the mortars going off. Other than that I had no fear, maybe because I was just twenty years old.

Louis Kutac: We were building some roads around the 93rd Evacuation Hospital to keep the dust down.   A helicopter came in with some dead soldiers and they asked me to help them unload. I still shake when I think of having to carry those dead GI's. I don't know why. I get so emotional about it, even today. They were the first casualties I had seen. I couldn't understand how you could have so much blood on the blankets; just soaking with blood.

We were going through some little villages up near the rubber plantation and there were rumors of VC in this area. They warned the people that they would burn the village down if there was any trouble. And they did burn it that night. The next morning I was on my roller and there was this mother nursing her child, sitting on what was left of her porch, just staring. It kind of got to me. I was so ashamed that we would come out there and hurt innocent people. We blew her house up. It stays in my mind.

William Wyrick: In 1965 we were mortared at Ben Cat quite a bit. And we ran over a lot of land mines on the road. I was in charge of the work crew one night in 1966 and one of the guys on the crew told me they had just seen "Charlie" running across the road with back packs. I reported this to the battalion CO. He said the infantry had just swept that area earlier that day and found nothing. About 7:30 the next morning they blew the ammo dump up.

I was at Camp Bearcat in 1967. Troops had already been living there for over a year but they sent me there with a wheeled entrenching machine to dig a ditch two feet wide by six feet deep to serve as a septic system for their mess hall. After this task was finished I went back to check on it and it was working very well for them. It was probably one of the first systems like that.

At An Loc (1970) they were trying to mortar the helicopters but they always overshot and came near us. The fire bases were hit a lot. One night we lost 66 killed and 40 wounded. The company commander was one of the men killed. They breached our wire, killed the guards – they went to sleep or something – and were throwing grenades and satchel charges into our hooches, which were out on the perimeter.

One of the enemy tricks was to plant mines at night after we had finished smoothing out our road during the day. They would put an unexploded 105mm shell under the mine. When the mine went off it would set off the much bigger 105 round.

When they started winding down the war it was very difficult to get replacement parts for the equipment. We had to cannibalize a lot of our equipment. We had .50 caliber machine guns with us when we carved LZ's out of the jungle, but because the drawdown was going on ammunition for the .50 caliber was not made available to us. But it was available for the ARVN so we had to go through MACV to get it. There was no paperwork involved. It usually involved a trade for beer or something.

I received a Technical Service Vietnamese decoration and the Cross Palm from President Ky in 1970. The medal for excellence as I understand it was only given out six times during the conflict. The other award was for saving some people during that big March 19, 1970 attack at An Khe. We had an armor outfit in with us and they had been our security. They pulled out that day and some ARVN troops were moved in to be our security. I saved some Vietnamese women and soldiers during that attack and won the Bronze Star and Purple Heart for it.

Frank England: We got some small arms fire; I don't think we were a high priority target. When we left Pratt at the end of my tour we caught small arms fire on Highway YK where we were doing road work, and we took some random rocket fire. The rockets weren't bad until the 199th left and the 1st AirCav moved in. They parked a lot of Cobra helicopters around our place and that attracted more rocket fire. But what we dealt with most was land mines and booby traps. They were sometimes planted in the jungle, and now and then we'd need to get a new laterite dig going and we'd have to clear the jungle back. We'd run over a few anti-personnel mines and booby traps. This ordnance was probably left over from when the French were there.

Once in a while we would have a piece of equipment that would break down. We usually tried to be inside someone's wire at night, but when something broke down we would take a team of mechanics and some security to go out and fix it. I didn't really think much about it until I got home, but those trips could have become ugly; there were only four or five of us in a very dangerous situation.

The existing roads in Vietnam were characterized by insufficient subgrade and poor drainage.[xxx] They required continuous maintenance. The ARVN had very few engineers back in 1965 so we persuaded them to organize engineers in their armed forces and U.S. engineer advisors helped at the schools.[xxxi]

MECHANICS

*Spc4 **Don Cook**, Welder, C Company, 46th Engineer Battalion, Long Binh, USA*

*Spc4 **John Welty**, Mechanic, C Company, 46th Engineer Battalion, Camp Pratt, USA*

*Spc4 **Larry Willard**, Mechanic, A Company, 46th Engineer Battalion, Long Binh, USA*

Arrival/Duties

Larry Willard: I was working as a machinist when I was drafted. Military life was a big wake-up call for me, for sure. I flew into Tan Son Nhut in March, 1966 and then was trucked to Long Binh. As an engine mechanic I spent most of my time in our motor pool at Long Bing, but occasionally I would go TDY to Ben Cat and other places for a week or so. Naturally you have to drive the trucks in order to work on them, so I did some of that, too.

We worked 12/7. We had no hydraulic lift but we used to drive the vehicles onto a ramp so we could work underneath them. The hydraulic pumps on dump trucks frequently blew gaskets. But they were running 24/7, which explains that. I could fix most of the trucks that broke down out in the field right where they sat; sometimes we would have to tow them back to the motor pool.

Don Cook: I arrived at Tan Son Nhut air base in December of 1966, and spent the night there.. We went to bed at 10:00, and later it broke loose. We didn't have weapons, and I was scared. In the morning, a few of us went out and looked at some VC bodies, and they were young-ins; children. Later that day we drove to Long Binh, about thirty miles north.

I was the C Company night shift welder. We primarily did arc welding. We also did some gas welding in Vietnam. I think the welding I did in Vietnam was more difficult than the welding I did as a civilian after I got out. In Nam, we had to zig zag our welds sometimes.

My work was split between repair work on the trucks and other equipment; we welded on tailgates, fixed their bumpers and fenders, things like that. The guys could be pretty rough on their trucks. We also did construction work such as welding sewer pipes and working on bridges One time we put in 4" sewer lines for the officer's quarters. One time we built canine kennels. We did all kinds of stuff. Most of our work was done within the perimeter, but we did go out a few times.

We lived in pup tents for two months or so. Then they started building barracks, and we had cement floors.

John Welty: I was an aircraft mechanic assistant when I was fifteen years old so I was mechanically inclined from an early age. When I enlisted, I put in for Heavy Equipment. I flew over in November, 1970 to C Company, 46th Engineers. They were out in the field at that time so they sent a supply truck in to pick me up. The driver stopped in one of the villages on the way out to our camp and picked up a Vietnamese house girl, and she rode in the back with me. I'm sitting there with no weapon, just arrived in-country, and I'm wondering if this lady is on our side or not. Our base was called Camp Pratt. Pratt was named after a truck driver killed earlier in the war by a mine on a day when they decided they didn't need to do a mine sweep before the trucks started out. I was there for nine months. We were the only company in the battalion that was in the field constantly.

We repaired every type of heavy machine -- dozers, graders, trucks, plows, cranes -- everything that was needed to build roads or bridges. I didn't work in the Motor Pool, I worked in the mud. We didn't have a garage out in the boonies. When we changed motors or changed transmissions we did it in the mud. And we didn't have any dollies to crawl under the vehicles; we just wallowed in the mud. Despite the fact that we didn't have a Motor Pool or any covered facilities to work in our equipment was up and running more than any of the other companies! We traded a lot of parts with the 1st AirCav; they were located about a mile down the road from us.

Vietnamese

John Welty: We lived out of an eight-man tent at Camp Pratt. We broke up pallets to give ourselves a wooden floor. One of our guys, Ron Eike, was cutting up an ammo pallet for our hooch when a large cobra came out from under the tent. Ron killed it with a piece of wood and cut its head off and a papasan came running up and grabbed the snake for the dinner pot.

Ron also managed to nail a rabbit with a stone while out on the perimeter bunker. He brought it back to the hooch holding it by its ears and a house girl told me to clean the rabbit and she would cook it, and we would eat it.

"You clean. I cook. We eat." I cleaned the rabbit, and she had a bunch of bamboo shoots and a quart bottle of their really potent soy sauce, and she poured that whole quart over the rabbit. Ron came back from guard duty and he had a case of beer with him. One bite of that rabbit with all that soy sauce over it, and his face went white. He grabbed a beer and downed it. He looked at the house girl and said "what the hell did you do to my rabbit, woman?" Then he reached for my beer. He grabbed another can, and quickly downed that. He said "these people over here can ruin anything!"

Don Cook: We found a huge lizard in a tree. It was about three feet long. I was planning to shoot it, but one of the Vietnamese papasans told me not to. He said it was "#1 chop chop" (good eating!). He went up that tree and caught that lizard. I guess they took it home and ate it. I've never seen a lizard that big.

One morning I was going to work early, and I cut through the motor pool, and turned the lights on to see where I was going, and I was brushing these big, long bugs off the work benches and stepping on them, and this mama san just got all over me about that. Again, "#1 chop chop, GI." She didn't like what I did at all.

We did kind of train one Vietnamese guy to help us out a bit. And we had a house girl that cleaned the barracks and did the laundry and shined our shoes. They were pretty good about keeping your uniforms up. We had occasional inspections, and if you passed the inspection, you "made the man;" you would be given a day off from guard duty. I "made the man" four or five times over there.

John Welty: We had been working about 12/7 and we finally got somewhat caught up with the construction, so our commanding officer decided to give us every other Sunday off. One of our medics was enjoying his day off walking down the road and he saw a military tent set up in this small new village. It turned out to belong to a catholic priest who had walked there from Cambodia with about thirty children to get them away from the killing fields. He had thirty kids living in this eight-man tent. An ARVN artillery unit had set up just across the dirt path from where the refugees were now living. The VC threw some mortar rounds in at the ARVN artillery post but some of the rounds went into the refugees. A lot of the kids took shrapnel wounds. The kids never whimpered; they were just happy that somebody was there to take care of them. The oldest refugee kid had his arm cut off back in Cambodia; he was only about seven years old. He helped the priest keep the kids in line.

The medic, Doc Wells, got me, Mr. Mapes, Roger, and a few others, and we started building a little village around their camp. We used a dozer to help move some of the earth for their camp. We'd go down there on Sundays on a MedCap thing. Doc would round up all the medical supplies he could, and we'd go down there and take care of the kids.

Adventures

John Welty: Our camp had been a rice paddy before we moved in. Since the camp was put together in the monsoon, everything was water. Sometimes we had to carry our weapons on our head to keep them out of the water. Our CO took off for R&R to Hawaii right when we moved in and when he came back his camp was gone! The radio shack and one or two other huts were still there; everything else had been washed away. We kept on hauling dirt in there and we finally built the camp up. The laterite, that fine, powdery, Vietnamese dirt, just got in your skin. Some guys got laterite poisoning from that. They just couldn't get it washed out of their systems. Some of them still have that skin disease.

Don Cook: The monsoon did affect welding. Electricity and water do not mix. We waited for the rains to slack off to do our welding. Like when we were putting in that sewer line for the officers, it rained hard, and we'd just have to wait until it slacked off. The good part of the monsoon is that it kept the dust down on the roads.

John Welty: We got a new First Sergeant in. There was a lot of hostility between some of the groups in the camp, and one time a fire fight developed. This new top kick was headed toward the shooting to see what was going on; one of those guys threw a grenade at the others and it landed about three feet from me. The First Sergeant ran over, grabbed the grenade, and threw it outside the wire just before it went off.

We were under rocket attack three or four times. The JP bags each held several hundred gallons of fuel. The rockets were undoubtedly intended for the fuel pods. The VC weren't after us; they were probably happy with the roads and things we were building! We built QL-13 and QL-1; before we built those roads they had nothing but dirt paths. We improved their life style!

Mr. Mapes sent me out one night to recover a 5-ton truck. It had broken down somewhere on the dirt path between our camp and Saigon. I found the truck; the vibration had broken the fuel line off. I cleared the fuel line and rethreaded it, but as soon as I got it fixed a round came through and sheared the fuel line off. I had to put another hose on. When I returned to camp, Mr. Mapes asked how it went. I told him I thought I was under fire. He asked why. I told him there was a bullet hole there in the frame.

Don Cook: We were building revetments to protect the helicopters from mortar attack. This was in preparation for Tet 1968, the big one. My 1st Sgt asked me if I planned to take my crew out that night (the night Tet started, as it turned out). I told him "one night isn't going to matter that much. Let's proceed on the side of caution." It is a good thing we didn't go out, because we got hit pretty good that night.

Larry Willard: Our base was mortared once or twice in my early days, but the rounds didn't land near me. Towards the end of my tour the VC blew up the ammo pad. They probably did this with a satchel charge. I was just returning from fixing a truck out in the field, and as I was passing by a mortar round landed and my jeep was blown on its' side. There wasn't time to jump out but I wasn't hurt.

SURVEYOR

Spc5 **Frank Jackmauh,** *HQ Company/B Company, 46*[th] *Engineer Battalion, Long Binh, USA*

Arrival/Duties

Frank Jackmauh: Prior to entering the military, I worked as a field engineer on a 16-story addition to the AT&T office building in Boston, MA. I also earned an associate degree in civil and highway engineering. My AIT was at Fort Belvoir as a construction surveyor. From there I did four months of NCO training and emerged as a Spec5 surveyor. I landed by plane at Bien Hoa in early January, 1969. I was assigned to HQ Company, 46th Engineer Battalion.

I went over there as a surveyor but within a couple of months of my arrival, the NCO that was running the Carpenter Shop returned to the states on some sort of personal matter and I was asked to step in. There were a couple of small hooches down there and a shower, and I was required to stay down there to eliminate any theft of materials from the Carpenter Shop. Plywood and corrugated roofing, in particular, were in great demand and I needed to keep an eye on these materials.

We received orders from units in the field (artillery, infantry, or whoever) as to their needs, and we would prefabricate the modules. Once they received our product they would fortify it with sandbags for their protection against enemy fire. The Vietnamese at the Carpentry Shop worked about a forty-hour week.

After about ten weeks of Carpenter Shop duty a staff sergeant reported in and relieved me and I returned to my surveyor work. That is right when the survey work was beginning in the direction of Xuan Loc and I wanted to be a part of that. This was a stretch of road from the intersection of QL20 and QL 1 (Highway 1), through Xuan Luc to Gia Rey. This was a stretch of about 32 kilometers. It was somewhat up and down but not mountainous. There were gradual slopes, probably no more than two or three degrees. All the drawings were done in France and everything was in metric units. I was surveying, or what they call "laying out the road." We would be driving in elevation stakes every 25' or so along the road. We tried to take one day off each week doing the surveyor work.

Courtesy: Harley Brinkley

I returned to Vietnam after leave in February, 1970. I spent most of my remaining Vietnam time in Xuan Loc. I also had a 40-day TDY to Ham Ton (on the coast) to look for potential rock quarry sites. The Xuan Loc work was actually begun back in 1969 and spilled over into 1970. When I left Vietnam, in November of 1970, this work was ongoing.

Vietnamese

Frank Jackmauh: In the Spring of 1969 I had two hundred Vietnamese working for me in the carpenter shop. I also had an interpreter who spoke English very well and he helped me communicate with the chief Vietnamese foreman who ran things. Very few of these Vietnamese had any carpenter experience; they were villagers who just came in from the outlying villages. The plans for our modules (bunkers, latrines, showers, etc.) were drawn up in English but they were able to understand them. Most of the measurements were provided in meters. All in all they did a wonderful job. Every now and then we'd get visited by various higher ups and I'd tell the interpreter to have the workers bang their hammers and saw wood to impress them; just make a lot of noise!

I made some good friends at the Carpentry Shop; I got along with the Vietnamese people very well. I had a lot of visitors there. ARVN's would come to see me, some of them looking for scraps of wood. One time I befriended a Vietnamese Army captain who wanted some scraps to burn fires. I was invited to his home in Saigon one Sunday and he took me to the zoo with his wife and two children. I was an honored guest and the meal was chicken. Chicken over there was considered more expensive than beef. Some of the hors' d'oeuvres his wife served were a bit unsettling, sitting on a platter as they were with little feet sticking up, but I wasn't brought up to be rude, so I indulged.

We had mamasans working for us at Xuan Loc but we had no Vietnamese on the road crews. Back at Long Binh we had one Vietnamese working for us as a surveyor and he did very well. We trusted him with his readings.

Every now and then when we ran low on lumber we'd get a couple of planks cut by a local Vietnamese sawmill. These planks would be cut from rosewood, a hard, sturdy wood. This sawmill was run by a Vietnamese family and their band saw was run off an old jeep engine. We'd agree on a price with them and then bring the wood back to our carpenter shop to use for custom projects now and then. I learned about this place from the sergeant that I replaced at the carpenter shop before he went home on emergency leave.

Adventures

Frank Jackmauh: We seldom took fire as we were standing in a road doing our surveying. Sometimes, when we were standing in the middle of a road pounding stakes in the ground or whatever, we'd pick up sniper fire. But I enjoyed the work I was doing so I went along with that.

There was a lot of trading going on. I traded an Omega divers watch to a MACV advisor for a camera once. A mess sergeant from the other side of Long Binh would come to the Carpentry Shop to borrow four or five of my people. The Vietnamese were anxious to work for him because he would feed them. One guy drove up in a deuce-and-a-half and I didn't see anything in the back of the truck. I didn't understand what he wanted to trade. He pointed to the front seat where there was a Vietnamese girl sitting. He said "Her, you can have her for a couple of days." Another guy wanted to trade me a small Cuyese Light Observation helicopter. All I had to do was assemble it. I told him I couldn't do anything with that.

We were harassed occasionally during our work and we'd find mines in the road. Sometime you would be standing out in the middle of the road, silhouetted against the skyline while surveying, and we'd get plunked at. Thank God they were bad shots. The road we were working on had been cleared at least 100 meters on each side so the sniper had to hit us from that distance, but I hit the dirt more than once.

Sleeping at Ham Ton with the 25th Division Artillery unit there was outgoing fire all the time. One time on the Ham Ton recon we were in a remote area with a jungle canopy over us and we saw a group of Vietnamese approaching; about six of them carrying firearms. We didn't know if they were ARVN, VC or NVA. We just stayed quiet and let them go by. We didn't recognize them and they didn't recognize us. It was frightening.

As surveyors we needed paint brushes to paint our stakes for the road crews. We couldn't seem to get them so we ended up whacking branches off a nearby tree to do our painting.

The monsoon was pretty bad. We were working on a section of road between Xuan Loc and Gia Rey, and there was a small, vertical curve combined with a horizontal curve. This curve in the road required some fill to build up elevations. Surprisingly, French engineers did a good job because they actually put in proper banking on the turn, both for drainage and stability. The monsoon would wash off some of the fill when we put it in, but if we compacted it well most of it held. The soil engineers were responsible for determining what was needed.

ENGINEER ADMINISTRATION

*1st Lieutenant **Ed Hanke**, 104th Engineer Company, 554th/588th Engineer Battalions, Cu Chi/Tay Ninh, USA*

*1st Lieutenant **David Cass,** D Company, 46th Engineer Battalion, USA*

*SFC **Jim Kuipers,** C Company, 46th Engineer Battalion, USA*

*Lt. Col. **George Gray,** Commanding Officer, 46th Engineer Battalion, USA*

*1st Sgt **Dale Gott**, A/C Companies, 46th Engineer Battalion, USA*

*Captain **Philip Johnson,** Commanding Officer, C Company, 46th Engineer Battalion, USA*

Arrival/Duties

Ed Hanke: Somebody from my family had fought in every war including the Revolutionary War and the Civil War so when I was drafted I figured it was my turn. I opted for Engineer Officer – OCS. As a newly-minted engineer officer I flew from San Diego to the Philippines in September of 1968. We then flew to Bien Hoa; since they had an alert the previous night we went in steep and landed hard. When they opened the cabin door it was like walking into the back end of a garbage truck. The smell was enough to gag a maggot and the humidity was like getting slapped in the face with a wet barber's towel that had been dipped in some unspeakable muck. Welcome to Vietnam. Adding insult to injury, we were regaled by the Greek chorus of veterans going home, telling us how "short" they were.

While I was waiting for my orders I guy I recognized from OCS appeared. You could tell he had been in-country for at least six months; his fatigues were bleached almost white and his skin was almost black in comparison to my bright green, freshly-issued jungle fatigues and scarlet complexion. He had been with a Land Clearing Team; they use D9 dozers with a special blade, known as a Rome Plow, since they were made in Roma, GA. The D9 blade had a "stinger," a big spike on one end for splitting trees that couldn't be knocked down with the blade alone. He recommended I find something else to do as his job was hot, dirty and dangerous. The VC didn't care much for us clearing the forest and jungle back from the roadsides. Since they knew where we left off for the day, setting the next day's booby-traps was a snap.

Armed with my orders -- happily not to a Land Clearing Team -- I was soon in a ¾ ton truck with an M-60 on a swivel in the bed, and a hunk of angle iron welded upright on the front bumper to snag piano wire stretched across the road, on my way to Cu Chi. The exhaust fumes and garbage smells of Bien Hoa were soon replaced by the reek of the jungle and rice paddies as we churned through the dust toward Cu Chi.

Hardly two days were the same. My platoon's primary duty was hauling asphalt out to QL 22 to pave the road from Saigon to the Cambodian border. Little did we know that this road would later be used for the invasion of Cambodia.

Seven engineers were killed and 132 wounded during the Cambodian invasion.[xxxii]

Ed Hanke: Sometimes the asphalt, laterite or crushed rock came from Cu Chi, but it could also come from Saigon, or even Nui Ba Den (the Black Virgin Mountain), ten kilometers from Cambodia; a place that I would soon call home. There were runs to Vung Tau for sand, or from the Plain of Reeds to Duc Hoa with lumber and other building materials. This was the furthest accessible point at the end of a long isthmus. We were ambushed with sniper fire on the way back but nobody was hurt, just a little excitement for the new lieutenant.

After six months in-country it was time to move on to another assignment, as was the policy of the 20th Engineer Brigade, in order to provide multiple opportunities in the field to all the officers. Sure enough, Lt. Stone called me into the Company Office and handed me orders for the 588th Engineer Battalion at Tay Ninh. This would be my home away from home for the last six months of my tour in sunny Southeast Asia.

I was given the position of XO and platoon leader of the quarry platoon and soon found myself back in school once more, learning by observing and asking questions and trying to stay out of the way of some very capable NCO's. I met a Sea Bee assigned to us as a consultant to assist us with trying to quarry a jumble of house-sized boulders. That was the reason for all the drill steels sticking out of the quarry. The track drills would drill down into a boulder and then the steel would fall into a void and if the next boulder was at an angle, the steel would get stuck. This made for some tricky blasting, as a "shot" could send steel spears hundreds of feet into the air. Thank God for bunkers and not just for defense against the VC but as protection from our own shrapnel.

George Gray: I assumed command of the 46th Engineer Battalion in May, 1967, the fourth CO for the battalion since their arrival in Vietnam in September, 1965. We were based at Long Binh, a base that the 46th built upon their arrival. Our strength was usually 750 men but we were at 1200 by the time I took over.

The U.S. Army's 46th Engineer Battalion was constituted on 7 December, 1917. The battalion served in the East Indies, New Guinea and in the Philippines during WW II, receiving two Presidential Unit Citations. The 46th arrived in Vietnam in 1965 and would ultimately receive Meritorious Unit Commendations from the Army and the RVN Civil Action Honor Medal, First Class.

George Gray: The highest priority field assignments during my tenure in II Corps were the Bien Hoa bypass and Bearcat Road projects. These routes would improve the quick reaction forces of the 9th Infantry Division in their defense of Long Bing, which was the home of II Field Force, the largest ammunition and POL supply areas in Vietnam, and the Bien Hoa Air Base.

The Bien Hoa Bypass Road had made no progress in two months, partly because they had begun it in a deep and lengthy section of quicksand, rice paddies and rubber plantations. We began a night shift on this project which was frequently attacked by snipers. They had stripped junk yards of artillery shells, jeep bodies and everything else to try to provide a stable sub grade for the road and the pressure from II Field Force was intense and embarrassing. We started a new approach in May 1967. Using 25-ton Euclid dump trucks and every other truck we could find, we hauled very large rocks from the Bien Hoa quarry and dumped them in the quicksand. By the end of the first day we had 300 yards of stable grade! In November, 1967, the nine mile stretch of paved road was opened with great ceremony! Our success with the Bypass Road led to our employment on the Bearcat Road. This completed road provided the 9th Infantry Division quick access to Long Binh area.

David Cass: I flew out of San Francisco in late April of 1968 – Steve McQueen was filming *Bullitt* while I was in the airport. In Vietnam I had a lot on my plate and I loved it! I was the platoon leader of forty-five men of the 2nd platoon and enjoyed scores of other assignments. My first task each day was to coordinate with SFC Carter on personnel, materials, tools, motor vehicles, including sick-call list. Then I would visit all projects and make up a punch list of items needed. Around 2200 I would write letters home if I didn't have Officer of the Guard.

Jim Kuipers: I had just made Sergeant First Class (E-7) and anybody that got promoted back then was on their way to Vietnam. In the Army's way of doing things my MOS (military occupational specialty) was abruptly changed from wheel vehicle mechanic to tracked vehicle mechanic. I was sent to Vietnamese language school at Fort Bliss, Texas prior to going overseas.

I arrived by plane at Bien Hoa on 3 February, 1968. My arrival was delayed several days due to the eruption of the Tet offensive. I was assigned to A Company, 46th Engineer Battalion; wheeled vehicles. This would have made sense but the Sergeant Major who interviewed me told me the battalion commander would want to talk to me. I went to see Colonel George Gray and he started asking me questions about engineer equipment and I told him I knew nothing about it. He pointed out that I had advanced awfully fast to E-7 (six years) and I agreed, and I asked him if he had technical manuals for the Corps of Engineers. He said "Of course we do; you're about a cocky son-of-a-bitch." I told him I didn't get to be an E-7 because I was quiet. Anyway he sent me to Charlie Company where I was completely out of my MOS. Naturally their wheeled-vehicles were not a problem since I trained on those, but the dozers and graders and tractors and pans; I had no clue about them. They had manuals and I started reading them and they had some good men and I set about learning about engineer equipment in a short span.

When I first got to C Company they were running two crews. The equipment was being worked 24 hours a day by two crews, and that was a downfall in my opinion. Maintenance was being ignored with that schedule. I got the battalion commander to agree to at least one maintenance day a week where we could shut everything down and pull some maintenance on it. He finally agreed to it, much to his displeasure since his job was making progress on the roads, but we began to shut down on Sunday for maintenance.

After several months at C Company the unit moved to Camp Bearcat where I was acting First Sergeant. We had our own area at Camp Bearcat (Camp Castle); we provided our own security and we continued our mission of repairing roads and bridges blown by the VC on the way to Vung Tau, one of our major sea ports along the South Vietnamese coast. When we were at Bearcat sometimes the Company Commander and I would go out to recon the road. We'd have an infantry escort with us or sometimes we would be in a chopper if it was too late in the day to get there by wheel. The CO and I also went back to Long Binh for numerous meetings while we were out at Bearcat. We returned to Long Binh after a few months when a new First Sergeant came in. I went back to my Motor Pool where I was happy.

Dale Gott: I arrived at Long Binh airfield in June of 1969. I was the Acting First Sergeant of A Company, the Dumpster Company in Long Binh. I spent a couple of weeks up north around Xuan Loc but spent the majority of my time building sixty-eight miles of road (Highway 1) out of Long Binh. We had about sixty dump trucks and 180 men working on that road. We supplied all the rock and asphalt for that section of Highway 1. I spent my entire tour in Vietnam working on that road. I worked fourteen to fifteen hours a day. There were three or four month's work left on that road when I rotated home. I never made a USO show. I was too busy.

Philip Johnson: I was an engineering graduate from college. I entered the Army as an officer with a Construction Engineer job description. I flew into Tan Son Nhut in June of 1968 and was bussed to Long Binh. We had no weapons on that bus ride. For my first two months I was the Assistant Battalion S-3 (Operations). Then I became commander of C Company in the 46th Engineer Battalion.

The way the 46th was organized in those days, you had a Headquarters Company, Alpha Company (heavy equipment), and then Bravo, Charlie and Delta Companies, which were construction line companies with two vertical platoons, carpenters, masons, plumbers, electricians in them, and one earth-moving platoon, with road graders, bulldozers, bucket loaders, rollers, cranes, and earth movers, and the Headquarters Platoon had the orderly room, supply room, mess hall and the maintenance sections. We had a heavy maintenance section because of all the heavy equipment.

As engineers, we had built bridges in Germany as part of our training. This would come in handy. We were building stuff all the time or replacing what the VC had blown up the night before. We worked six days a week, or seven, depending. I would start off the morning with paperwork, and then I'd go out and look over the construction sites. At the end of the day the guys would come back in and we'd have dinner, and then we'd have a company operations meeting with all the platoon sergeants and platoon leaders to discuss what went on that day, what went wrong, and what we needed to do to get ready for the next day.

Vietnamese

David Cass: We used house girls for laundry and we bought lumber and electrical supplies from the Vietnamese. We rented sampans to be used as a pile driving platform and we hired a Korean barge with a crane to help remove a collapsed bridge. I coordinated with Vietnamese foremen to resolve any problems with the two hundred Vietnamese we employed.

Jim Kuipers: They had Vietnamese people working in our compound, some in the carpenter shop and I had two or three at the Motor Pool. They stayed out by the bunker when I first got there and I didn't even know I had them. When I learned that I had three or four Vietnamese mechanics assigned to work in the Motor Pool I brought these guys into my small office and took their ID cards away. I told them to come see me at the end of the work day and they would get them back. This is how I got them to work for me. Hell, they were being paid, they should work! When I first arrived the Motor Pool was like a junk yard. You couldn't even put a vehicle in the shop there was so much junk in there. And I only had three bays.

Dale Gott: We didn't have too much trouble working on Highway 1 because the VC wanted us to build that road for them! Our house girl took care of two of us for $10 a month. She was wife #7. Her husband had all of his wives working for the military, bringing money in.

Philip Johnson: We ran our own water points and we had a big purification unit. A huge constrictor snake got stuck in the water intake and it took three rounds from an M-14 to finish it off. We brought it back to the base and we had a thousand Vietnamese civilians attached to the battalion as laborers, and the head man supervised the butchering of that thing and they all had snake for dinner. The snake was about 18' long!

We were assigned a section of the perimeter for security of the base. One time, about the anniversary of Tet '68, one of our three-man bunkers got overrun. They hit it with an RPG and knocked the three inhabitants of the bunker unconscious. The VC or NVA assumed these three guys were dead, and I sent a platoon in to deal with the breakthrough, which they did. They recovered our guys, all of whom received a Purple Heart for their ruptured ear drums. We found out that there were spider holes (foxholes) in back of our bunkers already pre-dug. The only way that could have happened was by the Vietnamese work force inside our camp every day. They probably had better blueprints of the camp than we did!

Our battalion ran a cinder block shop and a carpenter shop, where we pre-fabbed bunker and latrine modules, and a culvert yard. We put the Vietnamese to work in our vertical platoons where they could do construction on barracks, mess halls, and things like that. When I first got there I noticed that they were driving nails with rocks. So I went out and purchased a bunch of hammers for them. The next day I notice that they are still using rocks to drive nails. I asked the Platoon Sergeant and he told me they had sold the hammers on the black market in Saigon. So I didn't spend any more money on hammers.

Adventures

Ed Hanke: I took my R&R in-country, at Vung Tau. I wanted to observe their quarry operation. Arriving at the BOQ I was assigned a bunk and given a quick tour of the operation and a chance to meet the other officers who were assigned to the company. Just as we had at the Mountain, this quarry company had a member of the sea bees assigned to it for specialized training and the extensive knowledge they were able to provide to the operation. The first time I saw this put to use was with a couple of the dozer operators who learned how to use the weight of the dozer to assist them in pushing overburden down a cliff. "The blade is your brake" he told the operators and over the edge of the cliff they went pushing huge mounds of sand in front of them with the mighty D7, lowering the blade to slow the descent and raising it to increase speed. I'm sure it was pretty scary for the operators at first but after that initial ride they had all the confidence they needed.

Besides fulfilling my Draft/enlistment obligation and doing something that I felt was the right thing to do, the thing that I am most proud of is that I never lost anybody in my unit and the two units that I was assigned to were able to overcome some seemingly insurmountable obstacles and replace a dirt track with a paved road from Saigon to Tay Ninh in the allotted time specified by USARV. This road was later used to spearhead the invasion of Cambodia to interdict the VC supply line. Sure, guys in my unit got hurt from enemy action and their own carelessness and some even got evacuated home, but in the year that I was with them not one of them died and none seriously injured. We survived ambushes and mines on the road, mortar and rocket attacks in base camp, an attack on the quarry, got cut off in an offensive and even survived an errant 155 or 175 mm artillery round that Division Artillery refused to admit to.

George Gray: Facilities such as our Carpenter Shop and the Concrete Block Shop received widespread attention and were frequently visited by dignitaries such as US Ambassadors to Nepal and Vietnam, General Creighton Abrams, Lt. General Bruce Palmer, the II Corps Commander, and General Harold Johnson, Chief of Staff of the Army. We understood why the VIP's came to visit our facilities but many did not listen. As we had done in Korea US soldiers and native workers routinely worked together productively, forming teams without bureaucrats or corruption, providing desperately needed facilities to rebuild villages and win the "hearts and minds" of the Vietnamese people.

David Cass: I had rocket close calls twice. A dud landed a few feet from me on a bridge one night. I was sniped at while on bridge projects, at the gravel pit and housing project. There was a fire-fight in the motor pool in Saigon while trapping thieves.

General Gus came out to visit our bridge site when his jeep was attacked by a water buffalo. His aide shot the buffalo with his 45 pistol. Later the General sent him back to pay the farmer for the loss of his buffalo but the farmer only laughed at him. The farmer showed him the buffalo calmly grazing in the rice paddies. Upon closer exam the buffalo was found to have a hole in its right ear and grooves on its forehead where the 45 rounds slid along its' skull temporarily knocking it out.

It was Sunday morning 22 September, 1968. Hershel Gossett was one of five men sent to evaluate a bridge outside Ben Hoa in respect to installing security lighting. Up till this time we had been lighting bridges in Saigon and highways north to Long Bien with American gasoline powered 5KW and 10KW generators at 60 HZ. We installed 1,000W sealed spots in a pattern designed to overlap, providing thorough illumination for bridge protection forces to spot sappers, especially those floating charges in the river towards the bridge abutments.

Our mission that Sunday was to evaluate, measure, and tag existing power lines on a high tension line supported by steel power poles that ran parallel and over the granite combination railroad and highway Song Dong Nai Bridge that spanned a river outside Ben Hoa. We were to evaluate the local 50 HZ (cycle) Vietnamese power available on the existing power poles. We had been on sight for an hour or so. Hershel and two other electricians had been taking turns climbing every pole in the area. They were short of breath and we were late for our next job so I went up to help Hershel on the last pole. The clay buildings across from us were higher than us with false fronts above the roof, some with clay tile decorations. The poles we were climbing were made out of angle iron and they had steel spikes closely spaced, pointing down so the kids wouldn't climb them. We would just lean out to get by them. I was holding Hershel's legs so he could lean out with an electrical multi-meter to measure and tag these lines when we were hit by a hand thrown concussion grenade (very few fragments). The blast knocked Hershel and me off the pole. He hit on his forehead and did not survive. Local

Vietnamese guards on the bridge were trading shots with someone on a rooftop above us. I was medevac'd to the 24th Evac. Hospital in Long Binh, paralyzed from the neck down. Hershel was a good soldier, a nice guy and a great worker. He was smart and could handle plumbing, electrical and carpentry equally well.

Jim Kuipers: One time the Company Commander and I were coming down the road at dusk and just before we turned off to Camp Bearcat there was a jeep that was hit by a mortar or RPG or something a hundred yards in front of us. The jeep was blown to smithereens. As we passed the jeep bullets came whizzing over us. You couldn't see them but you could hear them. When we approached the village there was a fire fight going on. Finally the infantry got it cleaned out and we were able to go on into camp.

In the middle of the night a mortar round came in and landed beside the bunker I was in. I ran outside and popped some hand-held flares so we could see if anything was coming in on us. Then I called battalion and told them I wanted some fire support in front of the 46th Engineer bunkers. They asked me if I was sure and I just keyed the button on the phone and they could hear the firing. They agreed that we needed some help. So they sent Puff the Magic Dragon and artillery put some illumination over the area. Puff did his thing and the firing stopped.

My main frustration was a lack of replacement parts. That Red Ball supply system, or whatever they called it, did not work well.

The Red Ball Express system was established on December 1, 1965[xxxiii]

Jim Kuipers: When you ordered a part you were supposed to receive it within a couple of days. That often didn't happen. My view was that when you ordered something they were supposed to check in-country for availability before that request went back to the states. I could usually go out and scrounge the part before it came from the states, which tells me that it was already in-country and they didn't know it. Their monitoring of the supply system really wasn't great. One possibility is that parts arrived in Saigon and got ripped off before anyone could get to it to distribute it where it was needed. I know that happened.

Many units didn't have all that they needed to properly support us. For example: Engineer units have lots of equipment that require hydraulic lines. Our support unit didn't have the lines or the machine that did the replacing of the damaged line. What I did was go to the Air Force Base at Bien Hoa and say to the young man there: "Son, I'm in the Army. I need hydraulic lines. What do you need?" He told me he needed boots and fatigues. I told him I'd be right back. I returned with a box of boots and fatigues. He asked me what I needed. I showed him my hydraulic hoses. He asked me what kind of pressure I had on those hoses. "Do they exceed 10,000 psi?" I said "Hell no!" He told me that everything he had would withstand 10,000 psi since they were used on jet aircraft. So I got all my hydraulic lines that way. This was one of the reasons I was successful running the Motor Pool; I went out of my way to get what I needed.

I had a stint as Sergeant of the Guard, supervising the perimeter defense. We had something like six or eight bunkers on the back side of Long Binh that were our responsibility. Normally the Officer of the Day and the Sergeant of the Guard remain back in the battalion area and don't go out there. But when I reported in for SOG duty the battalion XO or somebody told me that they were changing the procedure due to the fact that a sapper had gotten inside the perimeter and killed a few people the previous night. We had three men to each bunker, two of whom were to be up at all times. Up to that point the Rules of Engagement were that if someone wasn't shooting at you, you couldn't shoot. I told them that as far as I was concerned if they saw movement or heard somebody moving out there, open fire. Don't wait for permission. Because by God they got no business out there! I accept all responsibility. That's one of the reasons the battalion commander had me go out there. He didn't want any of his people getting hurt or killed.

Philip Johnson: During the night of November 6th 1968, the VC blew up the bridge over the Saigon River on the Main Supply Route (MSR) between Long Binh and Chu Chi Phu Cuong. The story goes that the bridge was a concrete pre-stressed T-beam design. The explosive charges were set off under water in the middle of one span, causing a geyser of water to go upward against the bottom of the span, which reversed the stresses (loads) on the bottom chord of the span, cracking the concrete T beams and the span collapsed under its own weight. Allegedly the demo team was led by a Cuban and composed of NVA sappers which were supposedly caught later the next day. Anyway the demo guys knew their business.

The 46th Engineers (Construction) got the mission in support of the 65th Engineer Battalion to put in a temporary float bridge to bypass the blown bridge starting from the near shore. The 65th was to start from the far shore. C Company of the 46th would build the near shore approach, roads, and deck the bridge. D Company of the 46th inflated the rubber pontoons and installed the saddle assemblies. The bridge was to be approximately 900-1,000 feet long, Class 60 (to allow tanks to cross) and guyed (anchored) on both sides because of the tidal effects on the river currents.

C Company did the initial recon and proceeded to mobilize the entire company with two bridge companies in tow. Traffic had stopped on the MSR and was backed up for miles in both directions. The MPs were having a field day trying to control traffic, get everything parked on the road shoulders and praying the VC didn't attack the stopped ammo and fuel trucks. I can only assume that the locals didn't know in advance of the demo effort. In the middle of the confusion, C Company comes charging to the rescue with almost 200 vehicles, barreling down the road and ignoring the MPs. They (the MPs) never did understand just what we were going to do for them. I can only assume that LtCol. Jordan (46th Bn CO) or Col. Bates Burnell (159th Group CO.) smoothed their ruffled feathers since they were really PO'd at us for ignoring their orders to park on the road shoulder like everyone else.

Jim Kuipers: Initially I wasn't even out there, but Captain Phil Johnson, C Company commander called me and told me to get my butt out there. "Hell, Captain," I told him, "I don't know anything about bridges." When I got there they had the approach started. All I could see was a bunch of colonels and captains and majors standing around talking about how this bridge should be built. I asked a guy from the bridge company how this should be done and then I told Captain Johnson if he would get all those officers off the approach, I'd get this thing done. We worked on that thing all night despite occasional sniper fire and a strong current.

Philip Johnson: We supposedly had infantry security but I never saw it personally.

Jim Kuipers: We had intermittent flares to illuminate the area. As the length of bridge grew out into the river we'd be driving one dump truck at a time onto the section to dump their loads of ten to twelve foot bulk for each section. As it worked out C Company built about 65% of that bridge, which is pretty good for a construction company that had never built a bridge before. That's because we had good men and we busted our asses that night. Around 0400 we came in contact with the other side of the bridge coming our way and a guy from the 65th told me, "You guys are done." It's tradition that the unit that builds the majority of the bridge doesn't have to get into the water to pin it at the end. So they had to get into the water and take their chances getting their fingers chopped off.

During the night, there were reports of VC floating down the river, hiding amongst reeds and brush, so we were constantly throwing grenades in the river. It was a pretty exciting night and I was very tired but I sure was proud of those guys for what they did that night. That's the only time I ever built that type of bridge. We had built bridges using cranes before where it took days and weeks to build but this was a new experience. And as often happens in a war we did it at night and under sniper fire. From the time the main bridge was blown until our replacement was completed was only twenty-six hours. And our bridge was only one-way but it would support a tank. The alternate route if this bridge was out was through VC-controlled territory and they sure didn't want that.

Courtesy: Philip Johnson

Philip Johnson: First traffic crossed the float bridge at 0830 on November 7th, 26 hours after the fixed bridge was blown. The entire company was committed to this project including all of the officers and NCOs, mechanics, cooks and clerks. First Sergeant Aubrey Redding conducted the M4T6 bridge training before the company left Long Binh for the site and coordinated all our requirements with battalion. SFC Jim Kuipers (maintenance sergeant) was the field first sergeant. The battalion provided excellent support and kept out of our way as long as we kept them informed of our progress. An interesting sidelight was the large number of Huey helicopters that kept flying overhead (must never have seen a float bridge under construction before) that a mobile air traffic control unit was sent in so that the aerial rubberneckers didn't hurt each other. Col. Jorden reported later that the transportation folks that used the replacement float bridge were extremely appreciative of the float bridge because it saved them a lot of miles over a VC infested detour.

Dale Gott: We had lots of holes in our vehicles but none of us was killed or wounded, although some had the devil scared out of them. When our trucks were moving on the road the VC couldn't keep up with us.

There were so damned many officers giving orders that didn't pertain to what I was doing. Somebody always wanted to be the chief honcho but I only reported to the battalion commander, Colonel Gray, a very good man.

Philip Johnson: I guess I was shot at once a week while driving down the road. They were pretty crummy shots. We had certain Rules of Engagement, and when I first arrived, I was driving around outside of Camp Bearcat with the man I was replacing, and we were shot at. The rules said you could not return fire unless you could see not only the weapon but the person who was shooting at you. He said "I knew we were going to get shot at because there was nobody on the street." Then we're shot at again. He asked me if I saw where the shot came from. I said no. He continues to drive around the village five times until he could see the person who was shooting at us, and when he did he nailed him with an M-79 grenade launcher. I wouldn't have done that but I was just a passenger.

The first Thanksgiving I was there I went down to Saigon and bought a case of wine for the guys for their Thanksgiving table. I put a bottle of wine on every table in the mess hall. One kid wrote home to his mother describing the meal, and she wrote to her congressman, complaining that I am contributing to the alcoholism of the troops. I had to answer a congressional inquiry through the ranks about the evil things I was doing!

We were tasked once to go out and build this very long culvert in the Long Binh ammo dump. As engineers, we used 24" of rain in 24 hours as a design standard. And we were building this huge culvert, 72" diameter barrels, but there were fourteen of them in a row with a headwall on each end. The Group Commander (a colonel) came out and I told him this culvert would not survive the monsoon. I told him it wouldn't last two weeks. I told him we needed to build a bridge. He said "Don't you go second-guessing my engineers up there at the Group HQ. Just charge on and build it."

Well, we built it. The real story is there were no bridge materials available. So you built what you could with what you had. I bet him a case of beer and two weeks or so after the monsoon started I went to see him and told him I wanted a case of beer. I took him out and showed him that 130 – 140 feet had been washed out by the monsoon. They just didn't understand how heavy that rainfall was. And 24" in 24 hours means nothing until you see it! The monsoon made earth moving impossible; everything turned to mud.

George Gray: The reputation of the 46th was unusually good because of the men. Handed some unusual and difficult challenges, the young men of the 46th -- boys in their late teens and early twenties -- rose to meet and conquer these challenges. Young leaders always came forward as needed and the young men responded to them with vigor. They were America's best.

Construction engineers were indirectly involved in the support of combat forces. Direct involvement (demolition, minesweeping, land clearing, etc.) were usually the job of the organic divisional engineers. Rome plows were used for land clearing; a land clearing company could clear between 100 to 150 acres a day, but over the course of a year, they would suffer about 70% casualties.

SEABEES

Utility Man 3rd Class **Tim Pfeiffer,** *MCB-7, USN*

Petty Officer 2nd Class **Vince Malaterra,** *MCB-3, USN*

Arrival/Duties

Vince Malaterra: After high school, I worked for a survey company while I contemplated college. The draft was rapidly approaching and I was advised to join the Navy, since they did a lot of construction-type work and that would keep me out of Vietnam. Of course I fell for it! Due to my experience I was able to go in as an E-4. I landed at Danang In October of 1967 on a commercial Pan Am airliner. We ran off the plane with the ground rumbling under our feet, grabbed our duffel bags, and were directed to a bunker. The airfield was receiving an attack of B40 (rocket) rounds. Welcome to Vietnam.

During my first tour we built bridges and roads between Danang and the DMZ. I was also a gunner on the 81mm mortar. Whatever we did and wherever we went, that mortar went with us. That was the first thing we set up when we got to a work site. With a full charge, the range was about a mile. It was a close support weapon. We fired quite a bit of HE (high explosive) out of that, but at night it was mostly illumination.

On the first tour we were just like a construction crew. We'd get to the site in the morning in cattle cars, and sometimes we pulled guard duty or you worked to dusk, and then they'd come and get us out of there. Many nights you'd end up pulling guard duty somewhere, so you'd end up with a twenty-hour day. The VC would come at night and blow up whatever we built and then we'd come back the next day and rebuild it. We'd also patch the roads; the mortar rounds would leave a big hole in roads. We had to keep the civilian population moving through there too.

Tim Pfeiffer: I arrived in Chu Lai by plane in July of 1968 and worked there until March, 1969. I was at Guam between tours and returned to Dong Ha in the fall of 1969. I had a variety of duties including running a water purification plant, CAP duty, security work and working at a boiler plant. I also deployed to various Fire Support bases and landing Zones, including Baldy, Stud and Vandergrift. To get enough to eat while at Dong Ha I also volunteered to work at the mess hall. On average I probably worked ten to twelve hours a day.

Vince Malaterra: After my first tour in Vietnam, I went to Guam and was working on the air base. They were gearing up for the use of B-52's. My job was to set up the coral crushing plant. They mixed crushed coral with asphalt for the runway. That's when the government found out that working with coral seemed to create all kinds of sores and eye and lung irritations from the coral dust. I returned to Vietnam for my second tour in September, 1970. We came in at Bien Hoa and from there we went to Ca Mau. Then we went to Chow Dunk.

On the second tour, we built LZ's (landing zones). We would take in our team of fourteen, and in a week we would have everything plowed under, air matting put down, fuel bunkers put in, ammo bunkers installed, generators ready to go ahead to rearm these choppers to get them back in the air. They were air dropping us all the machinery we needed to get the work done; earth compactors and things, and I'm watching them parachute this heavy equipment out of the back of a plane.

Vietnamese

Tim Pfeiffer: I worked for two months on a Civic Action Program in the Vietnamese villages.

Vince Malaterra: Some of the Vietnamese we were in contact with were *Chieu Hoi's* and they really made me nervous. And we were around a lot of civilians. Every place we went there were little villages. Some seemed friendly to us and sometimes not. We used the Vietnamese to fill sandbags, burn the shitters and things like that.

On my second tour riverboats would bring in loads of gravel and it would have to be unloaded by hand. The Vietnamese would carry a basket of gravel on their heads. There might be twenty or thirty people carrying the gravel.

Guys would come to Bien Hoa for steam baths and other things but outside Bien Hoa it was very remote. We had to drive through some unfriendly villages to get to a job site. It was the first time I saw a guy's head up on a pole. Scared me to death.

The damn ARVN soldiers were just a pain in the ass. In many cases they had better equipment than we had. Once I saw they had brand-new deuce-and-a-half trucks.

Adventures

Tim Pfeiffer: I was mortared, rocketed and received "friendly fire" from the Army in Quang Tri. While stationed in Chu Lai (1969 – 1970) the Seabee base camp was next to the P.O.L. storage facility (fuel farm). We'd occasionally receive incoming rocket fire from the mountains but due to poor marksmanship from the enemy the safest place to be was in the fuel farm. The VC would hit everything but what they were aiming for.

I had some adventures while running daylight sweeps with the marines while attached to the security detail. I also had confrontations with rock apes and water buffalo. The monsoon was a problem; I still suffer from fungal infection on my foot. I lost my best friend (John Van Dusen) in a bunker explosion.

Vince Malaterra: We had so many mortar and rocket attacks, after a while you didn't have to wait for the siren. You could just smell the arrival of the rounds. When the nearby villages were completely dark and you didn't even hear the dogs barking, you knew it was coming.

We were sitting around somewhere and we had a bunch of body bags near us waiting to be transported to Saigon. Suddenly, we noticed movement in two of the bags. Rats had gotten in there at some point.

The government can be so wasteful. Sometimes the machinery and tools that were parachuted to us would be damaged and we would just blow it up so the VC couldn't use it.

I lost some friends on my second tour, and my life changed, and I decided not to get close to anybody after that. Those feelings took a long time to go away, but it's getting better.

During the busy years of 1968 and 1969 alone, the following structures were built in South Vietnam:

Schools	1253	Churches	263
Hospitals	175	Dispensaries	422
Marketplaces	153	Bridges	598
Roads (km)	3154	Dwellings	7099

South Vietnam had existed for centuries, but in terms of how things looked when we left we might say: Built by the USA. We certainly left a better country than we found.

ENGINEER SUPPORT PERSONNEL

Dave Cass

Jim Kuipers

Ed Hanke

George Gray

Frank Jackmauh

CHAPTER FOUR

MEDICAL SUPPORT

BACKGROUND

Military planning for the next war is usually based on learning from the last war, however different those experiences may have been. Data from Korea and the China-Burma-India and Southwest Pacific theaters in World War II helped planners anticipate the needs for Vietnam.

Prior to our buildup in Vietnam the nearest U.S. hospital to the Vietnam War Zone was Clark Air Force Base, in the Philippine Islands – 1,000 miles away.[xxxiv] Initial medical requirements for American personnel in South Vietnam called for one 100-bed hospital and one ambulance detachment. The hospital became operational in April, 1962.[xxxv]

One of the early concerns prior to insertion of our ground troops was the Vietnam environment; there were fears that indigenous diseases would cripple our troops.[xxxvi] Vietnam's high temperatures, humidity, monsoon climate and dust-rain cycle were expected to create lots of problems.[xxxvii] As it happened, the biggest obstacle faced by the medical support group was administrative -- the decision to place medical units under larger military commands; this caused major problems in the medical supply system.[xxxviii]

PREVENTION

During war the three primary causes of hospital admissions come from (1) Disease, (2) Battle Injury, and (3) Non-Battle Injury. While injuries - both battle and non-battle -- can be reduced somewhat by the exercise of caution (wearing helmets and flak jackets, safe operation of machinery, etc.), disease is both the biggest problem and the most preventable. Between 1965 and 1969, disease accounted for 69% of hospital admissions in Vietnam (battle injuries were only about 17%),[xxxix] but this figure is only one-third that of WW II and 40% less than the Korean War.[xl]

Among the diseases met in Vietnam, malaria was the most difficult. Combat and support troop alike swallowed pills to help prevent the disease and/or lower the relapse rate.[xli] Once contracted, aggressive treatment regimens greatly reduced the number of days lost.[xlii] Malaria was found to follow both cyclical (weather-related) and geographic patterns.[xliii] Over 80% of malaria occurred in combat units.[xliv]

Infectious hepatitis, often caused by unsanitary field and mess conditions or use of bad water[xlv] occurred at lower rates in Vietnam than either WW II or Korea,[xlvi] and was often connected with the level of interaction with the civilian population.[xlvii] Rest and avoiding the sources of contamination were the cure.

Diarrheal diseases were found to be only a fraction of that seen in previous wars and hospitalization for these problems declined steadily throughout the war. The average hospital stay was 5.5 days.[xlviii]

Skin diseases such as fungus and foot immersion were more common to units operating in flooded areas such as the Delta. Some antibiotics proved to be effective but staying out of the water was the best cure.

Psychiatric problems increased in 1969 and 1970 despite our reduction in combat activity.[xlix] This increase, however, simply mirrored conditions back in the U.S.

Overall disease prevention and treatment programs showed better results than in previous wars. A six-week acclimatization period was effective against high incidence, short-duration diseases but, as in many other areas, our twelve-month rotation policy worked against us.[l]

DOCTORS

1st Lieutenant **Robert Knuff**, Flight Surgeon, 1st Marine Aircraft Wing, Danang & Chu Lai, USN

Captain **Bill Richardson**, Flight Surgeon, Phan Rang AFB, USAF

1st Lieutenant **Lewis Moss**, Flight Surgeon, Marine Aircraft Group 16, 1st MAW, Danang, USN

Flight surgeons are responsible for the mental and physical health of flight crews and their support personnel.[li] They may also participate in flight operations and serve on aircraft investigative teams. The most common challenge facing the flight surgeons – who never numbered over one hundred at any time during the Vietnam War – was detecting flyer fatigue among the pilots. Pilots flew 100 – 150 hours per month[lii] and were routinely exposed to a myriad of stresses, particularly during the period 1967 – 1968. A study in 1968 noted that 70% of aircraft accidents traced to pilot error, and pilot fatigue was at least a contributing factor in many of those instances.[liii] Flight surgeons also conducted clinics in the villages. The recommendation to reduce flying hours was never acted upon.

Until early 1968 aircraft accidents caused more injury and death than enemy fire.[liv]

Training

Robert Knuff: I took the Senior Program to cover my expenses in medical school, which meant I owed the military four years after graduation. I went into the Navy as a Flight Surgeon.

Bill Richardson: I had just completed my Internal Medicine Internship and I had to take the Jungle Survival School to get on flying status for Vietnam. This school was held at Clark Air Force Base, in the Philippines. The first thing I learned was that if you weren't rescued within twenty-four hours you were NOT going to be rescued. The thinking was: Don't hoard your food or water; carry it in your stomach. You needed to be alert. We were told that the jet fighter had the glide ratio of a brick!

The pilot's yellow ejection lever would eject him and the co-pilot in the rear seat. The ejection pulled 14 G's, at which time you would hit the sub-freezing atmosphere at 500 knots. If you were lucky you would miss the canopy, wingtip or the exhaust jet. Then you had to disengage yourself from your lap belt and double shoulder harness, which took a crew chief's help to get into. Wearing the bulky flight suit and heavy leather gloves, this would not be easy. As you plummeted to around 3,000 feet, your parachute should deploy.

It was recommended that you bail out over water. Our navy owned the water. This was called feet wet. Water is no more compressible than cement so knees-together-toes-pointed-down was the drill. The VC owned feet dry. In the feet dry scenario, you keep your legs together and ankles crossed if you were heading for trees. If you landed in a field you bend your knees and roll to knee, hip, shoulder and back, hit the parachute disengagement panel, gather the chute and run for the cover of the jungle. After Day One in the classroom, we bussed to the jungle part of the exercise, ominously over the same road taken by the Bataan Death March.

Wearing flight suits and adorned with canteens, knives, flashlights, water purification tablets and other junk we were ready for the jungle, which appeared as soon as we left the base. Lush, thick green trees and bushes grew right up to the road. The road was narrow and winding and we saw signs saying "Mile 25 of the Bataan Death March". Reaching the top of the last mountain we had an unobstructed view of Subic Bay; twenty-five warships of all sizes sitting majestically at anchor. We de-bussed and formed in groups of eight to ten led by an NCO instructor and a Negrito guide. The Negritos were the "jungle people"; as a tribe they had not integrated with the Polynesian/Spanish main culture.

We walked and we walked until we could officially consider ourselves "lost". We now had to become survivors. Finding water and using our water purification tablets was our first priority. We then learned how to set a trap to capture a monkey. Signaling with metal mirrors, using camouflage, and hiding from the enemy were other things we practiced under the watchful eyes of our instructors. By the way, you're harder to find if you hide up a tree rather than staying at ground level. We practiced evading and hiding. I was found in two and a half minutes. So much for my 24-hour window of possible survival if this was the real thing.

We were then given a piece of a parachute and some mosquito netting and told to set up a hammock to sleep in that night. You had to be at least a foot off the ground to avoid the creepy crawlies. I'm glad I did this because that night I heard all kinds of funny noises around me and all sorts of shiny eyes scurrying around my campsite. I decided very early that night that I would pee in my pants rather than get up to take a leak if the situation arose. In the morning you were warned to shake out your boots because the creepy crawlies found these a comfortable place to set up housekeeping.

Now back to the monkey trap. We did catch a monkey. We killed him, put him on the fire to burn off his hair and then skinned and gutted him. This doesn't sound pleasant when you write about it, but it seemed perfectly appropriate at the time. We then roasted the monkey and boiled our rice. We had an absolutely delicious picnic dinner topped off with chlorine tasting water. You can't beat hunger to improve the taste of food.

After dinner we hung the remains of the monkey from a tree branch. Nightlife isn't too exciting in the jungle so we went back to our hammocks early to catch up on our beauty sleep. Much to our dismay, our nannies left us for the night. The next morning they reappeared and we could become tough guys once again. The remains of the monkey were taken down from the tree branch. It was covered with flies and other assorted insects. We threw it back on the fire, roasted off the bad stuff and ate a hardy breakfast. Again, hunger trumps squeamishness.

In the early afternoon we learned how to call in rescue helicopters. Remember this event occurred sometime between smoke signals and the development of GPS's and cell phones. We first attracted the attention of the rescue planes with mirrors. With a short range line-of-sight walkie-talkie we talked to the plane. We established our authenticity by answering a series of questions and answers which we had left behind just like the passwords on computers today. After all, the VC was smart enough to flash mirrors into the sky too. The helicopters were then allowed in. We guided them right over us. In a real rescue situation time would be critical. Then they lowered rescue harnesses and we learned how to put them on. We were then officially saved!

Arrival/Duties

Robert Knuff: On our flight to Danang, we stopped at Pearl Harbor; we were in our green fatigues and the civilians had their brightly colored tourist shirts on. There was fun to be had there but we were under orders. My brother was in-country with the Montagnards when I arrived in Vietnam so he had to leave due to the Sullivan law about two brothers serving in the same combat zone.

Our day was pretty lax. We had enough staff to deal with our clinic, although the clinic was on call 24/7. At Phu Bai, we just had a staff of three flight surgeons. At Danang we had four, plus a chief. We had time off during which we flew when we had the chance or went on MEDCAPS.

Lewis Moss: We did physicals, and we did testing on the Vietnamese women for venereal diseases. And we also had a lot of free time.

Bill Richardson: Fully trained I reached Vietnam October, 1967, and I was surprised upon arrival to see mostly mama sans working at the airport. Where were the men?

We had a general medical office at Phan Rang AFB. We received very few casualties. We mostly handled outpatient stuff at our clinic. We were overstaffed in anticipation of casualties, so our workload was not heavy. We also did an outreach clinic for the nearby Vietnamese village. We had Vietnamese people working on the base. They seemed nice enough but the language was a barrier. The worst thing they did to us was steal our silverware. The older mamasans did this.

Clinics

Robert Knuff: I spent the first half of my tour at Phu Bai, running a clinic and flying heavy duty helicopters. We also did some clinic work in the nearby Vietnamese villages. When we'd go, Kitty, our Vietnamese assistant, would be there to tell us what was wrong with each person, and we'd listen to their lungs and things, and administer antibiotics. We learned to say "take one four times a day" in Vietnamese! When we were finishing a dozen or two young men would come forward. They would be looking very malnourished. They would have injuries, wounds, infections, often foot infections. Foot infections were our main problem. Eighty per cent of the non-critical medical problems we saw were foot related. And some of the necessary medication would run out. We knew these young men were different than the villagers because the picnic atmosphere and all sound would stop. We would treat them but we knew who they were. The villagers would be surprised that we took care of the VC but we would say, "Why wouldn't we? They are your children, aren't they?" "Yes," they would answer. "They take them away." "Well, we'll still take care of them. We don't like what they're doing but we'll take care of them."

One of my nominations for hero would be the Civic Action Program guys; the greatest, greatest guys. I went to one MEDCAP unit out of Danang, and I looked at them and said, "You guys are all black." These guys lived out there with the Vietnamese people 24/7, and it was a dangerous place to be. "Why do you do it?" I asked. "During the day we take care of them," he responded, "and during the night, they take care of us." "But why do you do it?" I asked. "Because if you were black, you'd know why," he answered. He just pointed to the main base and said "Whitey is really hard to get around, especially some people from the south." I said "you're kidding me. It's still like that?" "Oh yes," he responded. I told him they were my heroes. "You're doing more good just showing what's right about the United States than all the rest of us back in that base are."

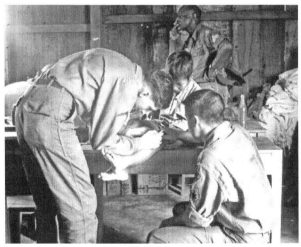

MedCaps
Courtesy: Harley Brinkley

Lewis Moss: We did a clinic at the base. The dentist at Danang showed me how to extract teeth. So when I went out to the villages I would do dental extractions along with our other medical services. I am proud of my service in Vietnam. I am also proud of the work we did in the villages.

We actually won the highest non-combat related medal from the Vietnamese government. The Vietnamese nurse Kitty was wonderful. A lot of the support people were great too.

Bill Richardson: Tet meant things changed. We cancelled our outreach clinic to the Vietnamese village. There was no more R & R.

Flying

Robert Knuff*:* I went to Phu Bai initially, then when my squadron (MAG-11) rotated back to Okinawa, since I had not been in-country that long they sent me down to MAG-36, at Danang. When I first got there I told them I wanted to fly. They told me the guy I was replacing was flying rear seat in the OV-10, and his pilot was shot in the head. He's sitting in the back seat, and he can't see anything because of the brains all over the cockpit and his wingman was able to talk him down, but the guy climbed out of the cockpit in the middle of the runway, covered in his pilot's blood and brains, and started taking off his flight suit, saying "I'm leaving." He did.

At Danang I flew OV-10's, a propeller-driven two-seater plane that carried a massive amount of ordnance. In the OV-10 we used to take out two planes, flying one high and one low. The Flight Surgeon was always in the lower airplane. I asked why the Flight Surgeon always had to go in the lower airplane since that was the one they shot at. They told me it was because they figured we didn't know enough about shooting the guns, so we would be used to draw the fire.

At Phu Bai, we were flying along the coast in our helicopter, and we were hit with some sort of thick weather thing and forced down. Our pilot landed and each one of us stood guard at one corner of the chopper. I was glad I had a .45 instead of a smaller caliber handgun. As it turns out he landed in a very safe place. Just after we landed we see a large group of black-pajamas guys coming our way. They start yelling "American," and we realized we were right near the ARVN compound. We were only two hundred yards from their compound but couldn't see it from the air. This was the scariest thing that happened to me.

Bill Richardson: You were probably being shot at a lot when you flew in the back seat of a jet plane but you didn't know it.

Lewis Moss: I was a Flight Surgeon, but due to a mishap in training (my flight instructor forgot to lower the landing gear; we had a fire in the cockpit that may have distracted him), I never flew solo.

Adventures

Robert Knuff: Just before the Tet 1969, a man who became my hero emerged. Several of us got a message to report to the commanding officer. There were several high-ranking Marine officers in the room when we entered. We were not introduced. The leader told us that we were there to witness something: At 0830 hours, we are going to lose contact with Washington D.C., we were told, and we will be out of communication with them for twenty-four hours. He went on to say that there was an arms and ammunition cache over three miles long sitting right over there in Laos, on the Ho Chi Minh Trail, that we weren't allowed to touch. Well, we're going to bomb that arms cache. The leader said "I'll be damned if they're going to kill my boys this year." He said "My career is over gentlemen, and in twenty minutes we'll start the bombing." It just ripped my heart out when he said that. And the American press deplored his actions, saying "The Americans bombed a neutral country." The leader made it clear that this was his decision and the rest of the chain of command in-country were not involved in it. He would take the blame. And his career was over.

We had rockets every night at Danang. We were occasionally walking around the edge of the Danang base, in sight of Dogpatch, and we'd hear ping, ping. We knew it was sniper fire. None of us were ever hit by this fire. Somebody would say, "Relax, it's not your bullet."

We decided to go swimming at Marble Mountain after the rain stopped. The monsoon had washed up a lot of sea snakes onto the beach. We must have pulled a hundred of these things back into the South China Sea.

The Vietnamese were telling us they were dangerous and would kill us. They had tiny little mouths so we figured they wouldn't be able to eat us.

The mayor of one of the villages we did the most with (it was his wife that questioned why we were treating the VC) came over to us with a bottle of Tiger beer, not ten or twelve ounce, but a big bottle, and he wanted to thank us, he said, because we would be leaving shortly. We told him we weren't going to leave him but he said "your papers don't like us. You're going to leave us within a year." We denied we would leave but he told us we had no choice, because "the people in your country are against us. When that movie star sat on the tanks up in Hanoi we knew everything was over." He thanked us for "helping them put in the well." He recognized that we didn't do it for them, but we got them the supplies to do it themselves. He remembered that we showed them how to build a bridge in an area where they always had to use boats. He told us his village had never been so proud! I asked him if he would be okay when the communists came back. He told me yes, "but Kittysan die." Anybody that helped us would have to die and the rest would be re-educated. They needed the farmers, but first they would have to re-educate them. He figured the communists would give them enough rice to survive and they would confiscate the rest. He said that while we were there it was the first time in his life that they had a little money left over to buy those things that they needed. He said he wanted to thank us before we went home and heard all the bad things from Americans back home.

Kittysan was irreplaceable to us. Here we were in the middle of a war zone and every village had a one-room schoolhouse. The kids had their uniforms; perfectly clean uniforms on each child, blue uniforms with white blouses or skirts for the girls and shorts for the boys. There were different levels of instruction; one group would be speaking in Vietnamese, one in English, and one in French. A rural schoolhouse in the middle of a war and they're learning three languages!

Bill Richardson: I felt perfectly safe at our base. We had no trouble for the first six months of my tour, but then they lobbed some mortar rounds into the base. After it stopped the commander came on the radio and assured us it was over and no one had been hurt. "The rounds fell about 100 yards short of the runway," he told us. A few minutes later two rounds came in and cratered the runway. The Viet Cong were monitoring the radio.

Lewis Moss: I was never much into guns. Some of the guys told me they would show me how to shoot "the right way." We went out to a rice paddy and they asked me to hit a particular plant in the paddy. I couldn't even hit the water!

We had flown down to Chu Lai and I was with several of my fellow officers. We were kibitzing and having a few drinks and one of the guys had a tank of laughing gas. So we're telling all these gory stories, and we're passing the tank around, and everyone is taking a couple of inhales, and a rocket attack starts. We laughed our way through it!

One frustrating thing is just being on the Marine Corps side of Danang. On the Air Force side you have paved walkways, air conditioning, but on the Marine side, there was no pavement, just dirt, mud, air conditioning that only worked some of the time, and metal hooches that leaked. But we were Marines. And even at the officers club the amenities stopped at mosquito netting. There was air conditioning on the Air Force side.

Another frustrating thing is the knowledge of how many guys were doing drugs. It was amazing how much heroin and speed was being used before guys went out on flights. A lot of the grunts did drugs. Speed and heroin were really popular then. All I did was smoke two packs a day, which I guess is bad enough.

The irony of the Vietnam experience is that it might be better off now, in spite of our effort, than it was before we got there. A Vietnamese pharmacist that I patronize occasionally now said that he thinks Vietnam is not communist; "more capitalist with a socialist flair!"

After their quick and often courageous rescue from the battlefield, and their prepping by the nurses, the wounded servicemen were in the expert hands of the surgeons – often aided by equipment as advanced as that found in any stateside hospital – who routinely performed complex surgeries. The World War II hospital mortality rate was 4.5%, Korea 2.5%

and Vietnam 2.6%. The rapid retrieval of casualties in Vietnam meant some mortally wounded men reached hospitals alive whereas they would have been KIA in earlier wars.[lv] A better comparison is the ratio of deaths to deaths plus surviving wounded (or "deaths as a percent of hits"); in World War II the ratio was 1:3.1, in Korea 1:4.1 and in Vietnam 1:5.6.[lvi] This ratio of KIA to WIA is also sometimes used to estimate total enemy casualties based on known dead.

There were not enough dentists in Vietnam[lvii] but the Dental Effectiveness Program, a 20% increase in dental officer strength[lviii] and the introduction of a stannous fluoride phosphate paste improved conditions by 1968. Oral surgeons were available for the first time in our military history.[lix]

TECHNICIANS

Spec4 **Don Classen**, Psych Tech, 67th Evac. Hospital, Qui Nhon, USA

Sgt. **Floyd Jones**, Medical Admin. Specialist, 100th Medical Air Evacuation Sqdn., USAF

SSgt **Bill Roy**, Environmental/Occupational Medicine, 14th Combat Support Group, USAF

Spc4 **Clem Blazewick**, Medical Lab Technician, 93rd Evac. Hospital, Long Binh, USA

Arrival/Duties

Clem Blazewick: We flew out of San Francisco on Christmas Day, 1965. We had to make an emergency landing on Wake Island (2.38 square miles). We spent the night there playing ping pong; the Filipino in charge made us put a $20 deposit on the ball since they sometimes lost balls in the ocean. We landed at Tan Son Nhut on the 29th and a few days later a sergeant woke me and told me to be at the helo pad at 0500 to go to a Marine base near Quang Tri. I told him I wasn't a Marine but he just told me to be there. At 0430 an army clerk woke me and told me to stay put. Lucky me!

I was assigned as a Medical Laboratory Technician at the 93rd Evacuation Hospital in Long Binh, about nineteen miles north of Saigon. As a lab tech my duties were to draw blood, perform hematology, immunohematology, chemistries, urinalysis and bacteriology on wounded troops. Sometimes it was necessary to assist the pathologist with autopsies, which were necessary to determine if foul play was involved in the serviceman's death. We also did guard and latrine duty.

93rd Evac. Hospital, Long Binh
Courtesy: Clem Blazewick

We didn't pay attention to the time of day or the hours worked in the lab. We were too busy. If there were casualties – I can't recall a day without them – or other demanding tests to be done one or more of the lab techs had to be there. Our work load may have averaged thirty to thirty-six hours out of a forty-eight hour period, especially during the first months of 1966. We were also on call during our off hours.

Bill Roy: I worked at both Pleiku and Nha Trang during 1968 and 1969. My job was environmental and occupational medicine. I would inspect work sites to ensure compliance with health and safety regulations. I was doing most of the things that OSHA does now. For example, I found welders not wearing proper safety attire, or people sawing through asbestos during hooch construction, and I would see that things were fixed; among the things that came under my wing was giving the new arrivals a VD bracelet and conducting a lecture on the types of venereal diseases they could contract in Vietnam.

Don Classen: After basic I went to Chicago for food inspector training. By mid-1965, Vietnam was starting to break open. Somehow the military had found out that I had worked at a state hospital for the mentally retarded back in California. They actually changed my MOS (job description) to a medic, a psych tech. I transitioned into that, and a friend who was in charge of procurement of people to fill Army needs told me one night that he was getting a lot of calls for my MOS for Vietnam. He said he figured he could protect me for a month or so, but eventually they would get me. I told him not to bother to protect me. If they needed me, I would go.

I went home on leave around Christmas, 1965, and reported back to Fort Carson, CO for jungle training. In January! We were doing night field problems in the snow up to our ___. And I never actually received any medical training in the military. I was on the ship with the 67th Evacuation Hospital unit but when I arrived at Qui Nhon I was told to report to the 1st Sergeant at the 42nd Evacuation Hospital unit, which was already there. I reported and was told that they had no need for my job description, they already had too many people, and to report back to the 67th.

One interesting thing about the cruise across the ocean; there were guys who originally boarded the ship back in the U.S. with only thirty days left on their hitches. So, after the 16-day cruise, they only had two weeks left to do in the Army! There was such a gigantic buildup going on, they wanted everybody I guess. So some of the guys that just arrived they started processing to go back! I had eight months to do and one of the sergeants I worked for told me about the early out for school program so I only spent six months there. Anyway, when I reported back to the 67th the 1st Sergeant decided to use me as his driver.

I never did work as a psych tech in Vietnam. In fact, I did nothing in the medical field at all. Nor did I work as a food inspector, for which I had been trained. I picked things up and dropped things off for the 1st Sergeant; it was a very casual job.

After the war started to wind down there was an increase in psychiatric problems.[ix]

Floyd Jones: My military classification was "medical administrative specialist." Our squadron had two work shifts, 1) The Administration Section would communicate to our office the specific needs, diagnoses and number of patients scheduled to be moved. We alerted our sister units at Clark AFB, Philippines. They would configure the C-141 aircraft to fit the needs of our patients. We would visit the hospital ward of outgoing patients and brief them about their departure. 2) Medical Staff placed patients in a pre-planned section of the "am-busses". Many carried IV bags or had other special needs. They had to be firmly in place to ensure nothing moved or came loose on the flight. The aircraft held four medics and one nurse. The transfer process took three or four hours of manual lifting, twisting and bending to ensure stabilized positioning.

It was the responsibility of the Admin Section to inform the wounded servicemen what would transpire the day they departed Vietnam. The task was more like "overtime" as it was performed at the hospital after dinner, usually around 8pm. Most of the guys felt it was a pain in the rear but I was touched by the response of the wounded so I volunteered for the job every night once I started working the day shift. The departing wounded were housed in a special ward prior to departure. I would enter the ward with a large megaphone (battery operated) and give the following speech: "Ladies and gentlemen, I'm Sgt. Jones from the 100th Aeromedical Evacuation Squadron here at Ton Son Nhut AB. Tomorrow morning at approximately 0600 you will be loaded on ambuses and transported to the flight line where our team will load you onto a C-141 aircraft for your journey to your assigned treatment facilities in the U.S., the Philippines and Japan." It never failed I would always be interrupted by applause and cheering. The joy, happiness and tears would rise up on so many faces as I looked across the ward. I would conclude by saying "this aircraft travels at altitudes of 32,000 feet and speeds of 400+ miles per hour so rest assured you are getting to your destination quickly. It is staffed with the best medical supplies, doctors, nurses and technicians to ensure each and every one of you receives the best medical treatment available. I will be walking down the aisles to answer any questions you may have in regards to your journey and what can and cannot be carried on the aircraft. Thank you!" I then walked the aisles giving instructions and chatting about home. One soldier touched me more than any. I approached his bed and he had just finished opening a present. It was in April of 1969. I asked him if it was a birthday present, and he said, "No sir, it's a Christmas present that's just caught up with me!" Lying on his stomach were tee shirts, socks and underwear. He looked up at me and said, "Sarge, would you like some socks? I only have one leg now so I'll only need one of each color!" I had to hold back the tears but jokingly told him, "Look at it this way. You know how easy it is to lose a sock? Just think how lucky you are to have "spares" when that happens! You have twice as many as the rest of us for the same price!" He quickly responded saying I was right and that he had to start thinking differently about shoes and socks. This young man was an example of the character I witnessed while meeting with these men and women. We truly have the best fighting soldiers and support troops in the world.

All out-of-country evacuations were handled by the U.S. Air Force[lxi] and reached 36,000 by 1969. The decision to evacuate was predicated on the length of time the patient would be hospitalized. If a patient could return to duty within thirty days he was usually hospitalized in Vietnam.[lxii]

Floyd Jones: Our primary role was simple: Move our wounded troops from primary in-country treatment facilities to the best American military hospitals around the globe that best fit their treatment needs. The most popular destinations were Brooks Army Hospital in Texas, for burns, and Walter Reed Army Hospital in Washington, D.C., for surgery. If no military hospital had the facilities or staff to treat wounded heroes they were then sent to civilian institutions. This was rare as nearly all injuries and diagnoses were treatable through the military system.

During my tenure, Aug68 to Aug69, over 17,500 wounded GI's were moved through my unit. Of course many recuperated and returned to the field. Every day was satisfying and sad. It was satisfying to see the troops happy about going home, but sad to see their many injuries, particularly amputations or gunshot wounds.

Adventures

Bill Roy: We picked up frequent mortar fire from VC in caves in the mountainous area around Nha Trang. There was talk of bringing in the battleship *Missouri* to shell the caves. I guess the assumption was that the trajectory of naval gunfire would be more effective than bombs or artillery. I argued that the risk of short rounds was too great. They decided to bring in Korean troops, who got the job done the old-fashioned way—boots on the ground. When they finished, they showed us all the neat stuff they dragged out of the caves.

Clem Blazewick: As a teenager I was always squeamish visiting hospitals, often leading to fainting. When the Army drafted me in June 1965 I fainted when my blood was drawn. Ironically, I was trained as a medic and a medical lab technician. I was responsible for drawing blood each and every day throughout my military career.

I saw many soldiers with serious injuries. Pints of fresh blood expired in fourteen days; if a supply didn't arrive and we had heavy casualties it became necessary for lab technicians, nurses or doctors to donate their blood, which I did four times during my tour. The war was escalating in 1966; we cross-matched 661 units of blood in January but averaged 856 units per month thru May.

Floyd Jones: Nothing made me prouder of my country than the night an Australian flare dropper called in an emergency. These flares were very powerful -- one million candles. One of their flares had jammed in the launch cradle. With no regard for his personal safety, the Australian airman physically grabbed the flare and dislodged it, freeing it from his aircraft in a matter of seconds and saving the lives of his crew members. He had 3rd degree burns over 50% of his body. His pilot landed at the closest medical facility, who notified us of his emergency. We called Clark

AFB in the Philippines and within two hours a C-141 was dispatched to Saigon to pick him up and transport him to Brook Army Burn Center in Texas. Within twenty hours the Australian hero was being treated by the best burn unit in the world. Sadly, he passed nine hours after arriving but the crews transporting and caring for him during those twenty hours did the impossible keeping him alive. His burns were so severe he could not have survived had he been injured in the immediate area of Brook Burn Center. My pride still swells today knowing that the United States of America would dispatch a single C-141 aircraft configured for "one patient", and, more importantly, a wounded soldier from another country. No expense was spared to ensure that we make the best effort possible to save a life. The USA takes care of its own and its friends. I am proud to be from a country with this philosophy.

Don Classen: We never had any sniper fire. There were occasional rumors of impending mortar attacks, but we were never issued our rifles. I paid a guy a nominal fee each month to clean my rifle but I never actually had a weapon. We did have bunkers to go to in the event of attack, but we never did get hit while I was there.

In my first days there, we used to sun ourselves outside the tents. We would find this black stuff flying through the air; it was like a black snow or soot. For the life of us we couldn't figure out what it was. We finally realized that this black snow was coming from a burner behind the medical dispensary. When guys had wounds that required amputation, they were burning the limbs and causing this black snow! I think somebody wrote their congressman and this practice was stopped. It had probably gone on for a month, and the aroma in the air was terrible.

Clem Blazewick: Relationships were often established with patients through discussions about home, family, military life, etc. Sometimes the soldier did not survive the injuries. It was not easy to accept that they were no longer alive. There was one soldier from Colorado that I will never forget. He was med evacuated to our hospital with one arm completely gone and the other arm missing from the elbow down. He was missing both legs below the knees and had shrapnel throughout his body. There wasn't much left of him! After 66 pints of blood and his will to live he left the hospital alive. I often wonder about him. I have checked the Vietnam Memorial Wall website and his name is not there. I thank God and feel he must have survived his injuries.

THE BATTLEFIELD

Unlike previous wartime experience our hospitals did not follow the advancing army.[lxiii] Due to the enclave nature of the war, our armies did not advance. But getting the battle casualty into the capable hands of a physician is the keystone of combat medicine; the two-step process involved retrieving the casualty from the battlefield, almost always under fire, and then air-lifting the casualty to a medical facility, again usually under fire. And despite the inherent danger in braving enemy fire to rescue a wounded soldier and fly him to the hospital our combat troops expected nothing less. Nor should they.

Once the casualty was removed from the battle field he was taken to a landing zone. In the early stages of the war returning cargo aircraft were used for evacuation.[lxiv] By 1968 116 air ambulances (helicopters) were in use.[lxv] Six to nine patients could be transported and each of these helicopters had medical personnel to evaluate the patient and provide the hospital with his condition over a dedicated radio network.

Jungle operations sometimes required the use of a hoist if a landing zone did not exist. The helicopter was a great target for the enemy as it hovered for several minutes while deploying a seat or litter but 1,735 casualties were retrieved in 1968 and 2,516 in 1969; men who otherwise could not have been rescued.[lxvi] Hoist operations included, the number of patients (including Free World and Vietnamese) needing aeromedical evacuation rose from 13, 004 in 1965 to 67,910 in 1966 and peaked at 206,229 in 1969.[lxvii]

MEDICS

Hospital man First Class **Alexander Phillips**, *USS Cleveland*, LPD-7, USN

Hospital man Chief **Al Kotrola**, *USS Joseph Strauss* DDG-16, USN

Airman Second Class **Pat Griffin**, Medic, 3rd Tactical Dispensary, USAF

Hospital man Third Class **Scott Squires**, 2nd LAM Bn, 1st Marine Air Wing, USN

The steps that produced excellent medical care in Vietnam were (1) Rapid evacuation of the wounded (2) Readily available whole blood, (3) Nearness to hospitals, (4) Advanced surgical techniques and (5) Improved medical management.[lxviii] The process began on the battlefield, where courageous medics initiated the life-saving steps by moving the casualty to a safe place to treat the wounds and begin the evacuation process.

Training/Duties

Al "Chief" Kotrola: I came from medical admin school and worked as a lab tech. The only experience I had in suturing was on a corpse in lab school and I never had any hands-on experience with emergency room work. I had been a lab tech on my first ship, an APA, and I only got to assist at one appendectomy, and then only because I asked to scrub in. The surgeon that we had on board had two blood donors on standby during all surgeries and I was standing by in case blood needed to be drawn. I wondered why blood would be needed just for an appendectomy but then I was watching a surgery through a porthole and I saw a stream of blood shooting up about three feet. Then I understood.

When I was in Portsmouth at the Naval Hospital I went up to the ER one time I asked them to call me the next time they did any suturing and they said "we'll show you how it's done." I watched how they did it and after that I was qualified to do sutures. I boarded the *Joseph Strauss* in May of 1964 and I left the ship in April of 1967. I asked them to put me on a ship where I could observe and learn some procedures but they told me I was needed on the *Strauss* so, for the first six months aboard the destroyer I wore out the medical manuals. Just to be prepared I showed my assistant on the *Strauss* how to suture and he and I ended up doing a lot of suturing. I usually had an E-3 working with me, and for a while a machinist's mate was helping me in Sick bay.

Pat Griffin: Unlike the other services Air Force medics did not deal with casualties on the battlefield. I helped run the VD clinic at Bien Hoa (lots of gonorrhea). It was boring. When we got to Bien Hoa, they weren't even expecting us. There wasn't any room at the medic's quarters so they said you're going to stay in the navy area for a couple of days. We went there and after two days I realized that I hadn't seen any sailors. I asked about this and was told it was called the navy area because, when it rained, this was the first area to go under water. It was just a transit area; flyers that came in at 2:00 am and would leave at 6:00. It was nasty; people would leave food lying around, it was crawling with rats; it was a terrible place. When I went back up to the medic's quarters there was not much to do. I'd take my turn running the VD clinic, sit in this Quonset hut, and every morning there'd be a big line of GI's with a sad look on their face. Every one of them almost to the last man had gonorrhea. We'd fill out the lab work; it was boring as hell, and of course none of them said they did anything. But gonorrhea doesn't come from toilet seats! Officers didn't catch gonorrhea, although we sometimes dealt with their Unspecified Skin Conditions in some of the back area tents.

We worked ten to sixteen hours a day/6 ½ days a week at Cam Ranh Bay. They tried to get you off Sunday afternoon, but not everyone could be off Sunday since we were running a hospital and didn't have a Closed time. Bien Hoa was overstaffed and you might get eight to ten hours a day. Cam Ranh was go-go . The combat casualties we had there were pretty much on the mend. When the hospital was up and running, on my second time there, it was a 400-bed hospital which had slowly evolved from being in tents, to Quonset huts, and air conditioned surgery, then air conditioned surgical wards, then the psychiatric wards, then the medical wards, then it was all Quonset huts. However, I was gone by the time it was finished. When I was there some of it was still tents. We always had more malaria patients than anything else. Our combat injuries were mostly on the mend. We always had a full psychiatric ward too. We had one psychiatrist who wasn't worth a damn, Dr. Gill, and all he tried to do was keep people sleeping until he was ready to leave. He just knocked them all out with Thorazine. Later we had a psychiatrist who came in and started setting up programs and getting things turned around. It was a full scale hospital. Everything you have here we had there, guys with the flu, a lot of dysentery, strange tropical diseases, an occasional case of local people with cholera.

Scott Squires: Training for corpsmen was a six-month program; the other services didn't have anything that comprehensive. I think Army medics went for four weeks or something like that. I joined the navy not as a Seaman Recruit like most guys, but as a Hospital Man Recruit. When I first arrived at Chu Lai there was a veteran corpsman there that had seen action in Korea. He was with Charley Med in Korea and the Chinese overran their unit. This guy sprawled on a stretcher, atop a dead guy, and pretended to be dead himself. The Chinese bayoneted him repeatedly, but he stayed still and survived. He left the service after Korea and they called him back for Vietnam. He was the unhappiest person I had ever seen! Another corpsman had once been kicked out of the navy for stealing an X-ray machine and they called him back because they were so short of corpsmen.

I was the junior corpsman in our battalion so I got every job that nobody wanted or that they thought was dangerous. There is no time clock on sickness or injury so you were on call always. There were many days I would come back to my bunk and collapse with my boots on, and then I'd wake up in exactly the same position four or five hours later when reveille sounded.

Doc Phillips: Prior to departing for our WESTPAC (read Vietnam) tour I attended VD Contact Interviewing; it was explained to me that finding all the contacts was important in the containment of sexually transmitted diseases. We left port on April 5, 1967. The work was easy at first since Sick Bay consisted of one First Aid Box with a bottle of Bayer aspirin and a package of J&J Band-Aids. Everything else was sitting in a warehouse somewhere. When the medical gear arrived it was smeared in Cosmoline, which required lots of Acetone to make the equipment ready for sterile surgery. But soon enough I was dealing with shipboard injuries, a suicide attempt and a man overboard.

The *Cleveland* had a sixteen-bed ward, a laboratory, a Sick Call area. A Medical Officer's Exam Room, a Dental Room, though we had no dentist, nor the prospect of ever having a dentist, an Operating Room and a Central Sterile Supply. We also had three storerooms; our supplies were divided among them, in case of a catastrophe in one location, we would still have supplies available.

Once we reached Vietnam we did Medical Civic Action Programs (MedCaps), Rescue Operations and PsyOps. My day was tending to the sick and wounded and assisting in surgery.

Scott Squires: My last tour was aboard the *USS Charles Berry DE 1035*, a destroyer escort, from June of 1972 to the fall of 1972. It was a Navy WestPac tour which lasted about six months. I really hated to accept $65/month combat pay for the easy duty we had. After living in the field with the Marines, having hot food and clean sheets didn't seem like combat to me. On the *Berry* I had what was called Independent Duty. The Navy doesn't have enough doctors to have one on every ship, so some of the smaller ships had a Senior Corpsman instead of a doctor. I reported directly to the captain of the ship. The ship could get underway if the captain wasn't aboard but by law, the ship couldn't go to sea without the medical person on board. One of my duties was food inspection on the ship to ensure that the quality of food was acceptable. As Master of Arms I also went through everybody's quarters to make sure their bunks were made and they had clean linen.

The *Berry's* job was protecting aircraft carriers, picking up downed pilots, things like that. The problem with the *Berry* is that it was too slow; we couldn't keep up with a carrier when they were really going all out. It was embarrassing. We ended up selling that ship to the Vietnamese.

MEDCAPS

The Medical Civic Action Programs were the best known of the medical assistance efforts made in Vietnam. MEDCAP began in January, 1963 and was intended to provide medical care to Vietnamese civilians through a

*one-day visit in outlying areas.[lxix] Some training of Vietnamese medical
personnel also occurred. Participation of American and Free World forces
in MEDCAP was often on a voluntary basis. By 1970 about 200,000
patients were being treated each month. Dental care, in a country where
betel nuts were chewed to help with the pain from bad teeth, was
conducted under the sobriquet DENTCAP and averaged 15,000 treatments
per month.[lxx] Not to be outdone, our veterinary personnel treated and
vaccinated sick and wounded animals under the VETCAP banner.*

*Additional medical assistance became necessary as the war intensified.
The Civilian War Casualty Program allotted 1,100 beds at Chu Lai, Da
Nang and Can Tho to civilians in 1967;[lxxi] eventually treatment of
Vietnamese at U.S. military hospitals was increased.[lxxii]*

Scott Squires: At Chu Lai we were going out and doing MedCaps almost
every day. I delivered a lot of babies and sewed a lot of Vietnamese
people up on these trips. We usually went out to some remote spot via
helicopter, and sometimes spent several days out there alone, with very
little security. Our side pretty much controlled things during the day but
things were riskier at night. There would be just three or four of us out
there. It never occurred to me that I was in a particularly bad place; I
didn't much care for the food though.

What bothered me the most was the kids. They were kind of forgotten
over there. We'd arrive for the MedCap and set up shop, and it was
always the old people that showed up first. They would have teeth
problems, or they were chronically ill or had wounds that hadn't healed.
The wounds would have to be opened up and drained and treated. Our
battalion doctor was a surgeon. He had taught all of us how to do surgical
procedures. We were all adept at it. We dealt with the stuff their
primitive folk medicine couldn't handle. Sometimes the enemy would
show up for treatment too, and sometimes the enemy would punish the
villagers for accepting our help. We couldn't solve the politics; we just
treated anyone and everyone that sought help.

Pat Griffin: We did MedCap (Medical Civilian Aid Program) which I think
was instituted by LBJ. We would take an ambulance, and the army would

supply us with an escort (a jeep with a machine gun and a couple of armed soldiers), and we were armed. And we went out with the engineers and they built a little one-room schoolhouse and we worked the village with the medical civilian aid. We would pass out antibiotics and vitamins (the Vietnamese were all vitamin deficient; we would turn the kids eyelids over and they were all white, a sign of a severe vitamin deficiency) in the village. Apparently the VC would just come in and take the medicine. I heard later on that they had found dead VC with some of our bottled medicine marked Clark Air Force Base.

Adventures

Al Kotrola: While operating in the South China Sea (in 1965 or 1966), in company with another destroyer, the Medical Officer on that ship had diagnosed a young sailor with appendicitis. He notified the *Strauss* that he requested evacuation of the patient by seaplane early the next am. The seaplane landed but they popped a seam while trying to get airborne and started taking on water. The patient was moved to the *Strauss* and the appendectomy was performed in our Sick Bay by the Medical Officer, assisted by the Air Force Medical Officer and the *Strauss* corpsmen. The young man recuperated in the XO's stateroom and the seaplane which could not lift off had to be deep-sixed by the other destroyer. The cost of this appendectomy was about $150,000 (cost of one Air Force issue seaplane) and probably the only appendectomy ever performed on a Navy destroyer during the Vietnam era, and probably the only one on a smaller ship since WW II.

One night I was awakened by a guy complaining of severe stomach pains. After examining him I told him I thought he had appendicitis going. I did a blood count on him, and sure enough it was elevated and I got an indication that there was an infection. I told the XO I thought we were facing an emergency appendectomy. We were about fifteen hours out of Subic Bay at the time and we wouldn't get there until the next evening. He went to talk to the skipper and I went back to my patient. About fifteen minutes later I heard the engines roaring; they kicked it into high gear. We pulled into Subic about 1100 hours that morning. They took the patient to the hospital by ambulance. I saw him at a reunion in San Diego in 1999 and he told me the pain quit when he reached the hospital. I said

"It busted, didn't it?" He said it did. When they opened him up it had leaked all over the place and he was in Intensive Care and on antibiotics for about ten days, until the infection cleared up.

I actually filled teeth on the *Strauss*. We always made sure guys got their dental and medical checkups when we were in port. In this guy's case, when he opened his mouth, half the tooth was rotted away. We had a formula we made up of zinc oxide and cotton fibers and something else, and I filled the tooth up, and when we reach port I sent him to the dentist. The dentist told me that they ruined three drill bits dealing with that tooth when they got at it. He told me I did good work and to keep it up. I am proud that we never lost anybody during my three-year tenure aboard the Strauss.

When my three-year tour on the *Strauss* ended, they choppered me over to the *Enterprise* and they catapulted me off that night. You talk about a kick in the pants! You sit backwards for COB (carrier on board) flights and one of the crew came by and looked at my seat belt and said "Chief, you're not in there tight enough." I said "I can barely breathe now," and he told me to tighten it some more. I did, and then he told me to take off my glasses. It is quite a jolt getting blasted off the ship and for a second you seem like you're stopped, but then you start moving again. It was a blast!

Pat Griffin: At Bien Hoa, there was a terrible explosion on the flight line. We got two stories about what happened. One, that a mortar had hit one of the alert planes sitting on the runway waiting for any emergency, and it, in turn, detonated two more alert planes. The second story was that a primer went off on one of the alert planes. All I know is that it was a helluva explosion. Of course we thought the base was under attack. We had been issued M-16's which were kept at our HQ shack. We also had a .38.

Hospital administrators were partially graded on how fast they returned men to their units. The recovering patients became tenser as their wounds healed, and you could see the tension in their eyes and when they asked if you had heard anything about them. The way I felt about it they had already done their part.

I took great pride in the gratitude of the doctors and nurses with whom I worked, and mainly from the wounded themselves, who were sincerely appreciative of our help. One time I volunteered to help a pathologist do his work, a grisly job. I didn't know anything about what he was doing so I just handed him things and helped where I could. When he finished he told me he appreciated someone helping out with such a difficult task.

At Bien Hoa, we were picking up a GI to take to Saigon for evacuation home. We had to drive through this big walled compound, and we saw a big stack of aluminum caskets, and the ground was sloped toward a central sewer. They were doing autopsies behind these canvas walls. We went through two sets of double doors, and found ourselves in a room full of multiple amputees. (*pauses here*) Okay, so our kid had no arms or legs, and his head was shaved; apparently he had some head injuries as well. So we took him back to Saigon like that. He was medicated; he just laid there and moaned. The whole ward was full of people like that. It changed me and my whole view of the war, the whole deal.

Scott Squires: I also spent a lot of time riding the weekly convoys between Chu Lai and Danang, which is about a 55-mile trip up Highway 1. We'd spend a couple of days at Danang and then drive back. There had to be a corpsman every fifth or sixth truck on those trips. We were usually on a truck that had a .50 caliber machine gun and the seats in the back were sandbagged. On those trips, you'd be driving along, and everything was quiet, and then a truck would take fire. If they disabled a truck on the road the whole convoy was at risk so they gave the truck thirty seconds or so to get things working. If not they just pushed it out of the way and went on. Everybody was always nervous on those trips.

Among the differences between Vietnam and the Korea/WW II comparisons were the type of wounds. The type of war being fought in Vietnam contributed a higher percentage of casualties from small arms, booby-traps and mines, and conversely, a lower percentage of bomb and artillery wounds than WW II/Korea.[lxxiii] The high velocity enemy weapons (AK-47) left larger holes and did more tissue damage. And weapons fired on full automatic often left multiple wounds.[lxxiv]

Doc Phillips: Assault Craft 11 didn't have a corpsman so I volunteered. My first trip with them was a Psy Ops (Psychological Operation). This was on December 10 and we pulled out of the well deck for a routine trip up the Cua Viet River, a fairly narrow body of water. Our job was to cruise up and down the river as far inland as Dong Ha, blaring messages in Vietnamese. I thought the mission successful since we returned without incident, but the military planners probably thought otherwise.

We were doing another PsyOps on December 22 when we were sniped at from shore. I stayed low and counted my morphine in the event the SOB got lucky and hit someone. Just as the sniping quieted down I heard a loud "boom" out to sea. I didn't see anything out there that looked like a destroyer. Then I heard a freight train go overhead and explode inland with only a "thud." This went on for five or ten minutes, then it stopped. We learned later that the battleship *New Jersey* was doing the shelling, but we never saw her. We certainly heard her!

The sniping resumed in the afternoon, interrupting our box lunches. We returned fire from our .50 caliber machine guns. Despite all the shooting I decided to take a peek at what was going on. I saw mortar rounds walking towards us. Someone yelled "Mortars," and we started evasive maneuvers. The mortar fire stopped and we returned to the *Cleveland* to report. Two of our gunwale-mounted speakers had small caliber bullet holes. I don't know if this was excellent shooting on Charlie's part or just pure serendipity hits; I prefer the latter explanation. Anyway it was over, and it came to a draw.

We brought a casualty aboard on December 17, a man with a fractured leg. We splinted the leg and airlifted him off the following day to the hospital ship. This event pointed out that the LPD's, because of their design with no direct access to Sick Bay, cannot be designated as casualty receiving ships. We had to lower this young man into Sick Bay with a winch. We learned this limitation of the LPD's after building seven of them. The planners also probably never considered our medical personnel limitations.

We executed a medevac of one of our injured sailors on the aft end of a PBR in the middle of a tossing sea. It was difficult to see, as I wear glasses, and the rough sea was churned up further by the helo's rotors. However with the cooperation of the PBR's CO and the expertise of the helo crew, we pulled it off.

The Tet Offensive was all about the explosions at the Cua Viet River mouth. The *Cleveland* served as a helo haven during this time, embarking gunships overnight so that they did not get hit during the offensive. The danger that they faced inland was from mortar attacks.

I served with a wonderful bunch of young kids, especially the crew of the Assault Craft embarked aboard the *Cleveland*. They worked hard and they played hard. One of the young engineers was the first casualty we treated aboard the *Cleveland*; he was struck by one of the exploding shells at the mouth of the Cua Viet River and recovered enough to stay with the ACU. Dr. Michael J. Levine made several trips with us to the staging area of Dong Ha and he was also impressed with the professionalism of the ACU crew.

Scott Squires: Units that didn't have a corpsman attached would come and take one of us for their missions. We went out with Recon a number of times, and other specialty units. The grunts had their corpsmen attached but we went a lot with these other units. The helicopters were always short of corpsmen for the MedEvacs for instance.

The Marines gave me a lot of flak for working on the Vietnamese -- the enemy. At that time we didn't see many VC in this area; we were fighting the NVA. I had no problems treating a wounded enemy soldier; I figured there was no reason why they should suffer any more than anyone else. I had no problems with us shooting to kill them because they were soldiers, but once they were hurt I figured it was my duty to treat them.

We had a First Sergeant at Chu Lai that had actually been in the cavalry in the Marine Corps before WW II. At the time he had over thirty-five years in the Corps. I think he needed congressional permission to stay in that long because after thirty years they make you get out. I was planning on extending my tour there in Vietnam but he is the one that persuaded me to leave. He explained that if I extended they would transfer me to another unit. He said it was bad enough how much combat I was seeing now, but if I stayed in I would be in it every day until I was killed. I thought about it overnight and decided he was right. The old First Sergeant did me a big favor. With all that went on nothing ever seemed to change. I never really felt that we were winning over there.

NURSES

1st Lieutenant **Fran Janki**, Nurse, Tachikawa Air Force Base, Japan, USAF

1st Lieutenant **E. Jane McCarthy**, Nurse, 95th Evac. Hospital, Danang, USA

1st Lieutenant **Edie Meeks**, Nurse, 3rd Field Hospital/Saigon and 71st Evac. Hospital/Pleiku, USA

Doctors and nurses usually completed their medical training at U.S. hospitals. In many cases the military paid for the training in return for several years of military commitment.

By 1967 Operating room courses for military nurses back in the States were shortened from twenty-two weeks to sixteen.[lxxv] The one-year tour in Vietnam created a problem in that most hospitals arrived with a full complement of nurses. When their tours ended, complete re-staffing was necessary.[lxxvi]

Training/Arrival

E. Jane McCarthy: The Army paid for my last year in nursing school, and then I owed them two years of military service as a commissioned officer in the Army Nurse Corps. After nursing school I went to basic training in Texas, and then I spent ten months at Walter Reed Hospital working in the ICU recovery room there. I got orders to Vietnam in September, 1970.

Fran Janki: I had finished nursing school and eighteen months of work in the hospital I had graduated from and I just needed a change. I decided to join the Air Force. I worked at Moody AFB in Valdosta, Georgia from February of 1969 and then we heard that they wanted volunteers for Japan. They wanted two nurses to go together under the "buddy system." One of my nurses and I volunteered and flew into Yokota AFB in December, 1969. This was only ten or fifteen miles from Tokyo. I bought myself a small Christmas tree to decorate.

<u>Duties</u>

Edie Meeks: When I arrived, the chief nurse asked me where I wanted to work. I went to 3rd Field Hospital in Saigon, in the ICU, for six months. We were supposed to be the medical showcase; we wore white uniforms, white nylons and white shoes. And yet we got the same patients that the people out in the field got.

I had done emergency room nursing and intensive care nursing before and I opted for ICU, not knowing what it was going to be like. It turned out to be nothing like the United States. It took me years to figure out what the difference was. In the U.S., when somebody comes to the ER, for drunk driving, or a sports-related accident or whatever, everything made sense! Over in Vietnam, you would have a perfectly formed young man come in and he was blown to pieces. It didn't make sense.

E. Jane McCarthy: We were a typical ER and we treated walk-in problems. I dealt with a lot of drug overdose and drug withdrawal. Heroin was the worst. Some of those on heroin that were due to rotate home soon knew they had to get off that stuff. We also had malaria and we delivered babies for Vietnamese civilians. We had no OBGYN. The hospital wards wouldn't take these Vietnamese women who were about to deliver so we had to do it.

About 50% of our casualties were Vietnamese civilians, mostly women and children. And babies. With frag wounds. I remember holding a baby that came in dead with frag wounds. And we had a lot of kids running around. They'd come in in the morning, and they'd have a laceration of the hand or an infected foot. So a few of us nurses started what we called the Pediatric Clinic. These are the days before nurse practitioners. We were not nurse practitioners! We didn't ask any doctors or anybody about this, we just started doing it. And I've got some very precious pictures of those kids. I don't think we ever started a chart on them or anything, but they'd come in and we'd just do the best we could.

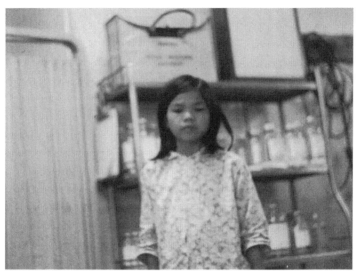

Much of our medical effort was directed to the civilian population.
Courtesy: Jane McCarthy

Edie Meeks: After six months in the ICU, I transferred to Pleiku. I just felt like a change of scenery would help me. Plus with the normal rotation of people, many of those with whom I was working were going home. Since we didn't go over there as a unit you'd find your friends were going home and you still had six months to go. You didn't have that backup that you needed just to hold yourself together. So I transferred to Pleiku, to the 71st Evacuation Hospital. We wore fatigues there in a bunker mentality. At night you brought your flak jacket and helmet to work because that is when the rockets came.

We worked six twelve-hour days. We rotated for both day and night shifts. We weren't staffed as well at night. When the patients got to us they had already been through the operating room and we would begin taking care of them. We would send our patients from Saigon to Japan or sometimes to the Philippines when they were stabilized, whereas at Pleiku we kept them longer. If they had malaria, for example, they were not going to be shipped out. I never got the feeling that we were shipping guys out of the hospital back to their units before they were recovered.

MACV wanted 40% of the hospital beds empty. They set up a 30-day evacuation policy; casualties who were expected to be hospitalized over one month were sent to Japan, the Philippines and other facilities.

Fran Janki: Based on their expected recovery time some patients were sent to Japan. I worked on an all-male surgical/orthopedic floor. Our patients were from Korea, Japan, and of course Vietnam. There was a "clean" ICU and a "dirty" ICU, distinguishing between wounds and no wounds. I worked in the clean ICU. The patients in the "dirty" ICU were isolated to prevent germs from spreading. I did work there a few times. It was all about routines: Come in to work, look at the paperwork, collect the medications, etc. We worked eight hour shifts five days a week.

Patients capable of being transported to the States would leave, but if not, they would stay with us for a month or two. Some of our patients did go back to Vietnam when they were ready. We had one Marine with broken bones in casts for quite a while. Some of our patients had malaria. The psychiatric patients went to another area.

About 11,500 women served in Vietnam, most of them in the medical field. [lxxvii]

E. Jane McCarthy: If I had night duty, there would be a radioman nearby, and two corpsmen, an XRay person, a Blood bank person, a physician, and they could all go off and go to sleep. I had to stay up all night, and if that radioman went to sleep and I heard a chopper I would have to go and tell them. The way we usually found out about incoming was when the helicopter pilot called in to our radioman, which gave us a few minutes to get ready.

We also had to inspect the KIA's in their body bags to look for ID and ensure there were no live grenades still on them. We tagged them. From that point they were taken to our morgue. I don't know if they did autopsies over there or not.

Over 11,000 women served in Vietnam, mostly as nurses.
Courtesy: Jane McCarthy

Edie Meeks: I was in ICU for about a month at Pleiku when I decided I couldn't do this anymore. I transferred to Medical ICU where you would get really sick malaria patients. I wonder what ever became of those guys who suffered such bad bouts of malaria. In the Medical ICU we weren't dealing with guys who might bleed out, they were stabilized and we were dealing with things like getting their temperature down, etc.

Vietnam may have been the first war where we had ventilators in the hospitals in a combat zone. We had some in Saigon and one at Pleiku. These were big, cumbersome machines that you wheeled around, but they kept a person breathing if they couldn't breathe.

OR

E. Jane McCarthy: My duties at Pre-Op were to meet the incoming casualties, put them on gurneys, begin a chart on them, get their blood pressure, get some history, assess their wounds, start IV's; I got really good at starting external jugular IV's and this was a very important part of my job. I would get them to XRay if necessary, determine their blood type (to do this we used a syringe and a stick in the femoral artery -- we didn't rely on the blood type that was on their dog tags), call the surgeon that would be needed for this type of wound, and prepare them for surgery.

We would also get the necessary blood from the blood bank that would be needed. If the guy was in shock we would get two liters of O neg blood right away. O neg is kind of a universal blood type. I would start pumping the O Neg in from the blood bags we used and by the time I had the O neg used up the blood bank guy would be back with his specific blood type. We also had to assess their air way; if the guy was asleep we would bring someone in to intubate them. All this was done to stabilize the patient. But sometimes we didn't have time to get them to XRay; we'd have to move them straight to the OR.

As the war heated up the demand for whole blood increased. From donor to patient, whole blood has a life expectancy of twenty-one days.[lxxviii] The whole blood requirement climbed from 100 units/month in 1965 to 38,000 units/month by February, 1969.[lxxix] A valuable donor was our Pacific Fleet. In fact the Vietnam War was the first time in U.S. history that every unit of whole blood used was donated by the military, their dependents and civilians working on military bases.[lxxx]

Edie Meeks: In Saigon, there were usually two RN's on, one for the recovery side and one for the ICU side. One night the gal who was supposed to be with me couldn't make it back from R&R, so I was alone. We weren't all that busy and I had a couple of corpsmen so I figured we'd be fine. Then we were told we were getting nine patients in. There had been an ambush. This was about 9:00 at night. I told one of the corpsmen that he was responsible for everyone in the ICU but that if he needed me to come change IV's or anything, to call me. I would be on the Recovery side with all the guys coming in. As the evening went on a lot of the other corpsmen started dropping by, just to say hello they said, and they started working. By the end of the rush that we had, around 2:00 the next morning, these guys who had probably worked all day were all there. They "just happened to drop by" and they'd ask me what I wanted them to do. That was our camaraderie; they would back you up no matter what and we did the same for them.

Fran Janki: A young man came in with shrapnel in his left arm. He was on our floor. The problem with shrapnel is that it moves. This patient had a sharp piece of shrapnel close to a nerve or artery so they left him with us so we could observe him. It did move and hit an artery but we were just a few feet from ICU so she whisked him in there and he made it.

Edie Meeks: We had a young patient with abdominal wounds which were so bad because of all the infection. He got a letter, and he was from a farm in Kansas. All my relatives from southern Minnesota were still farmers. This was in Fall and his mother wrote that his father and some others had just returned from pheasant hunting, with Spot the dog, and I related to that so much. And she wrote about how proud she was of him. I still think of that moment. Three days later he was dead.

When I went into the ICU our boss was an Army Major, and this guy was not an Intensive Care nurse. But he was bright enough to know that the nurses below him knew what they were doing and he let them do their jobs. In terms of making the military a career, with exceptions, it seemed like the most incompetent people stayed in! The really good nurses left. A lot of good nurses stayed in but I did see a lot of incompetents, people who fussed over the rules rather than the patients.

E. Jane McCarthy: If there was a backup in the OR, the patients would stay with me for a while. I would sometimes medicate them with morphine, but I didn't do that too much. In the case of head wounds the neurosurgeon would come down and look at the patient and determine if he could do something or not. If he couldn't help, that was what we called an expected patient and he would stay with me. I would set up an area in the back and sit with him until he died.

Fran Janki: One body bag in the morgue was moving. The guy was alive. He had been found face down in a puddle of water. This guy spent a lot of time with us and he was a lot of fun. He was fine. He was an Army guy. We saw Army, Marines and Air Force guys, but not many from the Navy.

We tried to do a lot of support for these guys knowing that it was not easy to communicate back to the States. We could use the MARS system or help them use my tape recorder. I would ask them "How would you like to make a tape message for your family?" And we would mail the tape.

Edie Meeks: I don't think I felt proud; I concentrated on the losses. Could I have done more? What did I miss? And most times, I didn't miss anything. The ones that really stuck in our minds were the ones we couldn't do anything for. But I did appreciate the sense of teamwork among the staff. If you had a busy night and you thought a patient needed some blood, you would just order it and the doctors trusted you to do that. I had absolutely fabulous corpsmen. If you told those guys that you needed something, all of a sudden it would appear. They'd say, "Don't ask," and I didn't. We never asked, and we didn't care, as long as we had it there for our patients.

Adventures

E. Jane McCarthy: At Pleiku, we lived in sandbagged hooches, six girls and a bathroom, with individual cubicles. The only air conditioning was in the ICU. We did have fans but it was so hard to sleep from the heat and the humidity. Our hospital was near the Air Base, which meant that we were rocketed fairly frequently. And the plan was for you to put the patients under their beds during a rocket attack, or if you couldn't move them, put a mattress on top of them. One night part of the ER was blown up and one night the CO's house was blown up. He was thirteen days past his rotation home date and he said "That's it. I'm out of here."

They built our beds a little higher in our living quarters, so that you could get under the beds during a rocket attack. The first time rockets came in I got under my bed, and three other girls joined me under my bed. You just didn't want to be alone.

The danger in Saigon when I was there (this was after Tet) was more the drive-by bombing kind of thing. You always had to be on guard. But in Pleiku, you expected to be rocketed almost every night. In Pleiku, when the first rocket attack came, I started to take care of my patients and the soldiers in the beds would say "Now Lieutenant, it isn't going to be that bad." And they started telling jokes so that I wouldn't be afraid. I thought that was the sweetest thing.

This general had been walking around the ICU handing out Purple Hearts. This one fellow had a trach and he had his eyes covered; we weren't sure if he was going to be blind or not. He was missing both legs and an arm. We were trying to stabilize him so we could ship him out to Japan. The general pinned the medal on his gown and I don't know if the guy even knew what was going on, and you think to yourself, is that an even trade? It was just so overwhelmingly bizarre.

We didn't need a neurosurgeon in Saigon because we were able to ship patients out so quickly. But in Pleiku, in the central highlands, we had a neurosurgeon. We had a patient one time with brain damage, and after his brain surgery he appeared to be getting better. For me, even as a nursing student, neurosurgery was the toughest, because you could fix so little. I had high hopes for this patient, but one morning I came to work and they told me he had spiked a temp during the night -- the temperature in his brain was off -- and he died. It was such a blow.

We had a patient in the 3rd Field Hospital, around Christmas time; he had been shot in the chest and it had just missed his heart, and he arrived at the ER fast enough that the doctors were able to save him. We had him in the ICU. At this time every ward had some sort of a party going on, and the medical staff would just go from ward to ward, and each ward had to have some libation available. The ICU nurses kept ordering 180 proof alcohol from the pharmacy to put in our punch. It was wonderful, but this fellow with the chest wound, who was still in ICU, asked us for a drink since it was Christmas. We talked it over and decided to give him just a little thimble-full; just a little taste. After his Christmas cheer he broke out in a sweat and turned gray and I thought we had killed him! He turned out to be okay. In fact, he is the only patient that we ever found out about after he left us. He wrote to us from Walter Reed Army Hospital saying he was doing okay. He had stayed with us for about two weeks; usually guys were shipped out after three or four days.

Over in Vietnam I saw what the will to live could do. You could see guys actually will themselves to live. You also saw guys who struggled and struggled, and then finally gave up.

Vietnamese

E. Jane McCarthy: My best Vietnamese friend was a nurse. Her name was Minh. She worked with me there as a nurse and an interpreter. She would log in all the Vietnamese patients and get their names. She was an RN trained in Saigon. Her husband was a minister, and just a lovely, lovely person. She wore her white uniform to work. And Sgt. Krang was there with me too. He was our liaison with the Vietnamese Army. If we received any ARVN casualties he was the liaison back to their unit.

When we worked on the Vietnamese casualties it was our job to stabilize them and then they'd be transported by bus down to the Vietnamese hospital. It was good for me to see what the Vietnamese hospital looked like so we would know where we were sending them. Their hospital wasn't much. As a result I tried to keep the Vietnamese kids as long as I could to give them a better chance to live.

Edie Meeks: We had Vietnamese working in the hospitals with us, and you didn't know if they were VC or not. They would come and do their job during the day but you didn't know what they did at night. You never trusted anybody. I found that I had to really work to be kind to the enemy patients we had. I had to will myself to remember that I was a nurse no matter what. The reality was, I had a limited amount of time and to whom do I allocate that precious time? My boys! I really had to work to give good care to the enemy. I had to choose if I was a nurse for everyone or if I would pick and choose. I realized that I could not pick and choose. But I did have to work at it!

I loved dealing with the Montagnards because they were short! Diane and I went into the town of Pleiku to see what it was like. We went to the local hospital. The Vietnamese nurses at the hospital worked just during the day and went home at night, because it was dangerous to be out at night. We were told, and I don't know if this is true, that if a patient was scheduled to receive, for example, three liters of fluid during twenty-four hours, they'd give all of it to them during their day shift. So a lot of the families came to take care of the patients, because there was no one else to take care of them at night. And they would bring their children, and they would bring their animals, because if they left their animals back at home they might never see them again.

The objective of our medical corps is to preserve the fighting strength of the troops. And despite the ever-growing lethality of modern weaponry, improvements in medical care outpaced the weapons in Vietnam. The death rate for wounded men reaching a medical facility in Vietnam was only 2.5% as compared to 8% in World War II and 17% during the Civil War.[lxxxi] Of the 194,716 wounded (January 1965 – December 1970) 31% were treated and returned to duty immediately.

Among the conclusions reached in Vietnam was there was no longer a need to assign medical officers to combat battalions. They should be assigned directly to the medical units. And direction of all medical units should be centrally controlled by senior medical commanders.[lxxxii]

MEDICAL SUPPORT PERSONNEL

Alexander Phillips

Floyd Jones

Jane McCarthy

Clem Blazewick

CHAPTER FIVE

ADMIN/STAFF SUPPORT

Some of the Hidden Army included staff and administrative personnel. In terms of visibility within the Hidden Army these support troops may have been the most transparent of all. Yet without a trained staff and an efficient administration an army is incapable of movement.

Military Assistance Command, Vietnam (MACV) was established in February, 1962. Our advisers were actively supporting South Vietnamese Army operations.

1st Logistics Command established on April 1, 1965. It consisted of seventeen officers and twenty-one enlisted men.

CLERKS

*Spc4 **William Harkins,** Ammo Specialist, 191st Ordnance Battalion, Long Binh, USA*

*Sgt **Rob Wiebe,** Personnel Clerk, 537th Personnel Company, Bien Hoa, USA*

*Sgt. **Larry Caldwell,** Clerk, H&S Co, III Marine Amphibious Force, Danang, USMC*

*Sgt. **Tim Smith**, Electrician, HQ, III Marine Amphibious Force, Admin Chief, MACS-4, Danan, USMC*

*Cpl. **Dennis Kapolka,** H&S Company, III Marine Amphibious Force, Danang, USMC*

Arrival/Duties

Larry Caldwell: I arrived at Danang by air in February, 1966, and after some re-organizations, ended up in III MAF. I was picked up by MSgt Orville Jones and we walked to a tent that was the 'Force Motor Transport Office, G-4' where I was now the only clerk. Looking back, that made me the 'Admin Chief', a title I wasn't totally familiar with just yet and certainly didn't adopt at that point.

MSgt Jones had been in the Marine Corps since WWII where he had been wounded twice during the Okinawa Campaign. He was Chesty Puller's driver during and after the Korean War and is mentioned in several books. I was impressed with his celebrity within the Marine Corps and that I got to work for him; he was now my boss!

Our office was a 'CP' tent where the OIC and several other senior enlisted managed the Motor Transport assets belonging to the Marine Corps in Vietnam. I had a field desk that served as my center of operation. I typed message traffic, memos, and other general correspondence that filtered through MSgt Jones, my direct supervisor. I also was the office runner and picked up U.S. mail, made deliveries to other offices and generally ran whatever errands anyone in the office required. Office hours were long, usually upwards of sixteen to eighteen-hour days, seven days a week.

Dennis Kapolka: After boot camp, where I was meritoriously awarded my first stripe, I went to Personnel Administration School at El Toro, CA. I learned about the new Unit Diary System that was coming in, where information was recorded on metal cards. This was in the days before computers. After the unit information was entered you pressed the handle down and the data were stamped on this metal plate.

I flew into Danang in February, 1966. Most of my work day was spent in G-5 typing up Situation Reports (SitReps) for the various sub units that reported to III MAF. This was an eight to ten hour day. These reports covered how many bars of soap, food or medicine this village received. Looking back, I think it demonstrates a very real attempt on the part of Marine leadership to win the hearts and minds of the Vietnamese people.

I flew courier hops to Saigon and helicopter hops up north to the smaller bases. I also stood occasional guard duty. I spent the first month as a clerk with the HQ Co., Sub-Unit 2, 3rd Marine Division and then the rest of my tour with H&S Company, III Marine Amphibious Force, Fleet Marine Force Pacific. My term of enlistment with the Marines ended while I was in Vietnam but I re-enlisted for four more years while over there.

Tim Smith: Headquarters, III MAF was disbanding in early 1970. My tour was not over so I was transferred to MACS-4, where I was the Admin Chief. I was in charge of the whole office. HQ III MAF was on the opposite side of the river from Danang so when I joined Marine Air Control Squadron-4 I moved to the top of Monkey Mountain. The Admin office at MACS-4 consisted of two clerks, a legal officer and legal clerk, and the First Sergeant.

William Harkins: I had a draft number in the middle but rather than waste time and money I volunteered for the Army and Vietnam, not because I was a hawk but because I thought it would be an adventure. I wanted to experience the real thing, not what Walter Cronkite presented on the evening news. Prior to writing *War and Peace* Leo Tolstoy went out on the battlefield to experience war. I landed at Cam Ranh Bay in September, 1971. I remember the heat and humidity and a peculiar smell in the air.

My primary duty was ammunition, storage, records, and operational specialist. I was a clerk at the ammo dump responsible for all the paperwork on our ammo. I worked sixteen hours a day with half a day off per week. I also went on some details when I first arrived; the one I remember most is spreading Agent Orange around our perimeter. I do not remember inhaling any spray but I do remember the defoliant coming into contact with my bare hands. I helped to interlink landing strip steel plates; this was during the monsoon and we were drenched. I flew courier hops to Saigon and helicopter hops up north to the smaller bases. I also stood occasional guard duty.

Rob Wiebe: I arrived in November of 1971, and was gone by April of 1972 with an early out for school. I spent my tour at Bien Hoa with the exception of three weeks we spent in Cambodia! I was a personnel clerk. In addition to the day-to-day record keeping I administered tests for promotion. I figured if a guy came close, because they were in-country I gave them the passing grade. Once a month we pulled perimeter guard duty. We worked an average day, 8 to 5. We were not overworked.

Vietnamese

Rob Wiebe: We had house girls that cleaned the barracks and did the laundry. They starched my underwear once. Number 10! I came into contact with Vietnamese people every day. I thought they were very competent. There may have been some "forced niceness" but I thought they appreciated it if you tried to speak their lingo.

Larry Caldwell: The local Vietnamese were provided jobs and through some checkpoint were allowed in to do an assortment of manual labor jobs. Some worked as maids to us who lived in tents. They were never a problem to my knowledge but we were ever vigilant to the fact that VC was known to work amongst them plotting, making maps and such. But they did their job and otherwise got along well with us. They chewed betel nut, a substance that would stain their teeth black. We would give them food we had taken from the mess hall or had gotten from home.

Adventures

Rob Wiebe: At 0600 every morning, we received three incoming rocket rounds. Our wake-up call.

I would have perimeter guard duty once a month. We were armed with M-16's but were not supposed to put a clip in the weapon without authorization. Earlier that month a couple of guys had had their throats slit. It may have been over drugs. Anyway two of us were on guard duty down near the motor pool and in the middle of the night we start hearing noises. The noises start getting closer and I finally sent the other guy for the officer of the guard. While he's gone the noises are getting closer and coming straight for me. I put a clip in the M-16. The other guy still is not back and the noises are too close for comfort. I emptied two clips in the direction of the noise. In the morning we find two dead water buffalo in front of my bunker. The officer of the guard is red-faced and furious. The word court martial is mentioned. I convinced them that leaving Vietnam for a court martial held more appeal than they realized.

Tim Smith: We also had a guy on guard duty try to Halt! Something, and the something didn't stop, and he fired, and the patrol the next morning found a dead wild pig.

Larry Caldwell: Everybody got shot at! The enemy was all around us. I remember a passenger window on a jeep I was driving being blown out once while driving towards Marble Mountain. Don't know of any other reason why it'd just give way. I was also on a rotating roster to deliver yellow postal bags of classified material to Chu Lai and/or Dong Ha via helicopter. I believe this was a monthly assignment for all or most of the corporal/sergeant '01's. The chopper would hug the coastline as it flew to its destination. Besides the crew I was the only passenger on all the flights I was ever on. I carried an M-14 and a .45 with instructions to protect the bags; they were not to get into enemy hands. Other than the weapons I had, I wasn't provided with a lighter, matches or flammable substance to burn them if it had come to that. It wasn't unusual to get a few rounds through the chopper at which time the door gunner would fire off a volley into the landscape below. I also made a couple of flights to Saigon to do the same thing, but that was on a C-130 as I recall. Never had any problems on that run and I might have been able to spend the night before returning the next morning.

There were a couple of times I was selected to augment a security team that would escort some convoys someplace. Those were fired on routinely and we got to fire back. The assaults didn't appear to be well orchestrated and probably were more to harass than to destroy.

Corporal Dennis Kapolka and I were on guard duty one night after HQ, III MAF relocated to the other side of the Danang airfield and across the river. We were in a trench dug out to accommodate this assignment. We were there all night. Our job was to ensure that no one approached the command from the water. We could see down a road and observe that people would come out of this one isolated house, get on a bicycle and peddle off. Quite a few would do this and it was our opinion that this house just didn't seem large enough to accommodate as many people as would leave the house. We contacted the Guard Supervisor and advised what we had seen. To us it was just odd that so many people would come out of the house one at a time over a period of a few hours but no one ever went in. No idea what became of our information.

Tim Smith: We were not bothered too much during the time at MACS-4 on top of Monkey Mountain. Our biggest enemy up there was boredom although we did have a few skirmishes with the rock apes. They were always around the perimeter because they liked to sneak in to our trash dump. One afternoon a group of these apes came strolling up and one of our guys threw a rock at them. They retaliated and he ended up with six stitches in his head. He tried to get a Purple Heart but we told him it was the wrong enemy.

When I was with MACS-4 we used to make a mail run to Udon Thani in Thailand in the C147 tail dragger aircraft. Some of us would occasionally take a day off and go over there to sightsee and what not. There were no seats on this plane other than the strap seats along the wall. We heard some alarms going off and the plane started shaking real bad, and they had us get up and put parachutes on. I had never jumped before and we're 10,000 feet above the jungle in Laos. We had no weapons and it was not where I wanted to be at the time. We made an emergency landing at Paxi, an old CIA air strip in Laos. We learned that the rear stabilizer cable had broken and was just flapping around in the breeze. The pilot said if he knew what it was he would have continued on to Thailand. But since we had landed they put us on helicopters and bird dogs for the rest of the flight to Thailand.

We were coming down Monkey Mountain to participate in a change of command ceremony and we lost our brakes. I was riding up front in the deuce-and-a-half with a corporal driving, and we had a bunch of guys in the back. Our driver tried to signal the driver in front of us by blowing his horn; we were hoping we could use his truck to slow us down but the leading truck didn't respond. As we neared the bottom of the mountain the corporal told us he would try to roll up on the right side of the road and then turn the wheel just as the truck was about to tip over. His plan worked and he saved us all. Everybody in that truck was terrified, including me. I put him in for the Marine Corps Medal.

Dennis Kapolka: On my monthly courier flight from Danang to Saigon one of our two engines was apparently disabled by ground fire. There were a few soldiers on that plane and some Vietnamese. All I heard was people praying, in Vietnamese, English and languages I never heard before. We were instructed to put our heads between our knees and our hands over our heads. I don't know how but the pilot managed to make an unscheduled landing at the Nha Trang airstrip. The flights I took after that didn't feel right. After I returned from Vietnam I never got on an airplane again! And I never will.

We received some random mortar fire at our compound and once, on a chopper ride up north, the M60 gunners started blazing away at something below us. I could see the dirt flying on the ground where the rounds were hitting.

William Harkins: We found one way to lock out the war. We were sitting in a room once with the volume so high on our music were unable to hear any shooting.

On the eve of my return to "the world" I was in the out-processing at Long Binh. About six of us were relaxing in the barracks, smoking marijuana and listening to the Moody Blues, just glad to be going home. An explosion and then a second one shook the barracks. I scrambled for the door in my underwear. Mortar rounds continued to fall. The explosions came closer and reminded me of the Giant stalking Jack in the nursery rhyme. I reached the long, thin bunker – open at both ends -- and scrambled for the middle. Sand filtered down on us as each round hit. I was nervous but I remember being more nervous having to speak in public. We had already turned our weapons in so we were defenseless. I worried that someone might enter the bunker with a machine gun and start mowing us down. I knew I didn't want to die this way. When the mortars stopped I heard shouting. We were safe but the air outside the bunker was heavy with the smell of gun powder. I was told a couple of men had been killed, but since I was in a different (processing) unit I didn't know any of them.

STAFF

*Cpl **Mike Holz**, Counter Intelligence, 5th Bn., 525 MI Group, Saigon, USA*

*1st Lt **Terry Monnie,** Operations Officer, 519th Military Intelligence Battalion, 525th MI Group, Saigon, USA*

*Captain/Major **Rick Spriggs,** Bn. Intelligence Officer, 28th Infantry, Deputy G-1, 1st Infantry Div., Lai Khe, USA*

*Captain **Paul Kaser,** Admin Officer, 3rd Security Police Squadron, Bien Hoa, USAF*

*Cpl. **T. J. McGarvey**, Co. A, 1st Bn., 9th Marines; G-3, H&S Co Bn., 3rdMarDiv, Dong Ha, USMC*

Arrival/Duties

Rick Spriggs: Between Vietnam tours I went to Korea and then I returned to the States for the Advanced Infantry Officers Course at Fort Benning, which took six months. Vietnam was heating up at that time and the rumor was that the 1st Infantry Division was going to be deployed there. I called my old company First Sergeant, who was now a Battalion Sergeant Major in the 1st I/D, and asked for his help in getting me back to the Big Red One. He came through in two days and I had a rifle company, A Company, in the 2nd Battalion.

My unit arrived by ship at Vung Tau in October, 1965. We climbed down cargo nets into smaller boats and waded ashore. We were then trucked up to Lai Khe, about thirty or forty kilometers north of Saigon. We were right in the bend of what they call the "fishhook" area of Vietnam.

I spent about seven months as A Company commander in the 28th. I tried to spend all my tour there but they had some regulations that officers only spend six months with a line unit so I transferred to a staff job. Because of my Korea background in Intelligence, I was made S-2 (Intelligence) within the 2nd Battalion, 28th Infantry. When the S-4 officer was killed in the re-supply mission to Bau Bang I was put in his place since I also had previous S-4 duty.

T. J. McGarvey: I arrived at Danang by troop ship (*USS Upshur*) in March of 1967. The night before we came ashore there was a lot of artillery fire flashing through the skies. We thought the world was going to end! We were pretty nervous. The next morning we climbed down the cargo nets into the boats – me with visions of Iwo Jima -- and we went ashore. Here are kids playing in the parks and selling Coca-Cola. Welcome to Vietnam! You drink Coke? Drink Beer?

I really had two different jobs over there. Initially I was a grunt with 1/9. They call 1/9 (1st Bn., 9th Marines) the Walking Dead. I lost my best friend from rocket fire at Camp Carroll. At Con Thien, we lost our CO, XO and chief corpsman, just after I left there. That was pretty traumatic. Then I did the Casual Reporter duty. At Dong Ha I identified KIA's. I went to the field a lot and went on some operations. I spent time at Con Thien, which was the big show before Khe Sanh. I spent time at Graves Registration. Casual Reporter was not good duty.

Terry Monnie: I arrived at Long Binh via Continental Airlines on July 16, 1967. I spent two days there and was then bussed to Saigon. I resided at the Meyerkord Hotel in Saigon.

Rick Spriggs: For my second Vietnam tour, I had orders to be an advisor to the ARVN. I had heard nothing but bad things about this kind of duty from friends over the years so I wrote to Major General Keith Ware, the CG of the 1st Infantry Division. As far as I know he was the only general officer in the Army at that time who was a graduate of OCS. Like me. I thought he and I had something in common and I was going to try to work that angle. I told him I wanted to do my second tour with the 1st I/D, and that ideally, I would spend some of that tour in the G-3 (Operations) slot, which was an important step in career advancement.

I didn't hear from him directly, but when I flew into Tan Son Nhut in January, 1968, and reported to the Replacement Depot I was told I wasn't going to be an advisor; I was going to the 1st I/D. I choppered up to Lai Khe. As I arrived at Division HQ they were receiving radio information from the field that Major General Ware, his G-4, and Command Sergeant Major had just been shot down and they all died. So I never had the honor of meeting General Ware.

The only job opening they told me they had was for HQ Commandant, commanding the Headquarters Company of the division. I knew all about that and wanted no parts of it. It was one of the easiest places in the world to get in trouble through no fault of your own. Most of the under-performers in the division would end up getting assigned to this unit.

I managed to wiggle out of the HQ job and became the Deputy G-1 (Personnel) of the division. The Chief of Staff told me he doubted that I had the background for that job but I asked him to give it to me for a month, and if he wasn't satisfied I would do whatever he wanted.

One of my responsibilities in G-1 was awards and decorations. One of the recommendations that came across my desk was for a young man from Auburn, NY, near my hometown. His name was Robert Striker. I thought the recommendation and commendation was kind of sloppy so I re-worked it. I ended up writing his commendation for the Medal of Honor that was approved and signed by President Nixon. He is now buried less than a mile from my house.

Mike Holz: When my draft notice appeared I volunteered at the last second. I was a lawyer before the Army claimed me so it was difficult taking orders from idiots! I flew into Tan Son Nhut, via Pan Am I think, in January of 1970. Our compound was about a kilometer from the air base. I was part of Detachment B, Counter Intelligence. We were like the FBI. My duties involved running background checks on the Vietnamese working for the Army, or girls that were planning to marry a GI. Our work schedule was 6 ½ days per week; I had Saturday afternoons off. We didn't have to deal with the usual Army BS; no formations, inspections or drills.

Among my duties was traveling to the nearby Army bases to ensure that they were following the correct security procedures. I had a Top Secret security clearance for this job. On one occasion we found a SECRET memo in the desk drawer of a Brigadier General. We had to write him up for a security violation.

Background checks were done on Vietnamese
Courtesy: Mike Holz

Paul Kaser: After doing mostly security work, in May of 1970 I was made adjutant to the base commander until my departure for home in October. During that period I was Chief of Administration for the 3rd Tactical Fighter Wing and commander of the Headquarters Squadron section of the Group. This period was mostly spent in the commander's office.

Vietnamese

T. J. McGarvey: The Vietnamese were not allowed on our base. I did see them on the infrequent trips to town.

Mike Holz: I was in frequent contact with Vietnamese. I worked with their interpreters and we also had house girls. Most of the guys I worked with were pretty good guys. The maids were all poor people from awful poor families. But it seemed like everybody else was trying to hustle; money changing, selling their sisters and stuff like that. Nobody tried to sell dope to me, though. I think you had to go looking for that.

Rick Spriggs: There was a Vietnamese village located **within** the perimeter in our sector of responsibility, so we came in contact with these people every day. Those people went out of their way to serve and protect our units. Our people were invited into their homes. I ate a rather unique dinner with them, with the fish with the eye and a cat and things. I guess I ran into their *nuc maum* sauce, I don't know, but there was a lot of hot stuff there! But you maintain your gratitude for their hospitality. I got so comfortable that I could walk from my quarters to the center of their village without a weapon, anytime, day or night.

On my second tour I jeeped to our location. I saw the Vietnamese village, which used to be within our wire, was now outside the wire and enclosed by an eight foot cyclone fence. Since Division HQ was now located at Lai Khe they decided they needed the fence for security reasons. And they couldn't figure out why they received sniper fire. They took everything away from these people; a human tactical error. There were not so many people in that village that they couldn't have been controlled.

Terry Monnie: The Vietnamese typically constructed buildings with every conceivable material scrounged from various sources: packing crates, Connex containers, lumber, and beer and soda cans flattened and used as wall coverings. Some were two-story buildings and I marveled that they would stand up to the monsoon, but they did. Many times they built their homes right against our buildings which, in itself, created some security concerns.

Paul Kaser: I really admired the doctors, nurses and dentists who made the weekly visits to the Vietnamese villages, orphanages and the leper colony. They were going into some areas that had just been secured. But not entirely secured. I was glad that I could contribute to the CAP's. I worked with some quality Americans in that role. That is what I liked most.

Adventures

Mike Holz: I am not aware that I was shot at, but I heard satchel charges going off many nights.

One Saturday afternoon I hitchhiked about twenty miles outside of Saigon just to take pictures. I did that on a lark; it was dumb. I didn't take pictures of anything that special; rice paddy's and things like that. While I was out there I was hitchhiking again and these combat guys picked me up. One of them had a 1,000 yard stare. He asked me what I was doing out there. I told him I was taking pictures. He said, "You'll die out here." I got the hell back to town!

One of my proudest moments was when Detachment A of our unit broke the story about the Cambodian coup against Prince Sihanouk before the CIA knew about it. If my group, Detachment B, was like the FBI, Detachment A was like the Army CIA.

Rick Spriggs: As part of my S-2 work we set up a base at Bau Bang, about twelve miles from Lai Khe, and we were running reconnaissance patrols and things like that. About the third or fourth night we were suddenly hit by a group of VC. It began to get pretty hairy and we learned that they were supported by a group of NVA soldiers. We began to run low on ammunition and I called the S-4 back at the base camp. I told them we needed a resupply quickly. Both the S-4 and his sergeant got a chopper loaded and told me they were on the way. I told them to let me know when they got near us as we were getting heavy fire. They agreed to let us know but the next thing I knew they were landing. Both the S-4, an officer named Gereaux, and a sergeant named Bennitt were on the chopper, and they began to throw ammo out of both doors. I observed both of them go down several times, hit by small arms fire. Each time they would get up and continue to throw ammo out the door. When they finished the chopper took off, but halfway back to Lai Khe it crashed and burned due to the many hits it had taken. I'm confident that both

Gereaux and Bennitt were dead before the chopper went down; I don't see how they could have still been alive after all the hits they had taken. We eventually drove the enemy force away and were allowed to boot up and go back to base camp. Both Gereaux and Bennitt were decorated for their heroism that night. I was awarded the Silver Star, the Bronze Star with Combat V and a Purple Heart. I thought those two men each deserved a Medal of Honor. One of our lieutenants was leading a recon patrol that night, and when the attack came it happened that they were trying to reenter our perimeter too. About half of them were killed. The platoon leader had safely come inside our wire, but when he learned that one of his men, carrying night vision goggles (which we didn't want the enemy to have) was still out there he went back to retrieve them and some of the wounded. He was also killed just as he reached our perimeter. His name was Robert Hibbs and he did receive the Medal of Honor.

T. J. McGarvey: During the time of Tet three of us stole an Army jeep and went into Dong Ha. We stopped at this hooch that sold beer and rock gut whiskey. A Vietnamese kid comes running up saying "VC come! VC come!" Well we got back in the jeep. We returned to the base and realized our buddy from Birmingham wasn't with us. So we went back to get him. We entered the hooch and they had an old Coca-Cola cooler against the wall. The Vietnamese kid kept pointing to it so we figure it is NVA. My buddy slid the top off, and I'm aiming my M-16, and it's our buddy from Birmingham.

We took a lot of rockets at Con Thien -- about 1,000 rounds a day of artillery, rockets and rpg's. It was pretty frustrating to take Hill 881, near Khe Sanh, then walk away from it and have to take it again. We took that hill three times.

During the Christmas truce of 1967, our recon people found 500 VC moving in the open in violation of the truce. Our requests to hit them went up the chain of command all the way to the president, who suggested we "use our discretion. Recommend **do not** engage." This message was repeated all the way back down the chain of command until it got to our commanding officer, who authorized us to "Pepper them." But the four-hour delay proved to be too long and they were gone when the order finally came through.

I had always heard that getting through the first and last months were the toughest things to do. We were on a convoy to Dong Ha and things were quiet. I had perimeter guard that night and I'm thinking "Boy, it's thirty days I'm in country and I'm fine. Where's the war?" Around 0300, we take 300 rockets. I was wounded lightly, and as they patched me up the corpsman said he would be putting me in for a purple heart. "What does that entail?" I asked. He said a recruiter would walk up to my front door and hand my mother a purple heart. So as not to worry her I declined the medal. Years later I would love to have a Purple Heart but I don't regret that decision for a minute!

There was no grass on our hill at Con Thien, so when the rain gushed and it washed out several bunkers. It was said that several marines were killed by falling timbers in the bunkers

They were a great bunch of guys. I never saw drugs or fraggings. We only had beer about three times during my tour. I think the Vietnam experience is most contingent upon what time period and what location you were at. I was at HQ during Tet and we got pounded. Dong Ha was rocket city. I returned home shortly after Tet and I was watching the news. It mentioned an outpost I knew on top of a plateau, very easy to defend, and they said it was overrun. I wrote to my friends and they said it had been quiet since I left. I started to wonder about the objectivity of the media.

Terry Monnie: By January 28, 1968, intelligence reports had indicated that something major was about to happen. My roommate Eli and I left our hotel in the Cholon (Chinese) sector of Saigon and walked around the corner to another BOQ (Bachelor Officer Quarters) where we joined some of our fellow officers and co-workers for breakfast on the top floor restaurant. Following a recent fire this restaurant had no walls, thus offering a 360 degree view of the city.

As we sat we noticed black plumes of smoke rising thousands of feet in the sky at a distance we estimated to be twenty miles. We were instructed NOT to proceed to the Center but to await further orders. With each passing hour the columns of smoke came closer and our levels of anxiety increased correspondingly. By mid-morning it was apparent that things had changed dramatically. We received reports that major Viet Cong and NVA forces were on the outskirts of the city. It was early afternoon when we observed groups of enemy forces carrying AK-47's moving en masse down nearby streets in the direction of the City Center. We learned later that their goal was the presidential palace and the US Embassy.

Our anxiety quickly turned to fear as we were all unarmed. General Westmoreland had long ago decreed that soldiers stationed in Saigon were not to carry weapons for fear we would get drunk and shoot up the town. We returned to our respective hotels where we remained in hiding for three or four days until order was restored in the city. While in hiding we looked for any weapon we could find. In a hotel with 120 officers there were maybe twenty weapons. The hotel was guarded by a lone MP stationed outside the front door in a concrete pipe turned upside down with a conical roof for protection from the elements. I finally located a 12-gauge pump action shotgun that had seen better days but it gave me a limited sense of security. It was this experience that fostered a deep and lasting resentment of my military experience, the sense of hopelessness and not having the ability to defend myself. The Viet Cong and NVA were aware that thousands of US service personnel stationed in Saigon were weaponless and that encouraged them to take over the city as we watched in hiding. My Vietnam is long gone but the memories are still there under the surface, ready to jump to the front of my conscious mind.

The May Offensive of 1968 was just as bad as Tet. My tour of duty was due to end in July and I was now considered a "short-timer". But we were all uneasy due to what we were hearing from prisoner interrogations. It looked like something "big" was again going to happen. On May 4 I completed my daily interrogations at the center and went to the enlisted personnel barracks near Tan Son Nhut AFB. I was scheduled to be the duty officer that night. We had received word that another attack on Saigon would occur early the next morning. We were all on high alert which meant that the enlisted men had located their weapons. Keep in mind that some of these men had not fired a weapon since basic training and most were highly educated nerd-types with multiple degrees. I recall one corporal who was a graduate of the London School of Economics. These men were great for running an interrogation center but not for fighting or defense.

I tried to sleep with little luck and at 0400 assumed my command post on the rooftop. I gave explicit instructions that no one fire their weapons except as a last resort. The next two hours were uneventful; we watched another brilliant sunrise in Southeast Asia. At 0600 a US Army Huey gunship flew over our heads at a very low level and fired several rockets into the housing area surrounding us and the open lands beyond. The noise was deafening and began twenty-four hours of chaos and confusion.

We spotted hundreds of black-pajamed VC moving in our direction, armed with AK-47's. I had my WW II/Korean War vintage M-2 carbine, which I had obtained after Tet. This was a fine weapon, unlike the troubled M-16. It was important that we not attract VC attention so we remained concealed and quiet. We spent the next few hours watching and on one occasion we captured a weaponless VC who was hiding in the garbage dump adjacent to our location.

It became apparent that the VC were not interested in us but were using the roadways to attack the air base and then proceed into the city center. But the Army sent in prop driven Sky Raiders to drop 450-pound bombs near our location. By late afternoon there was a commotion at the front entrance of the barracks. Some local Vietnamese had arrived carrying a wooden crate which contained a badly injured young girl. Her parents hoped we had a medic. I spent the next hour trying to help her with an IV with fluids to no avail. It seemed her veins had collapsed and she died in my arms.

Paul Kaser: One time we had an officer from back in the states doing an inspection. This officer is looking for dust and things like that. I was so mad. Where did this guy think he was? These guys were up all night and he is looking for dust?

We had some Army guys staying in the transit barracks waiting to go home, and one of the first rocket attacks I experienced we were trying to drag them out of the barracks to the bunkers. They had been drinking and it was hard to get them to move. At least one of them was killed during that attack.

After a rocket attack some of the nearby Vietnamese houses were on fire. Some of the Army guys were out there fighting the flames. A reporter was standing there watching. I got to where I hated to see reporters talking to our guys. And I was a Journalism major!

When Walter Cronkite announced that he didn't think we could win, American support for the war was over. But I think we were starting to learn how to fight and win that war.

ADVISORS

*Captain **Chuck Glazerman,** RFPF Advisor, Long An Province, USA*

*Spc4 **Pat Gallagher,** Advisor, 1ˢᵗ Special Forces Group, Airborne, Ben Het, USA*

Arrival/Duties

Pat Gallagher: I arrived by plane at Nha Trang in 1958 and, after a couple of weeks of training, was flown to Ben Het, which is 50 miles NW of Pleiku, near the Laos/Cambodia/Vietnam border. The French had departed in 1954, the year my unit first arrived.

I was part of a team of twelve advisors sent to train the Montagnards, tribal mountain people in the central highlands of Vietnam. The training included weapons, communications, construction, tactics, etc., and I was the engineering sergeant. I took part in some offensive operations, but those were primarily handled by the operations guys. We also planted sensors in the jungle. They looked like plants and were designed to detect movement

We worked about 12/7; longer when we were out in the field. My training classes on construction and engineering fundamentals were usually attended by ten to twenty tribesmen. When we could, we tried to teach them to use things that were readily available to them. I showed them how to build rope bridges; before this they would walk forty miles around and a rope bridge was a real help to them. We put up about fifty in my time there.

Chuck Glazerman: I came through the ROTC program at the Citadel so I entered the Army as a Lieutenant. After a tour in Korea I was assigned to Recruiting duty. This bored me so I volunteered for Vietnam. Before I went over I had to go to the Defense Language School to learn some Vietnamese. I was a combat arms officer with the armored cavalry, but when we arrived over there was little need for armored guys so they converted us to advisor roles. I flew into Tan Son Nhut around May of 1967 and, after a brief orientation, was choppered to Long An, SW of Saigon, in III Corps.

I was an advisor to the Regional/Popular Forces, a battalion size group in Long An Province. We actually had responsibility for more than Long An Province; we flew into several neighboring provinces from time to time. I usually had a radioman and an interpreter right beside me. I called in air strikes and artillery and medevacs. The Ruff Puffs took good care of me because if I would get hurt they wouldn't get the help they needed.

We would go to the field after breakfast and return at the end of the day. With additional planning and perimeter duties I worked at least 12/7. An American Brigade had a fire base near Long An and we sometimes coordinated action with them.

Vietnamese

Chuck Glazerman: The Regional/Popular Forces guys were somewhat derisively referred to as the Ruff-Puffs. They weren't like the regular ARVN army. As a comparison, maybe they were somewhat like our National Guard. They lived in the town they defended so they actually had an investment in its survival. They were always under-equipped; in my early time with them they were using the old M-1, and perhaps an occasional Thompson sub-machine gun. If better weapons were supplied to the ARVN they didn't necessarily filter down to the Regional/Popular guys. At the end of the day, literally, when the Americans were back in their bases and the Viet Cong were roaming the street, it was the Ruff Puffs who were right there to intervene. Were they good soldiers? Hell no, but they had a lot of experience fighting the French, and toward the end of my tour they started getting the M-16. When you got right down to it, it was the Ruff Puffs who had to defend their families and their village, and they did. During the night when the VC came to cut the head off a teacher, or savage the mayor, it was the Ruff Puffs who would respond.

My counterpart, a Vietnamese major, was killed. He was a proud man who had fought with the Viet Minh against the French, and he certainly hated the Viet Cong, He was leading his guys and it just happened to be his day, and he got shot. For his burial I was able to get a helicopter, put his body on board with his family, and took him to his final resting place. He deserved that. In a macabre sort of way that was my proudest moment.

Courtesy: Chuck Glazerman

Pat Gallagher: We lived with the Montagnards. In our location at Ben Het, there were about one hundred of them, including their family members. We lived in our own hut in the center of the camp, with barbed wire around us; an inner perimeter of the camp. I really liked the Montagnard people. And they liked us. They were primitive but hard working and fierce warriors. There were five Montagnard tribes and they all spoke a different dialect. We were with the Rhad tribe. Perhaps picking up on the Montagnard enmity toward the ARVN and Vietnamese, I ended up not really caring for those people. The Vietnamese had pushed the tribal people off their land along the Vietnamese coast centuries earlier, away from better land and food. These hard feelings were still very much top of mind.

We weren't really briefed on the Montagnard-Vietnamese relationship before we arrived at Ben Het. Consequently, when I first met the elders I said something about the Vietnamese, through the interpreter of course, that didn't sit well with them. They really got hostile over my remarks but we eventually got it straightened out.

As a gesture to how much they appreciated what our team leader was doing for them, the Montagnard chief arranged for his daughter to marry our boss! The boss was thirty-five, and she was about fourteen; he was also married and we tried to explain that this could not be done. They were upset but some sort of compromise was reached and a two-day ceremony that was supposed to be a wedding went on as planned. We ate much native food and drank ox blood, but there was no ritualistic throwing of rice! We kept the boss from becoming a bigamist.

The Montagnards were very appreciative of everything we taught them. They said thank you over and over. Some of the Montagnard customs could be very frustrating for us. But you had to respect their ways.

Adventures

Chuck Glazerman: The key road down to Saigon came right through us and there were a couple of strategic bridges on that route. We had to deploy several times in the middle of the night when the VC were threatening those positions. We were often exposed to small arms fire during ambushes. I had my Vietnamese counterpart killed during one of these fights. We had rockets, mortars and small arms fire on many occasions.

I was pinned down more than once by enemy fire where I got myself as close to the ground as I could possibly be, and I'd see stalks of rice above my head quivering due to the rounds whizzing by. That brings you a moment of Jesus!

A Ruff Puff standing next to me while we were getting air support during a fight was awed by the firepower the planes were throwing out. He was smiling from ear to ear one minute and knocked unconscious the next from an empty shell casing falling from a plane.

For the most part the Ruff Puffs were brave, brave enough to put on a pack and go out there and do it. They were also pretty savvy; they knew that come noon it was lunch time, and they would stop and go find a chicken to steal or a mouse to throw in a stew pot. The VC seemed to do likewise. And the war resumed at 2:00. These guys had been fighting this war for a long, long time, long before I got there. And the contributions that people like myself made, if we went out with twenty and came back with twenty, well, that was a success.

Pat Gallagher: The monsoon definitely had an effect on what I did. At times, a river would rise five feet in ten minutes; it's hard to build a bridge under those conditions.

Our team was mostly lifers (career guys), WW II and Korea veterans. We had two officers but there was no formality; we were on a first name basis. We wore no rank or patches. We tried to be inconspicuous.

MISC. SUPPORT

*Spc4 **Larry Gombos**, Graves Registration, Personal Property Depot, Saigon, USA*

*SSgt **Norbert Cheri**, Cook, 377th Combat Support Squadron, Saigon, USAF*

*Spc4 **Larry Holdredge**, Laundry/Bath Operator, 228th Supply & Service Co., 1st Logistics Command, Long Binh/Tay Ninh, USA*

Duty/Arrivals

Larry Holdredge: I was drafted right out of high school. I flew into Tan Son Nhut near Christmas of 1969 and was bussed to a repo unit at Long Binh, for a bit, and then to Tay Ninh near the Cambodian border, for about seven months. Then I was transferred back to Long Binh.

I had been trained to do the laundry/bath job back in the States but when I arrived they needed someone to do a Graves Registration job at Tay Ninh. There was nobody in the MOS in-country to do it. There was a guy with funeral parlor experience back home, but he wasn't working in the Graves Registration unit. It might be that he had problems with it but all of us had problems with it! The Cambodian incursion was on and they anticipated the casualties that would result. So with no prior training I was a Graves Registration person.

Graves Registration personnel did not have to stand guard or do other duties because we had a Section Duty Watch over the coolers which contained the KIA's. We rotated on that duty.

We had an area with nine or ten stacked refrigeration units. And we would get calls from the hospital in Tay Ninh whenever the KIA was pronounced dead, for us to come and pick him up. We would drive over with our deuce-and-a-half and they would have the body in a little shed on the back side of the hospital. We'd bring the body back to our section and if they weren't already in a bag, we bagged them, if there was any decay, we tried to stop it, using alcohol or peroxide and then we would refrigerate them. We would then cut orders and have them signed by the commander and then arrange a flight out of Tay Ninh to Tan Son Nhut, where the main mortuary was. There were three of us to do this job. We would rotate on who flew with the bodies. If we just received one body during a day we'd keep him in refrigeration because they didn't like us to schedule a flight for just one man. We usually transported three or four at a time.

If there was a question as to how the person died there would be an autopsy. Usually there was no question. A few who died around Tay Ninh were a bit suspicious whether they were suicides or whatever. Once we dropped them off at the main mortuary we'd catch a ride over to the transient barracks to arrange for a place to sleep. We'd get a hot meal, stay overnight, and head back to Tay Ninh the next day. Sometimes you would get a C130, sometimes a C123, sometimes a Chinook helicopter. Sometimes it was just a Huey. We took whatever was available to get back the next day.

With Graves Registration you were on call 24/7. When the call came, we went. Many of the KIA's that came to us had fallen in Cambodia and there was still some secrecy about us being over there. Also, some of those KIA's had lain on the field in the hot sun for a couple of days. Those bodies would be in bad shape.

After seven months doing Graves Registration work they began to close down the collection point at Tay Ninh and 1st Logistics Command was moving out. I was switched over to USA Vietnam and I told the sergeant I didn't want to stay there; I wanted to be someplace else. He listened and then sent me to a Fire Base near the Cambodian border. I never did know the name of this place. They had four guns: two 175's and two 8" guns. The Fire Base also had a small landing strip with fuel pumps for the helicopters. Here I was doing the job they trained me to do, providing and maintaining hot showers for the troops. There were about 100 – 150 guys here and they already had the shower units installed. We had a generator, a water heater, and five shower heads. This was more of a nine to five kind of job, maintaining the shower facilities.

Larry Gombos: I flew into Bien Hoa in September of 1969 with orders to the 43rd Field Service Company. I figured it was a supply depot since that is what I had been trained to do. I spent the first night there and then they pulled three of us aside and told us we were TDY (temporary duty) to Personal Property Depot, Saigon. The three of us got into a truck bound for Saigon. We had three other guys with us -- in body bags.

For the first few weeks of my Graves Registration duty I had to go by lots of body parts and sights that were hard to look at. Later I was responsible for the removal of jewelry and the packaging of personal items such as stereos for mailing home. After that I had the job of going through letters and personal items to determine what should be included in the shipment to next-of-kin. Finally I boxed additional things for shipment home. All of these tasks were done after the remains were identified, sometimes by forensic anthropologists. We only shipped things back to the States once the remains were identified.

There were about eighteen guys working in Graves Registration. We saw about forty-five dead a day. In my view some of the body counts were definitely understated. We also received coordinates on where the KIA fell. Some of our dead were coming from places we "weren't supposed to be" like Laos and Cambodia. I worked ten hours a day, six days a week. I caught guard duty about once every three weeks. The weapons were locked up until then.

We had four large, refrigerated trailers -- basically large, walk-in refrigerators. As the bodies were received they were placed in the trailers. When they were pulled out, if they could not be identified, they were returned to the trailer. Our team of about twenty forensic anthropologists was usually successful in their identifications. In cases of decapitations the bodies were shipped home in closed caskets.

The USAF Mortuary was established Tan Son Nhut in 1963 and expanded in 1965 to include other Free World forces. The mortuary was transferred to the Army in 1966. [lxxxiii]

Norbert Cheri: I flew into Tan Son Nhut in December of 1969. I worked in the storeroom of Big Bertha, the large dining hall next to the motor pool. We worked at least 12/6.

Vietnamese

Larry Gombos: We had Vietnamese women that processed the paperwork and we had a mamasan cleaning the hooches and laundry, and we saw the Vietnamese in the restaurants. At one of the houses near our Saigon base the mamasan had her kids rolling joints. The kids were very good at it. They would finish with a pack of twenty and it looked like it came off the shelf at a supermarket in the states.

Larry Holdredge: I had contact with Vietnamese civilians; we had hooch girls in Tay Ninh, and we occasionally ate in their restaurants. Civilians KIA's also came to us occasionally and we turned them over to the local authority in Tay Ninh City. They were using part of a blown-out building and they stacked the bodies out back.

Some guys drove over to us in a jeep once and they had four black-clad enemy soldier KIA's with them. I don't know if they were VC or NVA and we took them to Tay Ninh City also. Vietnamese casualties were just a small percentage of the bodies we dealt with.

Norbert Cheri: On one occasion I was trying to get rid of some pallets of outdated 1940's C-Rations. Behind the Dining Hall I had my truck backed up to a dumpster and I was opening up the C-ration containers and dumping the contents into the dumpster. The next thing I know we are surrounded by countless people, uniforms, weapons, jeeps, white mice, Rangers, God Knows who was coming out of the wood work, with weapons, telling us that the stuff on the truck belongs to them. We should not be throwing it into the dumpster! They are in charge of the dumpsters. I pull out my weapon and say "Great, but the stuff that is on this truck belongs to the Air Force and belongs to me until I finish putting it into the dumpster". They say we will do it for you. I say NO, we will do it. I tell my guys to go get ice picks and start sticking holes into every can, and also ask someone to bring me eight gallons of ammonia. After stabbing every can and pouring on all the ammonia, I told them "now it's your trash". There were people about a half a mile away reacting to the ammonia in the air; the dumpster was left alone.

Working in the Dining Hall it was not unusual to see the items we were cooking on sale at the main gate. Our Vietnamese staff came to work looking rather thin and left sometimes well endowed. Black Pepper was a popular theft item.

Adventures

Larry Holdredge: I ran into a very large snake outside the perimeter of the Fire Base. I shot at it; I don't know if I hit it. We did a lot of crazy stuff outside the perimeter, including going fishing with an M-79 grenade launcher. We stunned a lot of fish but we really didn't want them. We did a lot of stupid stuff there. I was issued an M16 and I also had a .38, a .45 and the M79.

We were mortared frequently at Tay Ninh. We had one round hit near our building but we were in our bunkers. Most of the sniper fire at the Fire Base was aimed at the perimeter bunkers.

I broke down at least once doing the Graves job. I had just received a letter from my mother and she had just lost her job. My father died when I was thirteen so I really felt badly. I was sitting in a corner in a fetal position, crying. I started sending money home to my mother at this time but she didn't use it. It was there when I got home. That's the way mothers are I guess.

The longer I stayed in the job the harder it got to look at these guys; some of them were younger than me and I was only 21. Some of these guys were only eighteen years old. If we had their personal effects you'd see pictures of family and letters. They might have letters hanging out of their pockets. Aw geez, it would get really bad. But we did it. We did a lot of joking around.

The Graves section was located right next door to where I should have been working, the laundry. One time we told one of the guys in the laundry that we had a full bird colonel in a bag, and for him to come over and see him. We covered one of our guys in a poncho and when the guy came in our guy in the poncho sat up. It scared the devil out of the guy. We did things like this to help relieve the tension of the job.

At Tay Ninh we always got mortared between 0215 and 0300. During one attack I jumped up and ran to the bunker. I entered the bunker and sat on a little wooden bench. I sat on a used condom that squished when I sat on it. That was kind of funny.

At the Fire Base we had a guy that would take our 5-ton truck and get into a convoy and appropriate things that we needed. He got hold of another generator, which we really needed. We were using this new generator when our captain told us that we had a colonel coming in to inspect us and we needed to get rid of the un-authorized machine. We took it down to the river and strapped a couple sticks of C4 to it and touched it off. The biggest piece we found was no more than eight or ten inches long. We got rid of it; I don't think that's what the captain meant, but we got rid of it.

Some of the troops stationed at Tay Ninh would go out into the field for a week, and then they'd return, get drunk, and throw tear gas grenades around. I was taking a shower one morning and somebody threw a tear gas grenade into the shower. The next thing you saw was a naked body running through the compound trying to get dried off; every place I was wet had that stuff burning me. That was kind of funny at my expense.

I never had any schooling for the Graves Registration job; it was on-the-job training. We thought we were doing a good job but the colonel told us we should not be collecting personal items and sending them along with the KIA's. He told us to leave everything on the body to help with identification. He said that may be the only way they can identify it.

A few months after I got home I got a folder from the Army containing a Bronze Star and the Army Commendation Medal for meritorious service. I guess they felt I wasn't doing too badly after all.

Larry Gombos: Some of the anthropologists screwed around with the bodies, posing them with cigarettes in their hands, drinks, things like that. I saw that seven or eight times.

Norbert Cheri: I remember the pains I had working, and seeing others working through pain made me a better person. I remember dislocating four fingers on my right hand and was sent to the field hospital. Seeing the carnage there I walked out and fixed my own fingers.

MACV was dis-established by the Paris Peace Accords in March, 1973. Speaking generally, the admin and staff jobs might not be considered the most glamorous or adventurous undertakings in the military, but, like all parts of the puzzle, they are important and necessary. An army goes nowhere without them.

ADMINISTRATIVE/STAFF SUPPORT

Mike Holz

Paul Kaser

Pat Gallagher

Chuck Glazerman

Norbert Cheri

William Harkins

CHAPTER SIX

BROWN WATER NAVY

Due to weather and terrain that allowed two harvests per season the twenty-six thousand square miles of the Mekong Delta produced 80% of South Vietnam's rice crop.[lxxxiv]   The Delta became a prime VC target in 1966. The American response was the creation of a mobile riverine force, our so-called "brown water navy," using flat-bottomed boats to navigate rivers and canals in the Delta.[lxxxv]   A brigade of the U.S. Army's newly-activated Ninth Infantry Division joined 1,600 sailors and a larger ARVN force to give the allies the advantage of mobility in the Delta.

Our planners studied the French campaigns in the Delta and the Monitor and the Merrimac during the American Civil War in order to understand what types of vessels were best suited for work in the Delta. The sailors that manned these craft were mostly volunteers from the Blue Water navy – our "hidden navy" as it were.

Arrival/Duties

*Boson Mate Chief **Don McMurray**, WFMB-17/USS Askari ARL-30, Dong Tam, USN*

*Engineman **Jim Fritz**, Mobile Riverine Force, Dong Tam/Nam Can, USN*

*Chief **Sidney Brown**, Hull Technician, USS Luzerne County (LST-902), USN*

*Ship fitter 3rd Class Diver 2nd Class **Steve Doak**, Harbor Clearance Unit #1, Clark AFB, Philippines, USN*

*Lt. Cdr. **Paul Gesswein,** Deputy Commander, Giant Slingshot, Ben Luc (Parrott's Beak), USN*

*Cook Third Class **Vic Griguoli,** USS Meeker County LST-980, USN*

Arrival/Duties

Don McMurray: I enlisted in August, 1960 and arrived by plane for my first Vietnam tour in February of 1967. There was supposed to be a truck there for us at Tan Son Nhut but of course there wasn't. We spent the night sleeping on the tarmac. I woke up with a face full of mosquito bites. Welcome to Vietnam! I went to Cam Ranh Bay for a month, building sewage trenches, and then flew to Yokohama, Japan to pick up our repair vessel (WFMB-17) which we towed to Dong Tam.

Dong Tam is about forty miles southwest of Saigon. It was created by dredging about six hundred acres of mud from the My Tho River and named by General Westmoreland. Dong Tam means United Hearts and Minds.

Dong Tam: Our major base in the Delta
Courtesy: Don McMurray

Our responsibilities at Dong Tam were basically to repair, replenish and service the river craft. So if the engine broke down, as the boson mate I was the one that lowered the hook down, grabbed the engine and pulled it up. I would swing the bad engine over and drop it into the engineering bay of our repair vessel, pick up a new one, swing it over and drop it into the boat. The average work day was ten to twelve hours. We worked on ASPB's, Monitors, and LCM's so basically I was a coxswain of all three; I had to know how to drive them.

There was a bar at the base at Dong Tam and I was the bartender. We always knew when the army was going out. They would come in and buy cases of beer. We normally sold a case for $3, but we sold it to them for $5 to $6 and they were paying it. We knew guys from the boats that carried them up the river; they were charging them another $5 a case to carry it. So much for the secrecy surrounding the move.

Jim Fritz: I arrived by plane in Saigon on May, 1968. We took a Korean ship to Dong Tam, in the Delta. We were ambushed the following morning and had four men severely wounded. I was an engineman on an ASPB. Our boat had two .50 caliber machine guns and a 20mm cannon. The ASPB's were listed as having a top speed of sixteen knots; the governor on the engine would be set at 2300 rpm. Our governor was set at 3000 rpm so we could probably do twenty knots. The ASPB's had a crew of five and were known as the "delta destroyers". The cost to build each of them was $325,000 and eighty-seven were built for Vietnam.

On the riverboats, everyone had to know everyone else's job. I was an engineman, gunner (.30 cal., .50 cal., and 20mm), radioman, and coxswain. We worked about 12/7 checking sampan traffic on the river and canals, looking for weapons and things. Every fifth round in the 20mm cannon was armor piercing but those rounds were slightly too big for the gun. We had to take these out of the belt.

Sidney Brown: I joined the Navy in 1954 so I was an E-7 (Chief) by Vietnam. In September, 1968, I received orders to join the *Luzerne County, an LST,* in Saigon. I flew to Tan Son Nhut and was greeted by

MP'S telling us to exchange all US currency for MPC (military payment certificates) down to the denomination of a nickel or face five years in jail!

We were billeted in a U.S. run hotel in the Cholon section of Saigon, near the racetrack. The smell from the racetrack each morning drove us out of the area! We ended up there for six weeks since the *Luzerne County,* our ship-to-be, broke down on the way over. This LST was WW II vintage and had to be re-commissioned to rejoin the fleet. They realized they would need a lot of veteran sailors who had some experience with the old vessels and the rumor was that they had emptied the brigs of old salts that had been imprisoned for one thing or another.

Meanwhile me and my future *Luzerne County* shipmates were being issued jungle fatigues, web belts, an M-14 and a .45; things that are normally worn by an infantryman. "But I'm a sailor," I protested, showing them my blue dungarees. "Nope, this is what you're supposed to have," they responded, checking their clipboards.

Finally we were bussed over to the pier and met the crew that had brought the *Luzerne County* from the west coast. They certainly looked the part of brig rats, what with long hair, shirt sleeves cut off, and menacing scowls. We exchanged conveyances; they took our bus and we boarded the ship.

I had eight guys working for me. They were electricians, ship fitters, pipefitters, metal smiths, etc. Our job was to keep that rusty old WW II ship running. We picked most of our cargo up at Vung Tau and hauled it up into the Delta. We hauled some of the first steel matting used to build landing strips. The first time we lowered the ramp in the Delta the elephant grass on the bank of the river was eight or nine feet tall.

Over time I was qualified as an officer of the deck and I stood watch just like the officers. Somebody is always on the bridge. Unloading cargo we'd work around the clock until that stuff is off there. A common cargo was bags of cement. They'd put twenty-four bags to a pallet and each bag weighed eighty pounds. They'd stack cement four pallets high. But the worst stuff we would haul was ammunition. At times we would have the tank deck stacked to the overhead (ceiling) with ammunition; 105mm shells, rockets, cordite. We stored lube oil in 55-gallon drums on the main deck because it would be slower to go off than gasoline. We laid 2x12 lumbers across the top to chain them down. If a round came in we got a lot of splinters but not shrapnel or a big explosion.

Steve Doak: I volunteered for gunboats in Vietnam. I never told my mom I put my name down, but they didn't pick me for that. I got picked for an outfit called Harbor Clearance Unit #1. This was a diving unit that was over at Subic Bay in the Philippines. I initially went over there in the summer of 1969 as an apprentice machinist. After a month I told them I'd rather be working as a pipefitter so they switched me over to another workshop where I started welding and doing pipefitting. I was brazing, welding and arc welding and things like that. Some guys in my unit were divers so I got into that.

I was what they called an "89-day wonder." They would fly us over to Vietnam, put us where they needed us but at the end of 89 days, no matter what we were doing, they'd fly us back to Clark AFB in the Philippines so we wouldn't count against the manpower total in Vietnam. This was a common practice. The Air Force also did this for guys coming out of Okinawa and Guam. Once back from Vietnam they'd give us a couple of months to rest up before we went back over there.

As part of Harbor Clearance Unit #1 we would go over to Vietnam and try to salvage wrecks, mostly our gunboats sunk in the Mekong Delta. We had a map that showed where these boats had gone down. Once we located the wreck we would determine which way it was facing. Then we would come up with a plan to bring it up. When we pulled it up we'd try to patch it and tow it back to the facilities for repair.

In the Delta where the rivers were maybe only twenty feet deep or so, we worked with what they call a Jack Brown rig; this was a triangular mask which fit across your forehead and came down around your chin. It covered your whole face so you could breathe and see. Even though most of our diving was done during the day it was so dark in those canals and rivers you couldn't really see anything. You could hold your fingers up against your mask and not be able to see them. It was so muddy everything we did was by feel. And you would get compressed air from the surface via a valve on your cheek that you could open and close. Most of the time we dove with just an old pair of cut-off shorts, maybe a long-sleeve sweatshirt as protection against cuts from sharp metal, and our combat boots. We didn't wear flippers. We would usually wrap an ankle or something around part of the boat to hold us in place while we worked. We didn't swim around much like you see in the movies. A number of times we worked through the night. We changed divers occasionally not so much because of problems from the bends since the water was not deep, but you would just get tired and water-logged after a while. On most jobs we worked until the work was done. We didn't want to become a sitting duck for the enemy. It was: Get in and get out!

Jim Fritz: My final five months in Vietnam were spent on Operation Sea Float down at the southern tip of the Delta. The camp was Nam Can and we had about a hundred guys there. Sea Float was a bunch of anchored barges on the Song Cau Lon River including a medical unit barge, a barracks barge, and a barge with 72,000 gallons of fresh water, one with 72,000 gallons of JP5 and another with 72,000 gallons of diesel fuel to refuel helicopters. We used to run patrols and ambushes off the barges. I also had two generators to take care of.

Don McMurray: Between tours I was stationed at Willow Grove, Pennsylvania. I went back in June, 1970, again to Dong Tam, which was growing by the day. We repaired, replenished and serviced the whole river craft, not just the engines like on my last tour. On the first tour we were inside the basin, this time we ran with the *Askari* from Saigon to Cambodia. The *Askari* maintained an inventory of over 4,000 spare parts.

We had a 72,000 ton A-frame lifting capability. We used a big hook; the boats either had river damage or shrapnel. We had two big ammis tied alongside the ship and we would put a 30 degree list on the boat to return them to an even keel. We would swing the ammis underneath it and sit the damaged boat down on railroad ties and the mechanics would do their thing, change the screws or whatever. We'd work ten – twelve hours then every two or three days we would move. This ship was self-propelled so we had to man our stations and move up and down the river so they couldn't zero in on us.

Paul Gesswein: On my second visit to Vietnam I flew into Long Binh in September, 1970. I was issued equipment there and met my boss, (who was in the hospital recuperating from a gunshot wound), the people to whom I would be reporting, and then I went up to Ben Luc to begin my job with Operation Giant Slingshot.   Ben Luc was an intermediate support base for Giant Slingshot containing probably less than two hundred men, including Navy, Seabees, Seals, ARVN, dust offs, sea wolves, psyops guys; a real military melting pot. I lived in a two-man hooch. I had a dog and a jeep.

I was the Senior Advisor to a CTG (Commander Task Group) stationed in the so-called Parrot's Beak area, the triangle between the Vam Co Dong and Vam Co Tay Rivers jutting into South Vietnam west of Saigon and east of the Cambodian border. The Parrott's Beak geography harboured significant NVA infiltration routes into the Mekong Delta, the breadbasket of Vietnam, and efforts to deter this infiltration had begun back in October, 1968.

We had five ATSB's (Advanced Tactical Support Bases) under our supervision. There were four on one river, and one on the other and they had PBR's going out on patrol. The Vietnamese, under the Vietnamization Program, were in charge. I was the Senior Advisor to them. I helped them plan the operations. I had a counterpart who was in charge of the security of the base, the supplies, the repairs, that sort of thing.

Vic Griguoli: After my first tour on the Cleveland, in 1967 and 1968, I went home for two weeks leave, and then they sent me back for duty on the *USS Meeker County LST 980*, down in the Delta, the so-called brown water navy. That tour lasted into 1970.

Vietnamese

Steve Doak: Shortly after we started the Vietnamization Program I lived on a boat. We were training Vietnamese to learn the salvage procedures and they would be given the boats when we left. We kept a couple of the old Mike boats (LCM's) for ourselves and the living quarters on that thing were just bolted onto the deck. They had canvas tops to keep the rain off us. Two of us built a plywood hooch up by the wheelhouse and we lived there on cots. Our shower consisted of dumping a bucket with a rope attached into the river or canal. We used that bucket for soaping and rinsing. That is the same water where you would see the floating dead pigs and things. I never pulled up a snake or anything in the bucket but one time I'm rinsing off and I notice an old mamasan over at the bank taking a crap in the canal. We also lived in the barracks at Cat Lo, down near Vung Tau. There we had regular beds, bathrooms and showers.

I worked mostly with their military guys and I had mixed feelings about them. When we first started sharing our boats with them during Vietnamization down at Cat Lo we'd be out there sweating and working all morning, and we'd go to chow and they'd be standing there in line. They hadn't done anything all day and they're ahead of us in line in their clean uniforms. There would be a hundred of them waiting for the mess hall to open. This went on for a couple of weeks. We almost had a riot on that one. They finally decided to put two lines together. The guys that were training as divers were pretty motivated and they were hard workers. The rank and file navy guys were not very motivated. The impression I had was they figured that if they stayed out of trouble for a while they would survive the war. They knew it was ending.

One of the things we noticed was if an Army base was closed down, within a couple of days it would be stripped clean. They'd take all the metal and everything and either use it for themselves or sell it on the black market. When we turned our boats over to their navy we'd sit by the docks and watch them take all the supplies we had just given them, and we heard they were offloading that stuff into their cars! Whether it was food, gasoline, anything, they'd just take it for themselves.

Paul Gesswein: Among the other functions at our ISB (Intermediate Support Base) we had repair facilities for the PBR's. The Vietnamese were taking over the repair function for the boats and they were rather proud of themselves for doing this. They were pretty good with the mechanical stuff but a bit behind on the electronics end of things.

One of our sailors was bitten by a dog. In hopes of avoiding the painful but necessary rabies shots, the corpsman suggested we find the dog to determine if it was rabid. We were unable to determine if the dog was rabid because the Vietnamese at the base had cooked the dog and ate it.

Don McMurray: The Viet's had weird ideas. Down in the delta would cut just behind your wake, as close as they could get to your stern, to get off any evil spirits they had on their sampan. And you weren't supposed to touch a Viet kid on the head because the evil spirits would be transferred to him. That was a no-no.

A lieutenant got in trouble and our government had to pay: We wouldn't let sampans get near us. We used water cannons to keep them away but they always wanted to come up and beg, and this time it wasn't working. He took this M79 to scare them, and it went off and killed a couple of people in the boat.

We had worked for 48 hours with Vietnamese advisors on a riverboat of theirs that was in a scuffle. The boat had holes in it and the Vietnamese said "Bad boat!" So they opened the sea strainers and sunk it. The water was twelve - fifteen feet deep. We had to pull the ship up, position ourselves, get the ammis in place, put divers in the water – it took two days for the divers to finally get belly straps around it – then we had to lift that sucker out of the water, all because they said it had bad spirits. That's some of the things we had to deal with.

Paul Gesswein: The first guy I had over me at Ben Luc was a South Vietnamese. He was kind of a plump, happy-go-lucky sort of guy who was not all that aggressive. He was fired about halfway through my tour. His replacement was from North Vietnam and he was a real go-getter. What a difference between the two. He stepped up the patrols and the ambushes. And he chewed ass.

One day the Vietnamese PBR's came into the pier returning from a mission. They are supposed to clear their guns before they get to the pier. The guy in the trailing boat cleared his .50 caliber as they arrived at the pier by shooting a guy in the lead boat in the head.

Jim Fritz: We saw the Vietnamese every day moving their sampans down the river. We gave them C rations and other things in return for information on enemy activity. They seemed to be good people who were on our side but I'm sure they just wanted to be left alone to do their farming. We learned to watch for signs of nervousness as we inspected their sampans for weapons, or we took note of the absence of birds in an area or a bunch of sampans hurrying in the opposite direction we were going, which could be signs of an ambush.

On November 1, 1968, we were tied up at Station 1 with the LST *USS Westchester County* (LST-1167), a supply ship and floating barracks. At 0300 two VC sappers evaded the patrol screen, maneuvered between the pontoons and the ship and placed satchel charges under the LST. We were tied up along the pontoons and sleeping at the time. Seventeen sailors were killed, the largest in-country loss of life at one time for the Navy during the Vietnam War. Eight soldiers also died in that attack.

Sid Brown: During December of 1968 we hauled several loads of cement to build revetments for helicopters. At the same time the US Aid International Development, which was an arm of the CIA, was trying to help the Vietnamese farmers grow more rice. The soil was so devoid of nutrients that we hauled bags of lime down to the delta and we'd drop a third at one place, a third at another place, and a third somewhere else. We unloaded this lime and at night we'd have lights on our surroundings with M-60's to protect us from sappers. We stacked all this lime on the bank and I don't know what happened to the guards that night but when we got up in the morning the only lime left was the row facing us. The five rows behind it had been pilfered during the night. So a few of us went into this little town to drink some of the local Tiger 33 beer and we were going to order some pork and fried rice. On my way through the kitchen I found out this pork was dog. They were cutting up these dogs. And then it started raining; it was the monsoon season. And we're watching these guys across the road building a cement wall. And I observed that I had never seen such white cement before. What it was, they had stolen our lime and they were mixing it with sand thinking they had cement, and we sat there for about two hours just watching the rain collapse their wall.

When we would go places to offload cement the forklifts would tear the paper cement bags open. That cement would get six to eight inches deep down in the tank deck. They would waste a third of the cement tearing those bags open. The forklift drivers didn't care. In January of 1969 we were in a local Catholic orphanage run by some Vietnamese nuns. They always had two or three men there that did maintenance for them. We'd tell them with very bad, broken English, that we had cement available for free if they wanted it. And they would come down and clean up all this stuff in the tank deck; they'd get a broom and sweep it up. You'd see these nuns in their black habits that would end up gray when they were finished. And they would cement playgrounds and parts of sidewalks; cement was like gold over there.

LST's: Delivery Service in the Delta
Courtesy: Sid Brown

Vic Griguoli: We trained ten Vietnamese officers on our LST in my final days. These officers left the ship just prior to an incident we had; it is possible that they passed the word to the enemy. The plan was for them to take over the LST when we exited, as part of the Vietnamization Program. The ship was to be theirs come July 31. But when the time came the LST was not given to the Vietnamese; it was instead sold to somebody in Europe for use as scrap metal. I didn't trust them.

Adventures

Jim Fritz: In December of 1968 our ASPB was on patrol as part of Operation Giant Slingshot with a PBR (patrol boat river); we came under heavy automatic weapons and rocket fire and our boat was knocked dead in the water. Our boat had suffered a direct rocket hit in the engine compartment, knocking out our electrical power to the .50 caliber machine gun and the 20mm cannon. We had to push off the bank of the river with bow hooks while under fire in order to get out into the current to float downstream until help arrived. After delivering a suppressing fire against the enemy I jumped into the river to lead our boat out into the current. Eventually our big guns began operating and we were then towed back for repairs. I was awarded the Bronze Star for this action.

ASPB's at work in the Delta
Courtesy: Jim Fritz

Sid Brown: We would have mud above our shoes when we went ashore during the monsoon. But it was worse on board. Our drains would clog from the cement dust that had been activated from the rains.

When we left Saigon for Vung Tau we got into an unusual tidal situation and we ended up high and dry at Vung Tau. We arrived empty and they started forklifting this steel matting for airfields into our ship. This stuff is 12' X 2 ½' and they had it stacked 18" high. This is the heaviest stuff you can carry on an LST. One stack is all a heavy-terrain forklift can handle. The stevedores would stack it three high on the tank deck and up on the main deck. The tide never came back in. We sat there with no water around us for six weeks! They took the steel matting off to try to float us but it didn't work. We were sitting there drinking beer and barbequing steak and walking around the bank. You could squat down amidships and look under the ship from one side to the other. They decided that a tug from the Philippines would pull us off. They tied this 4" line onto the big chock on the stern and the tug boat got a running start and it ripped off the chock and everything off the main deck so you could look down to the mess hall like it was a skylight. The LST never budged. After six weeks, with the Seabees digging a ditch alongside and washing the sand and dirt out from under us and the tide coming in, we slid into the ditch and finally got our butts off the bank.

Jim Fritz: Tet got our attention. We were on the Cambodian border and involved in numerous night ambushes. We noticed a lot more enemy activity after the bombing halt.

As part of Operation Sea Float we provided a floating naval support base for PBR and helicopters for brown water operations down in the Delta. One of the things they did on Sea Float was drop sensors into the countryside; when the sensors indicated activity they would put mortar fire in that area.

Living conditions were poor. We had seven men trying to cram into a 50' ASPB (Assault Support Patrol Boat) barracks barge on Operation Sea Float. The barge was in the Song Cau Lon River.

We passed a Vietnamese boat while going up river during Sea Float. On that boat a Vietnamese lady was holding a baby. Our boat bumped their boat and she dropped the baby into the river. I still feel badly about that.

Don McMurray: We'd work all day repairing boats and engines and about 0100 or 0200 we'd start getting incoming. The rounds would be falling every four hundred yards or so, walking straight toward us, then they'd hit the barge next to us; the next round would be us. But it stopped.

Sid Brown: We had a load of Air Force helicopter guys that were being shifted from Cam Ranh Bay to the Delta to build a new airstrip. The ship was crowded and we're transiting up the river with everybody up topside. Some of the Air Force guys are sitting in jeeps up on the main deck listening to Armed Forces radio and telling jokes and having a good time. Well you hear the rounds go by before you hear the pop. And when they hit the LST it was like putting marbles in a fruit jar and shaking it. It was metal against metal. Everybody started running for the ladder. Most navy men go down a ladder in times like this without putting feet on the rungs; you just grab the outside and slide down. Well the Air Force officer ahead of me was taking his time climbing down rung by rung. General Quarters is being sounded. The Air Force captain stopped in the middle of the ladder and I landed feet first on his chest. It knocked the breath out of him. I apologized but told him not to stop on a ladder during an attack.

A couple of weeks later we got stuck on a sandbar on a turn in the river. We were standing topside watching some of our jets really pounding something. Then we heard a whooshing noise from an RPG (rocket propelled grenade). It hit right near me against the edge of one of our lifeboats. The force of the explosion moved in the opposite direction from me, fortunately, and exploded into an armored bulkhead of Radio Central.

Steve Doak: There was some frustration getting spare parts since most of our repair work was done in the middle of nowhere. We simply had to make do. When we pulled the Zippo boat up the whole side of it was almost gone. This boat had hit a mine. We had some sheet metal flown in by helicopter and we had cutting torches and welding torches and I welded for eighteen hours straight. I was the only welder on that crew. Every time I'd strike an arc I'd get shocked since I was standing in the water. I had welding spark burns on my ankles where the sparks would go down into my combat boots. I still couldn't patch it up like I wanted; I didn't have the time or the equipment I needed. We patched it the best we could and got it pulled off the bank and it just barely floated. The water came right up near the top of the patch but I didn't have any more materials to patch. We hoped that if we went very slowly we might get it back. We threw off machine guns, ammo, anything heavy. We got it about three miles away and water started to come in over the patch. Within ten minutes it was listing and we cut it loose in the middle of the canal. We did get it away from the firebase, which was the plan, but we hoped to get it all the way back to the repair shop and we couldn't. Seeing that boat go under was hard to watch.

Sid Brown: Our drinking water came from machines called edulators, which we obtained from the US Army. The process spins the water around like a centrifuge and with the addition of chemicals purifies the water. It does not extract Agent Orange however. After you have seen dead water buffaloes in the river it is hard to be enthusiastic about drinking the "purified" water, or bathing in it, or doing anything with it. Our edulator broke once in March, 1969, and I was sent with three other guys to get some fresh water from the Air Force at their water purification plant. When we arrived at their location they told us to take all we wanted but that we should get out of that spot about a half hour before the sun went down. We were seven miles up the Basaac River, in a bad place. It was after dark when we left the place with only half the load of water we hoped to get. We came across a mass of military vehicles blocking the road ahead of us. There were tanks, APC's, halftracks, just about everything. They were manned by the ARVN. "What are you doing here?" they asked us. We told them. They thought we were crazy. "There is going to be a war here in a minute," they told us. We pressed on for the ship. After a while we could hear a lot of shooting behind us with red (us) and green (VC) tracers filling the air. Back at the ship one of the officers insisted we go back for more water. We asked him to look at how the sky was lit up in that direction. "You can court martial me, lieutenant" I told him, "but I'm not going back there." He went to discuss it with the captain and we heard no more about it.

Steve Doak: I got into a fire fight one time and earned my Combat Action Ribbon. There were a bunch of our boats -- all types and sizes -- on an operation, including a boat with a 30mm cannon, and a zippo boat, which shot flames, and another boat called the Monitor, that had a 60mm cannon, a couple of 50 calibers and a mortar pit on it. Our objective was the salvage of a Monitor that had been sunk. These boats are very expensive and we wanted to retrieve it if we could.

Knowing that the wreck was in a hot zone of the delta we went in with over fifteen boats. Many of the boats were manned by Vietnamese. We started receiving fire from the shore the night before. The next morning they spread out all the Americans amongst the boats. My boat was the last in line going in. I felt vulnerable. We were not in a canal; it was more of a river tributary. We were zigzagging. Our boat kept steering into the banks of the river, then backing out, and then repeating this move. The other boats were just losing us since they were not over-steering as our boat was. We found the wreck and we were diving over top of it. We had Vietnamese soldiers on one bank and they choppered in some ARVN to protect us from the other bank. Helicopter gunboats were above us for additional protection.

We dived on this wreck for about a day; at one point VC started walking mortars toward us on the river. We had a guy in the water and we pulled him up so he wouldn't get his eardrums burst. We cut our anchor line and all the other attached ropes; all the other boats had taken off and there were just two boats, including us, in the middle of the river. Each of us left in a different direction.

The next morning we returned but we were hit with small arms and P40 rocket fire from the bank. We had been authorized to spray the shoreline on our way in so there was a high volume of fire from our fifteen boats. Then we heard a different sound which we identified as P40 rockets from the shoreline coming toward us. My boat was again toward the rear of the column and I saw the rounds spraying the boat in front of us and I figured we'd be next. Another American, a chief petty officer, was with me in the boat and he and I were firing our M16's toward the shore. A

P40 round landed just short of our boat and threw shrapnel all over us. Both of us were knocked backwards into the boat. When I turned to look at him I saw he had taken most of the shrapnel in his left arm. His flak jacket had protected him from greater injury. He had a big tattoo of a leopard that he was very proud of on his arm. Half of it was gone. I had a little bloody string down the inside of my forearm. I dropped what I was doing and started bandaging his arm. A lot of firing was still going on but our ship was finally able to get out to the main river where we could lick our wounds and get organized. Medevac choppers were called for the chief petty officer and some Vietnamese guys in some of the other boats.

The medic was looking at the chief and he asked me if I got anything. I showed him the little trickle of blood on my forearm and asked him if it deserved a Purple Heart. "Nope," he answered. The chief told me if I got a Purple Heart he would kick my ass! "But I'm wounded," I laughed.

Vic Griguoli: I was on the *Meeker County* in June of 1970, and they sounded General Quarters at 0240 hours. We were tied up at the Vung Tau pier. Although it was night time, they had so many lights around it was like daytime. My battle station was in the captain's cabin wearing headphones. And we started to hear concussion grenades going off in the water. I was due to rotate home in three days (July 1), and this was making me very nervous. A voice from the pier came over the headphone telling us they had something under the ship and they didn't know what it was. I kept announcing that I had just three days left. No one seemed to care. They kept trying to rig some lights to look under the ship, but they call it the brown water for a reason; it was very muddy water and difficult to see.

One of my friends had the watch on deck, and he noticed that there was a light colored rope coming from a telephone pole on the pier to under our ship. All the other ropes around our ship were bigger, and dirty like the water. He had noticed this difference and it was him who sounded the alarm. Divers went into the water and they felt something underneath the ship, but due to the murky water they couldn't determine what it was. They could tell it had a Vietnamese timer on it, but they couldn't identify it for certain. The speaker from the pier told us to be patient. Then they told us to get all non-essential personnel off the ship. I asked the captain what all this meant and he told me that we apparently had a 40 pound metallic charge attached to the hull of our ship. This news caused me to remind him that I had just three more days in-country. The next thing I know someone is slapping me and taking the headphones off me.

The divers couldn't de-activate the bomb because they couldn't see the timer in the murky water, but they finally de-magnetized it and got it off the ship. The put the bomb in the captain's gig and steered it out to the mouth of the river, and then the captain's gig comes back to the ship, and I'm starting to cook for breakfast, and there is a mushroom cloud in the water; a huge explosion. Hiroshima-like. A few minutes later our ship is bouncing like a cork against the pier.

We were not supposed to be in either Laos or Cambodia, but our LST took supplies to bases in both countries. I think some of our guys must have blabbed something the night before while they were on liberty in the bars, about how we were going to be taking this big load of supplies, ammo and fuel up river the next day. Loose lips **do** sink ships! They found a plastic bag and a plastic pop bottle that they figured the sapper must have used to allow him to swim under water to attach the bomb. But thank god for the young man that turned in the alarm. His alertness may have saved over one hundred lives! For some reason, the after-action report recorded just one stick of dynamite in that satchel, but we knew it was forty pounds.

The effectiveness of the armor used in the river boats is apparent. Of the nearly 680 boats hit by either rocket fire or small arms, only thirty were temporarily out of action, and only two were scrapped.[lxxxvi]

Steve Doak: We were going to rescue a Zippo boat that had hit a mine next to one of our firebases. We had some support gunboats and started down this straight canal. There were six or seven boats and we also had helicopter support. It was easy to become complacent with all this firepower and we did! We started off with our helmets and flak jackets on and our fingers on the triggers of various machine guns. After about thirty minutes we started to relax. After thirty minutes more the helmets and flak jackets came off. A couple hours later there were four or five of us sitting on the top deck playing cards! When we reached the firebase a guy on the radio tells the choppers and duster planes overhead that they can go home. He thanks them and tells them this is the first time we've come up this way in over a month that we hadn't been hit! The card players just looked at each other!

All but two of our jobs were done in the rivers and canals of the Delta. In one instance two of us flew over to the western fringes of South Vietnam, near Can Tho and Ben Tui, to do a demolition job in support of one of the Vietnamese villages. There was a major ferry crossing used heavily by both military and civilians in that area and their ferry had hit a mine and sunk right there at the ramp. They wanted us to clear it out of the way so they could move a new ferry in. We did a series of demolitions on the sunken ferry and dispersed it.

On another occasion we did a job for the Coast Guard. One of their cutters had run across a Chinese trawler in the middle of the night and when it refused to stop when they fired across its' bow they sank it with gunfire. They wanted us to determine what the cargo on this trawler was. There were four or five of us for this mission. This job was in the South China Sea not some little canal. On the way out I got very seasick. I was almost incapacitated the whole time.

The cutter showed us where the wreck was and we made a series of dives down there to check the cargo. The Coast Guard guys were great hosts and they invited us over for dinner, showers and movies. We determined that the trawler was full of AK-47 ammunition hidden under the nets of the trawler. We also found the crew members of the trawler underneath the nets, dead of course. And one by one during the course of our search they started popping to the surface. The bodies were bloated and the fish had down their work on them as well. The Coast Guard was very pleased that we confirmed their actions with this enemy supply vessel.

In the 70's we had more guys that had come out of the fleet. Their mentality was still fleet sailor ("Keep your mustache trimmed, keep your hair short"). We weren't used to that. I ran into problems with some of those old timers late in the game. By then I looked like a pirate; my hair was long and I kind of clashed with that new generation of NCO's that came over and wanted to straighten things out. Our guys were hard workers. And they played hard. We had a reputation for hard drinking, womanizing and partying. We enjoyed that moniker.

Don McMurray: On the river I'm working a crane doing some loading on our Mike boat and the army was nearby offloading ammo and I see the army guys throwing the shells to each other. Just as I notice this, one goes off. Guys were killed. Mortar rounds have a large bursting radius, even when they're used improperly!

The VC started placing mines in the rivers and canals so we had to place a man with a rifle in the bow of our repair ship to shoot at anything floating in the water. It unnerved the villagers to hear shooting, especially if a mine blew up.

In the Delta we were close to Cambodia, where we weren't supposed to be. We got a call from an outpost that needed twelve engines. We had just finished working on these engines. This outpost was nineteen miles west into enemy territory. Along the way I found out that I didn't have a qualified coxswain when the ammis we were towing started taking on water. Then I'm told there would be an escort waiting for us, two Vietnamese and two American advisors. We met them and started our trip up the river. We got into the free fire zone and tested our weapons. All we had were .30 caliber machine guns. One of the Vietnamese wanted to get a drink of water. We had two jugs sitting there, one for water and one battery acid. Of course he drank the acid so he and his American had to split, leaving us with one escort. The other guy said his Vietnamese came down sick so that left us with no escort. We went seventeen miles with no escort, the enemy on both sides.

Coming back we left at 0400. We followed a lights-out freighter back down the river. I had to follow right behind them, following their wake since they had no lights on. I was six feet behind their stern. By the time daylight arrived I was beat. My eyes were all red. We returned safely and our XO, who was on the trip and had been drinking, fell into the river as he debarked. Somehow he was awarded a Purple Heart for this mission.

Paul Gesswein: We did get a couple of mortar rounds at least once. We were exposed to fire when we drove through Indian country once a month to our staff meetings, but I don't recall any problems.

Jim Fritz: We had two empty mike boats tow an empty barge down the river to the South China Sea for purposes of loading the barge with JP-5 diesel fuel. Chief Towery was in charge of this and there were about six of us with him. We recognized if we were hit on the way down river the barge would blow up due to the gas fumes; on the way back loaded with JP-5, the barge would just burn.

One of the enemy tricks was to spread straw across the mouth of the canals, which were only twenty or thirty feet across. When the PBR's went over the straw it would foul their engines. The straw didn't bother the ASPB's.

We ran a number of ambush patrols on a small boat out of Nam Can. There were three of us on the boat and we were looking for sampan activity. We'd cut the engines and hope to find something, but we never did.

I spent two years working and fighting in the Delta. I left around May of 1970. In that whole two year span I never really felt that there was any progress being made.

Early in the war General Westmoreland estimated that the enemy received 70% of his supplies by water.[lxxxvii] Operation Market Time was initiated on March 11, 1965.[lxxxviii] This effort covered 1,200 miles of the South Vietnamese coast and extended forty miles out to sea, and, in conjunction with efforts in the Delta (Operation Game Warden) effectively closed down that channel of supply. U.S. and ARVN forces sank over 1,400 barges and junks in 1967 alone[lxxxix].

Our riverine navy was given to South Vietnam as part of the Vietnamization Program. When Saigon fell in 1975 our enemies inherited the largest and most sophisticated brown water fleet in the world.[xc]

BROWN WATER NAVY PERSONNEL

Steve Doak

Jim Fritz

Vic Griguoli

Paul Gesswein

Sid Brown

Don McMurray

CHAPTER SEVEN

AIR SUPPORT

All five branches of the U.S. military had planes in Vietnam. It was said that the Army had more boats than the Navy and the Navy had more planes than the Air Force. Offensive operations against North Vietnam began in February, 1965 (Operation Flaming Dart) and attacks against the Ho Chi Minh Trail began a month later. South Vietnam's airfields became the busiest in the world.

AIR CREWS

Airman 1st Class **Tom Emmons,** Loadmaster, 374th Tactical Air Squadron, Cam Ranh Bay, USAF

Lt.Col. **Bud Might**, Pilot, Special Ops/Psy Ops, Saigon, USAF

Airman 3rd Class **Frank Towns**, Jet Mechanic, 436th Org. Maint., Dover, Delaware, USAF

1st Lt. **Claude Roberts**, Rescue Pilot, 39th Aerospace Rescue & Recovery Svc., Cam Ranh Bay, USAF

1st Lieutenant **Eric Dauphinee**, Helicopter Pilot, 1st Marine Air Wing, Danang, USMC

AT2 **David Greene**, Aviation Electronics Technician, Patrol Squadron 4, USN

Petty Officer 3rd Class **Dallas Johnson**, Air Ops/Aircrewman, *USS Enterprise* CVA(N)-65, USN

*AV1Boson **Ed Rodgers,** Okinawa/Philippines, USN*

Spc4 **Bob Janecek**, Crew Chief, US Army Support Command, Saigon, USA

Spc5 **Donald "Tip" O'Neill**, 3-Qualified, Detachment C-2, 5th Special Forces, USA

CWO **Norris "Woody" Woodruff**, Pilot, 229th Assault Helicopters, 1st Air Cavalry Division, USA

Spc5 **John Lawrence**, Crew Chief, 101st Aviation, Udorn, Thailand, USA

Spc4 **Ray Dougherty**, Crew Chief, HQ Detachment, USASCD, Saigon, USA

Sgt. **Jim Doute**, Aircraft Mechanic, 6200 Armaments/Electronics Squadron, 13th AF, Clark AFB, USAF

Spc4 **Daniel Kreynest**, Tactical Imagery Interpreter/Tactical Observer, 131st Aviation Company, Phu Bai, USA

Arrival/Duties

David Greene: I was stationed on Okinawa and was in and out but mostly high above the Vietnam area from 1961 to 1964. We flew a Navy P2H or P2D7 Neptune twin-engine patrol plane. Our job was to detect enemy radar systems and monitor enemy shipping in the South China Sea. We sometimes hopped the waves at 1,000 feet to monitor shipping or higher to detect the radar sites. It was an unpressurized aircraft so we couldn't fly too high. We had a crew of about eleven, four officers and seven enlisted, and the plane was crammed full of radio and electronic equipment. There was so much gear on board it was tough to walk the length of the plane. In fact, there was actually no place to stand up!

In addition to Okinawa, we flew missions out of the Philippines, Thailand, and Japan; even Saigon. In addition to the twin engines the Neptune had two jet pods which could help us on takeoffs. The jet pods could also help in case we lost an engine. Basically, the plane was built for anti-submarine warfare. When they realized we had all this electronic gear aboard they knew we were perfect for detecting the radar installations, and that is when we started flying those missions.

I personally worked all the positions in the rear of the plane including radar, anti-submarine detection, radio and other things. My job required a Top Secret security clearance. Our flights were evenly divided between day and night missions. We were on call 24/7 and usually flew every day.

Our work days were insane. But being on a flight crew we didn't have to stand any guard duty or KP. We could have a flight at 0400, and it could last from eight to sixteen hours. We were in the air a long time. Anything that went down on the plane – electronically, mechanically -- we had to fix ourselves. If we weren't flying we were working on our aircraft.

Bob Janecek: I arrived in November of 1964 as a crew chief on a UH-1B Huey helicopter. Later, when I joined the 12th Aviation Group, I was given the experimental 540 rotor head helicopter which was capable of more speed. A crew chief was assigned a helicopter and was responsible for all the maintenance, paperwork and inspections; everything. There were different pilots, different gunners, but only one crew chief. When the chopper flew the crew chief was required to be aboard. The crew chief sat behind the pilot and manned one of the two M-60 machine guns. We flew three or four days a week, nearly always during the day. When we weren't flying I was responsible for the maintenance of the Huey.

Helicopters were still an uncommon sight in 1964.
Courtesy: Bob Janecek

Ray Dougherty: As I neared draft age (20), I tried to enlist with a preference as a helicopter pilot, but was turned down because I was color blind. Later, I was drafted, which I didn't expect due to the color blindness, but they let me get into helicopter mechanics, so I was satisfied. I flew into Tan Son Nhut on Pan Am in November of 1964.

As a crew chief I had complete control over my helicopter. If the helicopter flew I was in it. I was the left machine-gunner. If we were flying my work day was eight to ten hours. If we weren't flying I spent six to eight hours cleaning and servicing the chopper.

Donald "Tip" O'Neill: I flew into Tan Son Nhut in June of 1965. I then flew to Nha Trang, which was the headquarters of my unit, the 5th Special Forces. I spent four to six weeks there, mostly rigging air drops and going up and kicking bundles. I also had to pull patrol duty. Then I was sent to Pleiku to replace their parachute rigger. I was the only parachute rigger in II Corps and the camp demolitions man. When I was in camp I always had old munitions to explode or I was asked to consult on rigging for other units. Special Forces were divided into three teams, A, B and C. The B and C teams supported the A team, the combat force. Because I was the lone rigger I flew 550 combat hours kicking supply bundles out to Special Forces A teams when they came under attack. I did my share of ground operations but more flying than anything.

Dallas Johnson: On my first tour in late 1965 I was an air ops supervisor on the *Enterprise*. I needed to go for FAA license for promotion and was asked to extend my term of enlistment. When I declined my advancement was blocked by seniors. I finally transferred to an air crewman job. This was more physical work involving flying combat logistic support missions, mail delivery, rescue of wounded, etc., in the Grumman C1A twin-engine plane. My responsibilities included loading the plane as necessary. We would take off from *Enterprise* – just the pilot and me – for Danang, Chu Lai, Tan Son Nhut, etc. My first time being catapulted off the carrier was really a jolt; it knocked my helmet off! Sometimes we remained overnight, sometimes we returned to the carrier.

Tom Emmons: In 1967 I was stationed in Okinawa. It was very regimented. While we were there we did training missions, dropped paratroopers, etc. We would go to Vietnam for a two-week stint to Cam Ranh Bay – an eight-hour pain-in-the-ass flight -- that was our duty station. And we'd go twelve on, eight off, and after two weeks you'd fly back to Okinawa for a week or so, then return. We were not included in the Vietnam troop count.

U.S. military personnel stationed outside Vietnam were not included in the number of troops "in-country". These personnel could operate in Vietnam for up to thirty days without being "counted". Their home bases included Thailand, Okinawa and the Philippines.

Tom Emmons: I was trained as a loadmaster. Our mission in Vietnam was to haul anything that the army needed to be moved from one place to another, whether it was dead bodies, soldiers, ammo, beer -- I carried a .38. We could check out an M-16 if we wanted to.

Our plane was a C-130A four-engine turbo jet that could land on an aircraft carrier. In fact, on 10/19/63 a C-130 landed on the *USS Forrestal* in moderately rough North Atlantic seas; the 132' wing span had just 15' of clearance but that was more than enough. The C-130 was a real workhorse. The Army used a two-engine version. We carried 32,000 pounds of fuel. We burned 4,000/hour, so we had about eight hours of fuel aboard. We were lucky to get four hours of flight time a day. We'd come back and you'd be met by the chief maintenance man. That was his baby. He would want to talk to the flight engineer. What do we need to fix? So then his work started. There was pride there.

The more landings, the harder I worked. Once we hit the ground my first job was chocking the plane. Then I'd load it making sure everything was tied down. Vehicles were the biggest pain. A deuce and a half was 8G's forward and 4G's to the rear, so a 10,000 pound truck was 80,000 pounds going forward. It took all kinds of chains and a half hour to secure it. I was never on the ground for less than half an hour to load vehicles. If I was lucky they'd just roll pallets in, and if it was all pallets in fifteen minutes you were loaded up and ready to go.

Usually from Cam Ranh Bay we'd leave empty. We'd go up -- unless we had something to move from there we'd go up empty -- and we'd fly to airfields from Khe Sanh to Tan Son Nhut. We landed on fields that were nothing but a dirt strip. We had a crew of five -- pilot, co-pilot, navigator, flight engineer and me. I was low man on the totem pole. I was the first guy to jump if we went down.

I served eighteen months, the middle six months was in Thailand dropping flares all night over the Ho Chi Minh Trail. I was kind of burned out on Vietnam at that point and I had heard that the Thailand thing was good duty.

Eric Dauphinee: We launched off the *LPH Tripoli* pre-dawn on May 23, 1967 in the world's largest helicopter, the Sikorsky CH-53A, and I got my first look at my new home. Upon landing at Marble Mountain my pilot and I were sent to Operations for a mission briefing. We flew the rest of the day into the night.

The CH-53A Sea Stallion is a Sikorsky-built heavy-lift helicopter that carried a combat crew of five, pilot, co-pilot, crew chief and two door gunners. The aircraft could carry internal cargo on pallets rolled in or out the rear ramp. It could be rigged to carry patients on litters or had seats for 38. At 72 feet in length and almost two stories tall at the tail, it was one very large helicopter. Our cruise airspeed was 170 knots or about 200 miles per hour. There is a hook at the center of mass used for attaching external loads such as downed aircraft, 155 mm guns or cargo nets full of ammo. The crew chief, lying on his belly, looked through a hole in the cargo deck to guide pilots into position over these loads. The only armor plating was in the pilot seats and a little around the two jet engines. Fuel cells were designed as self-sealing for small arms fire. Hydraulic, oil, electrical and fuel lines run throughout the aircraft. I have seen this helicopter land with so many bullet and shrapnel holes in it that you could recognize the individual standing on the other side, yet it flew home. Thank you, Sikorsky!

We did external load missions to lift ammo and artillery into fire bases throughout our area of operations, I Corps in the northern portion of South Vietnam. We did a little work in northern II Corps and some in points west. There was the occasional lift of aircraft downed by accident or enemy fire. Each of our aircraft had a silhouette painted by the door of these aircraft picked up and returned to base. There were Huey's, Ch-34's, CH-46's, O-1 Birddogs and an occasional jet. We brought beans, bullets and mail to the men operating in the field. Our Sikorsky hauled some unusual loads. We hauled lumber; we hauled a water buffalo. Both of those loads tend to shift around in flight and can be a hazard. Who would have prioritized a water buffalo over ammo and mail? I learned not to even copy down the information from a briefing for a "Routine" mission. "Emergency" missions were the ones we did every day.

Reliance on helicopters in a logistics support role freed the ground forces from dependence on surface transportation[xci]. Extensive use was made of the external sling load concept. Over 10,000 downed helicopters were recovered.[xcii]

Frank Towns: I enlisted in the Air Force in September of 1966. I did basic training at Lackland AFB. They told us in training that for every man in a combat role in Vietnam there were thirteen people in support!

Our usual trip consisted of flying cargo from Dover, Delaware, usually with a first re-fueling stop at Elmendorf AFB after about 3300 miles since we lacked the capability to refuel in mid-air, and then sometimes a second stop at Clark AFB, in the Philippines. We never knew where we were going until we took off and the pilot unsealed his orders. We usually flew into Cam Ranh Bay, then on to Tan Son Nhut. Then we flew to Bangkok. A one-way trip took about twenty-two hours. We usually spent a couple of days on the ground before returning, sometimes longer if major maintenance was required. Our last stop was always Cam Ranh Bay, where we sometimes backloaded medevac patients but always caskets coming back to Dover. We never came back empty. I was the jet mechanic on the flight. There may have been about thirty planes doing these flights out of Dover and thirty or more out of Charleston. Those were the two largest cargo bases. We carried about 280 caskets on a trip, twelve to a pallet. On the supply trips over we often carried beer (144 cases to a pallet); never premium beer, usually Pabst, Wiedemann's, Carlings or Ballantine ale; all stuff that had been donated from those breweries. We carried ammo, weapons, peaches and pound cake. Some peaches and pound cake would be snatched during the unloading process and maybe sold on the black market. Since there might have been eight or ten guys unloading the plane, usually with two or three forklifts, it was hard to keep an eye on everything.

The crew on the C-141 included pilot, co-pilot, flight engineer, navigator, cargo master, mechanic, radioman, and a few others. The cargo master was the most important guy; he had to balance the aircraft -- he used a plumb bob -- and he was required to have a Top Secret security clearance. Mine was Top Secret also. Only about 300 of the 6,000 military at Dover held a Top Secret clearance. Other planes flying out of Dover were high-altitude reconnaissance planes that did filming of various areas of Laos and Cambodia. This activity also required a high-level security clearance, since we weren't supposed to be in those areas.

The things that needed maintenance the most on the C-141 were seals and engines. The dusty conditions in Vietnam probably accounted for that. We always assisted the specialists on the big jobs. Changing the fuel bladders was a tough job; I don't know how those guys could breathe in there.

Jim Doute: I wanted to control my own destiny so I enlisted in the Air Force. The Air Force seemed to offer better food and a chance to travel. Looking back after forty years, I've concluded that we were the only smart branch of the service in that we sent our officers off to do the fighting for us. I can't march and I can't swim, so it seemed the only thing left was the Air Force. I flew into Clark AFB in the Philippine Islands in September of 1967. President Marcos didn't want combat troops stationed in his country nor would he allow combat aircraft to fly out of the Philippines, but support aircraft were okay.

I was an aircraft mechanic on combat aircraft but since the Philippines were not allowed combat aircraft I really did not have a job. I was in the 13th Air Force stationed in the Philippines; they chose not to transfer me to the 7th Air Force in Vietnam. So I tried to train myself to be something of a loadmaster. I helped maintain the aircraft and loaded supplies. Since I wasn't trained as a loadmaster I was always under the direction of those that were.

The plane I dealt with was a C-97, a four-engine Stratocruiser cargo aircraft with a crew of seven or eight, including two loadmasters. There were three of these planes in our squadron. We would spend a few days loading and balancing the aircraft for the upcoming trip; when we were ready, we'd notify Operations that we needed to fly to whatever location. We went to a number of different places including Thailand and several spots in Vietnam such as Saigon, Cam Ranh Bay, Danang and others. We might make three trips a week.

Upon arrival at our location we spent a few hours offloading the cargo. Then we would load anything being sent back, such as damaged equipment. The loadmaster had to keep a sharp eye on the weight of the stuff going on to the plane.

John Lawrence: I flew into Udorn AFB, Thailand, in January of 1968, just before the time Tet occurred in Vietnam. Udorn is very close to the Laotian border. I was assigned to the 101st Aviation. I was a crew chief on a Huey helicopter. I had four guys working for me. We flew over Laos and Cambodia -- places we weren't supposed to be. I did thirteen medevacs. We also delivered supplies and soldiers to places. I worked seven days a week, either flying or on call 24/7. During Tet I flew for thirty-one straight days. I often slept in the Huey. We didn't have a door gunner on our Huey; the guns were electric, wired to the pilot's helmet.

The 101st Aviation had two choppers, two turbo-prop planes and one bird dog. One of the choppers was a lemon. In September of 1968 they took both of them away and gave us two new models with full crews; we just couldn't keep up.

Daniel Kreynest: While in basic training at Ft. Leonard Wood I was given the option to go "RA". This was the designation for Regular Army or the guys that had enlisted voluntarily. The "draftees" carried a "US" at the beginning of their service numbers. It would mean an extra year of service but I could pick my choice of schools and not end up in the Infantry. I took the option and chose the Tactical Imagery Interpretation School at Ft. Holabird Maryland. The II School, as it was known, taught you everything there is to know about aerial photography and how to pick and plot targets. After graduation all but one of us got orders to Vietnam. The one guy that did not had orders to Korea; his dad was a full bird colonel.

I arrived in country the first week of January 1968. I flew in on a commercial airline with 200 other guys I did not know and landed at Danang air base. The war was going on when we got there and we had to circle the air field for about 45 minutes due to rockets and mortars. On my fifth day in a holding company a couple of Sergeants got me and my buddies, took us to Supply and had 1st Cavalry patches sown on all our uniforms. "Guess where you guys are going" they joked. Next thing we knew we were in a chopper and headed for some firebase. As soon as we got off the chopper we saw a couple of grunts with a VC prisoner. They called us over and said talk to the guy. I said "hey how are you doing". The grunts were pissed and said "no, talk to him in Vietnamese, ask him about his unit". I said I did not speak Vietnamese and they asked me just what kind of an interpreter I was and what languages I spoke. We all said we interpreted aerial photography and only spoke English. The two Sergeants that had snatched us from the replacement unit had made a mistake and grabbed the wrong guys. We spent the night sleeping on the ground and were taken to our correct unit the next day.

Since most of our missions were flown at night it was natural that the unit picked up the nickname "Night Hawks". The unit has a distinctive crest depicting a hawk with the unit name and "Night Hawk" underneath. The Army decided to outfit the Mohawk as a gun ship (JOV-1A) to take advantage of free-fire zone targets while en route to and from their recon mission objectives. The Vietcong nicknamed it 'WHISPERING DEATH.' The Mohawk was primarily designed as a forward observation aircraft and photo- recon platform.

The wings have six 'hard-points' numbered from the left wing-tip to the right wing-tip. Hard-points three and four normally hang fuel drop-tanks. Hard-points one and six could hang machine-gun pods or rocket pods. Hard-points two and five could also hang rocket pods (either seven or nineteen shot 2.75 inch folding fin unguided aerial rockets). Legend has it that a North Vietnamese MiG-17 was shot down over the DMZ (Demilitarized Zone) by a so armed Mohawk

Life with the Nighthawks was not bad. I worked mostly nights either flying SLAR (side looking airborne radar) missions up and down the coast of North Vietnam or working in the II (Imagery Interpretation) shop plotting targets and writing intelligence reports. We flew VR missions in Laos and Cambodia (we were never there) and in the Plain of Jars in Laos, along the Chinese border (not there either). It was not until the "68 TET" offensive that things got scary. The Nighthawks base was at the air field in Phu Bai just a few miles down the road from the city of Hue, the old imperial capital of Vietnam and a major enemy objective.

Bud Might: I had flown 35 bombing missions with the 8th Air Force over Germany in WW II and was involved in the Berlin airlift of 1949. I was in Iceland during Korea, but after my orders for Vietnam came in I went to Louisiana for training on how to drop leaflets and do "ground talking;" a new trick for an old dog, perhaps. Following some jungle survival training in the Philippines I flew into Tan Son Nhut in 1968.

Our job involved dropping leaflets and using a loudspeaker to talk to people on the ground. All these efforts were done in IV Corps, around Saigon and the Delta. There were six planes assigned to these tasks; two C-47's, including mine, and four smaller planes. The C-47 had a crew of about five, including the pilot, co-pilot, navigator, flight engineer, and a loadmaster, or interpreter, or somebody. We would meet with representatives from the Army and get our directions for the week.

The composition of our crew depended on the mission. If we were going to be talking to the ground with the loudspeaker we would have an interpreter who spoke English and Vietnamese. If we were dropping leaflets we would have a crew member, maybe a loadmaster, who handled the drop. We also did flare dropping missions and we would need someone to handle the machinery to eject the 64-pound flares.

In WW II we knew who the enemy was. In Vietnam, you had no idea who was who. Maybe the barber was a VC. In Vietnam we had more Chieu Hoi (surrenders) in IV Corps than the other three corps combined. So I guess we learned how to talk to the ground. And old dogs can learn new tricks!

Jim Doute: In January of 1970 our C-97 was replaced by cargo jets. The new C-5 had a larger load capacity. We spent the last months packing up aircraft parts for shipment back. I didn't fly much after 1970 started. The phasedown had begun. I came home in March, 1970 after about thirty months overseas.

Claude Roberts: We flew a C-130 out of Cam Ranh Bay in 1971. We had both ground and flying duties. Our rescue missions were mostly done over Laos -- over the Ho Chi Minh Trail – usually during the day. We flew up and down the Ho Chi Minh Trail at high altitude (20,000) waiting for beepers to go off or forward air controllers signaling a pilot down. We organized and directed almost all the air rescues.

Air Rescue was a very complex operation. Once a pilot went down virtually all the air war stopped and everything was turned over to us. In discussions with the FAC (forward air controller) we would determine what types of ordnance we needed to suppress whatever antiaircraft fire or enemy ground units were in the immediate area of the downed plane. If possible we also tried to establish communications with the downed pilot. The rescue choppers (usually on the ground in Thailand) would be alerted. After the rescue chopper went in and made the pickup, we would then refuel them. We would descend from our normal high altitude to about 4,000 feet to do that. The choppers always went in with a small amount of fuel so they needed us after the rescue. Our C-130 had a pod under each wing that the helicopter could access for refueling. Some of these complex rescue operations took several days or at least many hours. They were very tense operations. The choppers often got shot up pretty well. Most of the days we were up there no one was shot down and we had a relatively easy day.

We spent about three days a week in the air and as much time during duties on the ground. My ground duty, due to my history degree, was squadron historian. As historian, I would compile a quarterly report on the rescue mission activity. These reports were classified, sent on to higher headquarters and never seen again, at least by me. In addition we practiced on a mission communications simulator, primarily working with the new guys on the vital communications piece of a rescue operation. There could be dozens and dozens of people we had to talk to during a rescue mission and the training helped the new guys learn the ropes. Rescues were extremely intense communications problems and you had to know who to call at each step.

Ed Rodgers: After two tours on the *USS Cleveland*, I spent three years (1970 – 1973), covering two deployments, as a crew member on a P-3. I flew out of both Okinawa and the Philippines to patrol the Vietnamese coast.

On the *Cleveland*, as an Aviation Boson we had responsibility for a lot of things, mostly related to aviation. We dealt with helicopters, seaplanes; we were actually trained to launch and recover dirigibles! I was in the Deck Department and I supervised many of the newer men. At this point I was 20 and they were 17 or 18. Guys on the *Cleveland* from the captain on down really knew nothing of aviation. When I arrived as an Aviation Bosun they didn't know what to do with me, so they put me in the Deck Department. I became a boat coxswain.

On my third tour in the early 1970's, I flew in a P-3 Orion, basically a sub-hunter/killer four-engine plane with a crew of thirteen. We had twelve planes in the squadron. We flew maritime missions checking out the sampans and junks to try to determine if they were fishing boats or not. We took pictures of these boats for later evaluation. We were based out of Naha, Okinawa, which is actually a civilian airport.

I flew as an ordnance-man on the P-3. I dropped the sonar buoys and took the pictures of the sampans and junks. We flew very close to the water level. Our pictures were returned to the intelligence folks for them to try to determine what the boats were carrying. Vietnam was being supplied by water as well as by land and that was an important thing back then. The P-3 was capable of carrying rockets but we never did. We carried a torpedo for anti-submarine purposes. The P-3 may or may not have had nuclear capability.

I didn't fly continually on the P-3. When I wasn't flying I took care of the flight line. That was part of my job. Another part of the job was training the new guys that had never been there before. I was the leading petty officer for that and I did make E-6 while I was there.

We spent a bit of time at Diego Garcia, in the Indian Ocean. They were building the place up as some sort of submarine base. I did some firefighting training there so I had come full circle from the early Navy days as a firefighter.

A/A Fire

Claude Roberts: We kept a very detailed computer book on the locations of enemy AA (anti-aircraft) and SAM (surface to air missiles) sites. Our navigator was responsible for keeping us away from the heavy concentrations of AAA and SAM activity. And we flew too high for small arms fire. We still kept an eye out for enemy planes although our system kept us away from harm most of the time. When we went down to 4,000 feet to refuel we were subject to ground fire. Our plane was not hit but some of our other planes did take a round or two. One of the planes was hit with a 12.5, which knocked a hole in it. We also had to leave the area a couple of times because a Mig was approaching.

Jim Doute: We found a few indentations in the skin of the plane from time to time, which probably meant that we were shot at, but we never had any serious trouble.

Ed Rodgers: On the P-3 flights flying over the Gulf of Tonkin we were "painted" (locked on) many times by different warships, but never fired upon. Our sister squadron was involved in the *Mayaguez* incident; they were tasked to keep an eye on what assets were coming into the area and they were fired upon, and received some hits in their tail section. When we flew we did have jet fighter protection in the area in case of trouble.

Tom Emmons: You could see the fire from the ground. We would do a flyover routine. We would come down in a tight spiral. Sometimes you had to fly through a valley coming in and that was always a sticky wicket. We took lots of fire. The worst time was a night mission where we flew to a star base that ran out of ammo. It was a volunteer thing; that's how I got my DFC. We went in hot, dark and hot to almost a black runway. Guys on the ground provided suppression fire, we popped the doors open, our engines were screaming, we unloaded, cranked up and left. We were only on the ground five minutes, but it was a long five minutes.

And one night we were in Laos -- where we weren't supposed to be -- dropping flares at night. These flares weighed sixty-four pounds, so after a night of throwing them out the plane you were really whipped. They were shooting something at us that would explode. I don't know what it was, but it would come up so high then it would explode behind us. We're flying along dropping these million candlelight flares in a line so that the F4s could see and come do their bombing runs, but the guys on the ground were getting better. I'd be sitting there dropping flares, and boom boom, and I'd hit the mike and say "Turn right, **now!**" The guys on the ground figured it out; if you're dropping in a straight line they just have to lead you.

Bud Might: We took a lot of small arms fire. No ack ack, like over Germany. They hit a gas tank once. I made two emergency landings.

Dan Kreynest: We were flying just off the coast of North Vietnam on the second leg of our mission. I was fascinated by what looked like flaming basketballs coming up from the ground. The pilot noticed me staring out the window and asked me what I was looking at. When I told him about the basketballs he banked the plane so hard to the left that I swear we dipped a wing in the South China Sea. In so doing he missed the 37mm anti-aircraft fire (basketballs) coming our way.

John Lawrence: We were flying along one time in the mountainous part of Laos, and I happened to be looking at the ground. I saw this puff of smoke come out of the trees and told the pilot to bank right. If I hadn't done that we would have been hit. The Air Force should have told us not to fly in that area because they knew where the hot areas were, but they didn't warn us. During the course of our missions we were often shot at but never shot down. And I thank God for that because some of my buddies did get shot down. We had our share of bullet holes in the chopper.

Norris "Woody" Woodruff: We were having some difficulty getting chest armor through our supply channels. At one point, we were told that we'd be getting them "any day." In the meantime (this was late January of 1966) we were dropping troops into Landing Zone Quebec, and it was definitely a hot zone. We had eight grunts on our Huey, and Captain Phillips (my best friend) was flying. As we approached a red-hot LZ Phillips took a round through the chest, penetrating his flak jacket, killing him instantly. We were about twenty feet in the air and came down hard, but no one was hurt. The grunts went about their work and I was left there by myself. The other Hueys coming in were ordered to do their job and not worry about me. I had my weapon, a sawed-off shotgun, with me. A sniper was shooting at me from eighty yards away; I fired an occasional round from my sawed-off at him to let him know I was armed. My rounds fell about 75 yards short of him, but he got the message. Finally, an M-79 grenadier came along and I pointed out the sniper to him. He disposed of the guy with one round from his blooper gun. The next flight in picked me up and I went back to my cot to ponder the loss of a friend and the absence of chest armor. I was shot down five times on my first tour, and crash landed two other times.

Bob Janecek: It didn't take long to get shot at for the first time over there. On my second flight we were going north from Saigon, along the coast. My chopper had the M-60 machine guns. I told them I had been trained on the .30 caliber machine gun (vintage WW II), and I knew how to take that apart, but had never seen the M-60. I asked for a 30-second primer on the M-60. They told me they'd take me to the range later in the week, and then we took off.

It came up on the radio that there had been an ambush of a Vietnamese convoy in a rubber plantation. We landed and picked up a couple of wounded Vietnamese guys and took them back to their staging area and went on about our mission. On our return we flew by the site of the morning ambush, and the VC was in the process of ambushing the relief force from the first ambush, one of their favorite tricks. We approached an artillery position which was in the process of providing furious support fire for the beleaguered ARVN. It was dusk and I could feel the concussion of the 105's as they were firing. We were rotating down to their location and, as I looked out the window, I saw these red basketballs going past. When the pilot turned to where he could see these "basketballs," he said those are .50 caliber rounds aiming for us! He put us down hard and fast and we weren't hit.

Another time we were flying to Tay Ninh Mountain, known as the Black Virgin Mountain. This is west of Saigon, near the Cambodian border. There was a Special Forces Camp there and also a radio relay tower. This was one of those instances where we controlled the top of the mountain and the enemy owned the rest. This was a hot landing zone where we could see the tracers in the air.

Once we were flying over a convoy just to keep an eye on them, and we picked up ground fire. What we sometimes did in these situations is drop a smoke grenade where the ground fire was coming from. When we dropped the smoke grenade the convoy opened up on the location. We figured we should just stay out of there, since we were liable to get shot by our own guys. That smoke grenade probably started a small war there!

Ray Dougherty: We took a round through the bottom of the chopper. Fortunately it hit the toolbox, and no one was injured.

Engines Out

Jim Doute: We were flying from Clark AFB to Bangkok when we lost two engines. We were beyond the Point of No Return to Clark so we diverted to Tan Son Nhut, thinking that it would be easier to get spare parts there. Our plane was designed to fly on just one or two engines but it was a challenge for the pilots. We landed and were there for a week while they repaired the problem. As it happened we left the day before the big Tet offensive started. In fact, the plane that took our parking spot was hit on the ground during Tet. We avoided flying into Vietnam when Tet started. We may have flown a few more missions into Bangkok around that time.

Tom Emmons: We were dropping flares over Laos illuminating the Ho Chi Minh trail. This was the time I was the most scared. We had cut out the two outboard engines to conserve fuel and when we restarted the outboard right it flamed out. The other engine on that wing also went out. This was in Laos, very close to China, maybe fifteen miles away. I really thought we were going to have to parachute into the jungle. The pilot says "we're not going to make it, so start throwing stuff out." So anything that wasn't tied down I threw out the door. Then he said "I still don't think we are going to make it so the load master is the first one out the door." I was in the back, and I pushed the talk button and said "Bullshit!" I said 'I'm not going first. You guys can jump and I'll fly the damn plane!'" I think the entire crew was petrified.

David Greene: We were tracking a submarine once, and we had dropped a picket line of sound buoys in the water. We could tell by the signature it was putting out that it was a Chinese sub. It was a diesel sub. We were only about 300 feet above the water, and I was sitting in my position getting a read on the frequency this sub engine was putting out. We lost one of our two engines. The starboard engine went out. We were going down fast but our pilot hit the jets and got us safely back to the correct altitude. But because the jets were on we were now in danger of running out of fuel. Our Flight Engineer, an enlisted man, crunched the numbers to see how far we could go; we decided to try to make it back to Okinawa. It looked like it would be a close call and a backup plan was one of the nearby smaller islands of the Ryukus chain, near Okinawa. This smaller island had a crushed coral runway and they used smudge pots to light it at night. The runway there was also pretty short so our pilot really wanted to make Okinawa.

Finally, we saw the lights of Okinawa appear in the distance, and we were really low on gas. The pilot figured we had enough to make just one pass.

We went to lower the landing gear and they wouldn't come down; complete hydraulic failure! We were able to lower the wheels manually but the concern when you lower the gear manually is that you don't get a Locked light. I ran to the radio seat to be ready to send the SOS if we didn't make it. The pilot hit the runway on the first pass but we couldn't reverse props and we had no brakes due to the hydraulic failure. We knew from our many previous landings on this field where the runways turnoffs were and we kept flying past them. And the end of the runway was truly the end of the runway; it was ocean and rocks! Our pilot locked the emergency brake, which blew a tire. We did a sharp turn and slid onto the grass on one wing. We were safe! We used to have this trailing wire antenna and in the excitement I forgot to reel it in, but we were down and safe.

Ed Rodgers: We were on a training mission on the P-3, in the Philippines, flying at 30,000 feet, which is a lot higher than we normally flew. The smoke door between the pilot, co-pilot and flight engineer blew up and open. This door was right above their heads and could be opened with a handle in the event of a fire aboard the aircraft. I was at my station in the tail of the aircraft and over the headset they called me to bring a broom handle forward. About the time I started making my way forward the aircraft nosed over and started diving. This made my trip forward very dangerous. When I reached the cockpit I could see the smoke door open and everything was being drawn out of there. I couldn't breathe even though we were now down below where you needed oxygen. We had a rapid decompression and I was out of breath. I gave the broom handle to the engineer who bent it where the door closed and we started to level out. But when it was over we were down at water level. It was a near thing. Our squadron had lost a plane in a training accident in the Philippines about a year before. This accident killed the crew of thirteen and always made us a bit nervous on training flights. It was one of the scariest times I've ever had. That problem shouldn't happen that way, but it did!

Aviate, navigate...communicate: Dealing with problems aloft!

Ground Attacks

Claude Roberts: The only time I really felt fear was a couple of times on the ground at Cam Ranh Bay. In the first case, a sapper came through the wire and blew up the ammo dump. I was awakened by a huge concussion and my windows blew out and I found myself on the floor. I couldn't see out due to the walls around the Quonset hut so I didn't know what was going on. Large, secondary explosions kept going off and I wondered if we were being attacked or what. We finally realized what was going on but the noise was continuous. The explosions continued for 36 hours. We had 500lb bombs and 1,000lb bombs, going off one after another.

Jim Doute: During my nights in Vietnam we were never mortared.

Ed Rodgers: I saw the Vietnamese people a few times when we were in town. We did get to a nearby Seabee Club and that was very nice. We had a Red Alert while we were at that club and the rule was, if you had a drink in front of you, you could finish it. If not, you had to run to the bunker. When the incoming started most of the Seabees ran for their hooches and a few of us sat there and drank until we couldn't see!

Bud Might: I lived in a trailer with my operations officer. The trailer was sandbagged on all sides, but not on the roof. We got mortared three or four times a week at the base.

Frank Towns: Seven C-141's took off one night from Cam Ranh Bay. I was in the second plane. With planes that big, when they took off the first would go to the right after takeoff, the second to the left, and so on. Four mortar rounds hit near the first plane as it went down the runway. All the planes got airborne, but when that first plane reached Dover, they found that shrapnel had missed the fuel tank by less than an inch. If that plane had exploded, since we were right behind them, we'd have gone up too.

We picked up mortar fire during down time at Cam Ranh Bay, usually from the north or the west. The Marines guarded the perimeter to the south; they patrolled aggressively and kept the enemy off balance.

The Events at Plei Me

Donald "Tip" O'Neill: The war was starting to pick up in late 1965, and we had a lot of camps hit. I did a lot to do air drops. At this time, the Special Forces camp at Plei Mei was under a 15-day siege. They had a lot of planes shot up trying to get supplies; I flew supply drops for five days of that siege. It all started with me, a young, 19-year old guy, sitting in our little bar -- we called it the Bamboo Hut -- drinking a beer. This place was no bigger than 25' X 25'. I was a Spc4 at the time and I said I could get stuff into that camp. My remarks were overheard by a full bird colonel. He tapped me on the shoulder and asked me what I had said. I repeated my remarks as I gasped for air, and I told him my idea, which was to use high velocity drops. Not many people were using that technique then. I told him I would take a 500-pound capacity parachute overloaded to about 750 pounds. Pinpoint accuracy was a key on this technique. The colonel turned to his exec, a major, and said "Get this man an aircraft immediately." The colonel told me to get what I needed and try this plan.

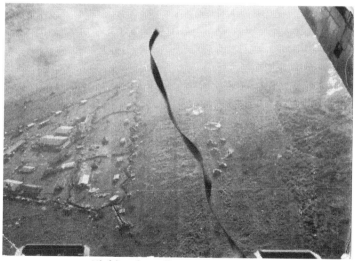

Kicking bundles over Plei Me
Courtesy: Don "Tip"O'Neill

The Caribou was probably the ideal aircraft for this type of mission since it was vital that we be able to fly at somewhat slow speeds. This plane was twin-engine and had a couple of good things and a couple of bad things. On the bad side, it was a wet wing aircraft with self-filling gas tanks. The slow speed was a plus. We went in that night at about 390 feet off the ground. The guys in the camp filled a can with gasoline and lit it, and that's what we aimed on. I would kick the load out when the pilot gave me the signal. I was on a safety tie-down strap and the cargo was on rollers. When the pilot gave me the green light he pulled the plane up, and I released the cargo out the tail. We dropped five chutes, three on the first pass and two on the second. All five chutes fell within friendly lines, although two of the camp defenders, Montagnard tribesmen, were killed when a load hit them. They had been instructed to stay in their bunker but they wanted to see the show I guess.

We took twenty-one .51 caliber rounds in the plane that night; it sounded like somebody smacking the side of the plane with a chain. They knocked off about a foot of the inboard fuel line. We had taken off from the new asphalt strip at Pleiku for the mission but due to the damage to the Caribou we had to land at nearby Camp Holloway, which had a much shorter runway. There were four of us on board, including the pilot, and when we landed, due to concerns about a crash on the short runway, and the fact that the pilot couldn't reverse props because of all the aviation gas pouring out of the wing, three of us jumped out of the tail at 35mph. We got bruises and scrapes but we were okay. I was awarded a Combat Air Medal with V for Valor.

I had free rein on these types of missions after that. I told them I could get arms and ammo, food and medical supplies in there, but not perishables. I flew in there the next few nights. After the battle I went in to the camp to retrieve my parachutes. The stench of death was terrible. There were loads of NVA soldiers that had been killed by bomb blasts or mortar fire, and in many cases the rats had eaten most of the meat off the dead. Not only did our Intelligence know that the NVA was in South Vietnam, we knew there were both Russian and Chinese advisors with them.

There were so many casualties in the Plei Mei camp there was a need for additional medics in there. There was this young, black medic who wanted to meet with the chaplain before he went in to Plei Mei. He said he didn't think he was going to make it. The chaplain took him off to the side and prayed with him. The Vietnamese Marines flew the helicopter taking the medics into Plei Mei. Twenty minutes after they took off for Plei Mei they were back and the medic was dead. He had taken a round that hit his flak jacket on the lace on the sides, and went straight through to his heart. Things like that got me to the point where I had seen enough; I just wanted to go home.

Bob Janecek: While I was flying for the 12th Aviation Group later in 1965, we were in the 540 chopper, and we had a pilot who preferred to be flying rather than pushing a pencil. He got the best co-pilot he could find and put himself in harm's way quite a bit. We were in the area of the Plei Me Special Forces Camp when they had a siege going on. Looking down on it, the ground was littered with multi-colored parachutes but most of the chutes were outside their barbed wire. The pilots had probably dropped their loads from too high up.

Over the radio, the commander from the Special Forces Camp was swearing that it had been three days and no choppers had landed to evacuate his dead and wounded. The commander saw two choppers, including us, above him, and demanded that someone land to help with his wounded. He said their morale was terrible and guys were dying like crazy. It turns out that the commander that was yelling to us was Norman Schwarzkopf.

Our pilot decided to go down and help out, and our co-pilot, who was a really good pilot, took over. We flew out about two miles and came in at treetop level right for the camp. We could see the VC as we flew over them but we were looking at their backs since they were facing the camp. They probably didn't hear us until we passed them because we were flying so low. Our rule was, if someone is shooting at us we shot back. We came in over the camp barbed wire and did a flare with the chopper, standing it on its' tail, and then flopped down on the ground.

We were immediately charged with twenty or twenty-five wounded ARVN wanting to get out. I was pushing them off the skids. A couple of Special Forces guys came and pushed them off the chopper and we started to make a run across the camp to lift off. Suddenly an empty body bag flew into our rotor blades, which threw the chopper off balance. I wasn't sure how I was going to die: Was I going to be thrown out, or were the rotors going to hit me, or what? At the last minute, the centrifugal force threw the body bag out and we were able to get up and out of there.

Tet

Dan Kreynest: In the early morning hours of 31 January 1968, a division-sized force of North Vietnamese Army (NVA) and Viet Cong (VC) soldiers launched a well-coordinated multi-pronged attack on the city of Hué. Their targets were the 1st ARVN Division headquarters in the Citadel and the MACV compound in the New City on the south side of the river. Their strategic objective however was to "liberate" the entire city as part of a country-wide popular uprising designed to sweep the Communist insurgents into power. We were shelled with rockets and mortar fire for 26 days and spent most of the time defending the perimeter around the airfield and building bunkers out of sandbags.

Frank Towns: Even though we were half way around the world from Vietnam, when Tet started in February of 1968 there was an order issued to our unit that no one could be granted leave unless their mother or father died. For the next 72 days we worked eighteen to twenty hours a day, or some days without sleep. Every plane that landed at Dover had to be re-fueled, and maintenance performed, and turned around to go right back to Vietnam. Working at that pace you get almost numb; it's almost like you're in another world. I had one date with a girl here in the States just before Tet; well, after seventy-two days of no contact, she's long gone! We were on tight security all that while.

The morgue in Dover had a capacity of 3,000 bodies. That capacity was exceeded twice during my stint, both during the Tet offensive. I actually was pressed into work there for two weeks during Tet. It became almost too much, bringing them home to begin with and then working in the morgue itself, watching what goes on. It was almost a different world; those people had a strange sense of humor which they said it was to keep them from going nuts! They would do things like moving an arm from one guy to another to make a whole guy. I don't know how I lasted two weeks on that!

Allies

Dallas Johnson: We came into contact with some who we thought (or hoped) were on our side. Once we were joking with some Vietnamese kids, and shortly after some of us moved away one of the kids just exploded. He had been wired with explosives.

Eric Dauphinee: We also worked with ARVN troops who seemed to be lazy, undisciplined and definitely ones to watch. Our favorites were either the ROK Marines or Aussies. They were well schooled in the art and science of combat. The Korean marines had incredible attention to detail and pride in keeping their area pacified. The Aussies, they seemed to do their job without all the trappings in rules. They were a fun bunch. I don't remember a time when they talked above a whisper because of their proximity to "the other guy." ARVN troops brought family members, animals and whatever else they could cram in. Never did figure these guys were going to do much combat if they brought home with them. They often left us little surprises. Crew chiefs would scour the helicopter as ARVN disembarked for grenades with pins pulled or such. You never knew which of their forces were working both sides. We found it best to consider them all dangerous.

David Greene: I came into contact with the Vietnamese people infrequently. I didn't feel that you could trust them. There was always the underlying fear of abduction, of being rolled, whatever.

Bob Janecek: I worked a lot with the Vietnamese military, especially in my early days there. Some of the farmers and villagers out in the field would provide us with information on the VC, but they started to be killed when they did this so their help evaporated. I just didn't sense that they were willing to stand up and fight for their freedom.

David Greene: I can't really confirm that I was ever shot at, but we did get intercepted by aircraft several times. Chinese aircraft. We usually flew about twenty miles off the coast in international waters. One time they forced one of our planes to land in China. That's the kind of thing we always worried about. Our plane was not armed. Their planes would come out and fly on our wing and we had these big cameras that we could stick out and snap their picture. The cameras were big enough to be mistaken for cannon! I was always worried that they might get the wrong impression.

We had contact with both Russian and Chinese submarines over my three years over there. When we found them we would track them, and we'd spend hours on station following them. Once we left station another plane would come out and relieve us. After I returned home some of our squadrons began dropping listening devices along the Ho Chi Minh Trail.

I liked what I was doing so much I extended my enlistment for another two tours. I was told one time prior to a flight that we would not be finding any radar sites on our mission. The CO promised us a case of San Miguel beer for each installation we uncovered. We found twenty! We never saw the beer but we did check out the R&R boat and got a nice tour of the Bataan Peninsula and Corregidor.

Claude Roberts: Successful rescues were the cause of much celebration back at the bases, but many missions failed. We might go through all the efforts and steps to save him, but sometimes the pilots were either captured or killed. Another frustration was our isolation from The World for a year. Communications (letters) were so slow you just kind of felt the world was passing you by.

Jim Doute: My loadmaster boss played a lot of golf with the officers back at Clark AFB. He also picked some of the better trips for himself. I didn't resent him since I enjoyed anywhere I went, but I did notice that he picked the more fun trips for himself. He was upset with me one time because he perceived my trip was going to be better than his. I told him he couldn't take it out on me since he was the one that scheduled it!

Four years of military just reinforced the work ethic that I always had. One of my proudest moments was meeting Lieutenant General Benjamin O. Davis, a black officer, in the Philippines. He came down to our squadron one time and was looking around, and complimented us on our work. We were always proud to do our jobs and complete our mission. In 1970, our mission was different; we were in the Phasedown mode, and we took pride in getting aircraft parts packed for shipment back home.

Ed Rodgers: When we were down at water level photographing and observing the sampans they would usually make some less-than-friendly gestures toward us. We in turn might pickle off a smoke flare over them if we determined that they were large enough to be carrying something.

Frank Towns: We never knew what our mission or our cargo would be until it showed up. One time we had eighty to one hundred officers show up in full dress uniform. They boarded the plane, folded down the seats, and I gave a puzzled look at the cargo master, then I asked the pilot if these guys were going home. "No," he told me, "They're re-enlisting." These officers had come from all four branches of the service -- and they were not combat-types -- to fly in a combat zone **above** Vietnam, to re-enlist in the military. By re-enlisting in a combat zone they received a combat re-enlistment bonus! We went up, circled, stayed up there about forty-five minutes, and then landed. They all re-enlisted in the air. You will never find that flight on a manifest or on any records. The lowest rank I saw was a major. There were even some generals.

Dallas Johnson: One of my biggest adventures was our night landing on the *Enterprise* with a pilot who was NOT night qualified! We were running late getting a passenger out of Hong Kong due to a head wind and, since Hong Kong has restrictions on when you can fly in or out we thought we might be spending the night there. We had our civilian clothes ready for a night on the town. But the *Enterprise* ordered us to return and as we approached the carrier, they advised our pilot that he was not night qualified. But he made it on the first pass. The air controller then told him, "Sir, you are now night qualified."

When the *Pueblo* was seized, the *Enterprise* was ordered to the waters off South Korea. Sort of a show of force I guess. Remember, I carried a .38. Once we reached Korean waters all our jets were in the air on various missions and reconnaissance, and we had just taken off. Shortly after takeoff we noticed two communist "bears" coming in on the carrier, just skimming the waves. We notified the carrier and the guy riding co-pilot, who normally flew a jet fighter, took the controls. He turned the Grumman on its' ear and dove in behind the communist planes "I need more power Hawkie," he told our pilot. "The wings are coming off already," Hawkie responded. When our F4's returned to the carrier area, each side spent a few minutes flipping each other the bird and taking pictures of each other, and then the bears left the area.

Two sailors were injured when a cable snapped as they were raising the anchor on a destroyer. We told them to give us forty minutes to get our Grumman rigged to transport patients. They brought the two injured guys twenty minutes early and one of them had a leg nearly severed at the knee. He was in an air cast, a clear plastic cast, and you could see more than I wanted to see. The guy was moaning like crazy. I had flown all day and I had had enough. Someone else took over and they finished rigging the Grumman and off they went.

Living conditions were not bad on the *Enterprise*. When staying overnight in-country I would sleep in the plane. However, one night at Ton Son Nhut I saw the wreckage of a helicopter hit the night before with a rocket and I changed my pattern. That night they trucked us to the filthiest hotel in Asia. Rockets or rats. Some choice!

Norris "Woody" Woodruff: We were given a mission to spray Agent Orange on the perimeter of a base, right along the concertina wire. We had 55-gallon drums of Agent Orange on our chopper. It had a motor and a sprayer on the top. This mission lasted three days. Each day as we finished we were covered with Agent Orange residue. So was the inside of the chopper. We would fly to a nearby river and ease the chopper down just below the waterline to clean out the chopper and ourselves as much as possible.

Bud Might: We would have a gunship in the air over Saigon at night. They would get a call for a disturbance somewhere and just after they left we would be mortared and our gunship wasn't there to spot the source of the fire. That first disturbance was probably a diversion. About the time you'd get another gunship in the air the mortars would stop.

One night we were up and our mission was scrubbed so we asked Saigon if they could use us. An army captain with a group of helicopter gunships asked us if we had any flares. We did. He said they had something going up the river and they couldn't identify it. He had eight choppers ready to go down as soon as we popped the flare. Our flare illuminated a bunch of heavily loaded barges. Anything moving at night was in a free fire zone and after they hit them there were secondary explosions rising higher than our altitude. The choppers were going down both sides of the river and I was in the middle. Anything that moved at night was fair game because our troops didn't move at night.

We had a flare ignite on our plane once. The crewman was able to shove it overboard.

Tom Emmons: Another incident, it was probably the moment in Vietnam that made me the saddest. It was the night we were doing medevac right out in the field. They were carrying bleeding guys on stretchers and loading up the plane, and we'd take off, and I was seeing people die on the airplane. There was blood all over the place.

I had a man die on the tarmac. That was a damn shame. We had about a hundred guys on the plane. There were no seats. They were brand new troops, different than the guys you brought back from out of the field. These were new green troops who were scared shitless. They had no clue. They had duffel bags; they had a weapon. They looked like they came out of supply. We had to sit there that day and it was just hot. I could hear screaming in the back. There was a guy who went down and they were screaming "water". Heat stroke. He died right there on the plane. By the time I got water back to him he was gone. You talk about some freaked-out troops. Kids. Kids. And pissed. Pissed.

Bud Might: I am very proud that in all of my time in the air, including thirty-five missions over Germany, the Berlin Airlift, and Vietnam, no member of my crew was ever hurt. Luck plays a part; one time over Germany six of our twelve planes either turned back or were shot down, but we made it.

Eric Dauphinee: On our re-supply missions, we always seemed to back-haul casualties or guys going on R&R or home. One time I picked up a body that turned out to be the son of my barber back in Maine, who was a grade or two behind me.

Along with proud moments came frustrating ones. I think frustration reared its ugly head far more often. I hated dealing with the media. They were demanding and always tried to get us to do more for longer than the assigned mission. They often interviewed troops and edited it to show a question asked while the answer given was to another question. They asked stupid questions of young men not equipped with life's experiences to give a sane answer. Some of the answers given exceeded my wildest hope, but I'm sure none of those ever made it back to the States.

Other frustrations included finding enemy troops in the open and being unable to get artillery, naval guns, attack aircraft or permission to fire upon them ourselves. There often didn't seem to be enough time or assets to accomplish what needed to be done, let alone some of the things you'd like to get done. Sometimes a medevac went from emergency to routine. You knew some loved ones back home were about to get the worst news they had feared.

Donald "Tip" O'Neill: I earned my Combat Infantryman Badge (CIB) with Mike Force in mid-December, 1965. I was inserted with four other Americans and about 100 Montagnards into Camp Playground. We then walked three days to hit an enemy village. The Montagnards were class people. The women were bare-chested, and the men wore loin cloths.

The Vietnamese really discriminated against these people. At one point, there was an uprising by the Montagnards and they were killing the South Vietnamese. In response, the ARVN were executing the educated Montagnards. The Montagnards would travel to Cambodia to see their religious leader, and they'd return with a bag of some secret stuff around their necks. They believed this made them invincible. They were great fighters.

The C-5

Frank Towns: On July 1, 1970, I participated in the maiden flight of the C5 Galaxy, from Dover, DE to Cam Ranh Bay. This was a test flight and it was like flying on a cloud. I had flown this mission for years on the C-141, and although the C5 and the C-141 both had four engines, the similarity ended there. When the C5 arrived they asked me to check the oil and things, and I told them I didn't have a tech manual; I didn't know where the oil was! Believe it or not you needed a Top Secret Security Clearance to change the oil on the C5.

The C5 could be loaded from both the nose and the tail, while the C-141 only had one load entrance. The C5 had sixteen tires, twice that of the C-141. The fuel and cargo capacity of the C-141 was 318,000 pounds, while the fuel capacity alone of the C5 was 318,000. I took pictures of the plane with me standing in front at Cam Ranh Bay. They told me I couldn't take pictures. I said "bullshit!" After that flight I came back and was discharged in September.

GROUND CREW

Our biggest technological advantage in Vietnam was often at the mercy of the most basic of conditions – weather and climate. Dust-ingestion problems plagued the helicopters.[xciii] The construction of aircraft maintenance facilities – tents, for example – was difficult or unsuitable in the tropical climate.[xciv] Lack of replacement parts were a problem for everyone but since air support demanded more resources (50%) than the other groups, the problem was exacerbated. The authorized aircraft parts list grew from 8,000 in 1965 to 46,000 three years later,[xcv] direct air shipment of parts from Corpus Christi, Texas was begun, [xcvi]aircraft overhaul time was increased from 2,140 hours to 3,300; [xcvii]the enormity of the air campaign surpassed anything in history.

SSgt **Daniel Kreynest,** Tactical Imagery Interpreter/Tactical Observer, 131st Aviation Company, Phu Bai, USA

SSgt **Jimmy Smith**, Air Freight, 15th Aerial Port Squadron, Qui Nhon, USAF

Sgt. **Patrick Ryan**, Jet Engine Technician, 3rd Tactical Fighter Wing, Bien Hoa, USAF

Airman 1st Class **Bruce Quinlan**, Instrument Repairman, 315th Consolidated Aircraft Maintenance Squadron, Phan Rang, USAF

Spc4 **Stan Clingerman**, Parachute Rigger, 383rd Rigger Detachment, Cam Ranh Bay/Bien Hoa, USA

Spc4 **Noah Dillion**, Aircraft Mechanic, 221st Recon Aircraft Company, USA

Pfc **Bill McGonigal**, Fuel Handling Specialist, 114th Assault Helicopters, 1st Aviation Brigade, Binh Long, USA

LCpl **Tom Gase**, Anti-Warfare Electronics Operator, Marine Air Control Squadron-4 (MACS-4), Danang, USMC

Captain **George Burk,** Chief Controller, 1972nd Comm Sqdn, Danang, USAF

Arrival/Duties

Stan Clingerman: I flew Northwest Airlines into Cam Ranh Bay via Japan in September of 1967. Before Christmas I was transferred to Bien Hoa, where I spent the rest of my tour. There were about a hundred guys in my unit.

When I first arrived I spent a month on guard duty at Cam Ranh Bay. After guard duty I was part of a team of cargo packers. We packed cargo chutes under huge packing tents. There wasn't much individual parachuting going in that war so all of our work was for cargo chutes. If we packed a hundred chutes by noon we got the rest of the day off. When I got to Bien Hoa we did our packing in large buildings. There was a shakeout building there where we would open up the chutes to look for damages from a previous drop. We had longer hours at Bien Hoa. We worked 48 hours straight through one time. We rigged a lot of 105mm shells, C4, all types of ammo and food. Some of those loads would take more than one chute. We could actually drop tanks! Our cargo was dropped from C130's.

George Burk: I arrived at Danang AB, RVN at 0130, 21 October 1967. For safety reasons we exited the rear of the plane. I still remember three things as I exited: The noise from departing fighter aircraft and the accompanying noise from the equipment around the airfield was almost deafening; the stiffing heat and humidity and the smell. The smell was almost too much to bear; never smelled anything that had the odor of an open sewage pond. Later, I discovered my initial impressions weren't far off.

I was assigned to the 1972nd Communications Squadron as the Chief Controller, Radar Approach Control (RAPCON). Due to several personnel issues, six months into my tour I assumed the duties as the Flight Facilities Officer....RAPCON and Control Tower.

The RAPCON was responsible for every plane that landed and departed from Danang. We coordinated approach and departures with the Control Tower located in the east side, the Air Force side of the base. During the period from October 1967 to October 1968, Danang was the busiest airport in the world with over 1.2 million take-off and landings. The aircraft that landed and departed from Danang comprised every type of jet and piston driven aircraft. They included the CIA's Plautus Porter to Air Force, Navy and Marine Corps fighter aircraft, military transport, civilian DC- 7, DC-8 and C-47 aircraft, to Boeing 727's 200's and military helicopters.

The RAPCON was positioned halfway between Runways 17 and 35. Both runways were 10,000' feet long, 150' wide with 1,000' overruns at each end. About 50 yards south was a Marine Corps MOREST Crew...they used the same type of cable system on board aircraft carriers. The RAPCON, TOWER and Precision Approach Radar Controllers (PAR) worked closely with the MOREST crew and Tower Controllers. When a pilot requested the "Cable" he gave the controllers his landing weight and speed. That allowed the MOREST Crew to set the proper tension on the cable and allowed the aircraft to land safely.

Tom Gase: Ever since I was old enough to know what Marines were all about I wanted to be one. My plan was always to get my high school diploma, join the Corps, and hopefully get a job that I could take outside the Corps when my enlistment was up. I arrived by Flying Tiger Airlines into Danang in January of 1968. We were expecting the worst when we landed and the people that came down to pick us up had their M14's locked and loaded and had real grim looks on their faces; they kind of freaked us out. I was assigned to MACS-4 at Monkey Mountain, and when we got there they told us it was the "safest place in Vietnam."

I was an Anti-Warfare Electronics Operator or, as we called it, a "scope dope." We sat in a hut with three different radar scopes and we controlled the aircraft when they took off from Chu Lai or Danang. As they got closer to their mission we would hand them over to a mission controller and then we'd pick them back up as they returned and hand them off to approach control.

There would be about twelve of us working each of three eight-hour shifts. Each time we went to work we'd get a different position on the radar scope. Someone there would be in charge of marking anything on the scope that the Navy didn't get. We'd have a Weapons Officer and his assistant. We had three air-conditioned huts for our working space. The huts had to be air conditioned due to the sensitivity of our equipment.

Between planes and helicopters there was a lot of traffic in the air every day. We had a way of distinguishing which was which and the Navy handled most of the helicopter traffic. We were primarily concerned with jets and we could pick up their signature via the radar squawk.

Of course I had guard duty and mess duty when I was over there. There would be two people on a post for guard. This was on Monkey Mountain.

Some of the people walked a post and some were assigned to do the honey runs.

After six or seven months with MAC-4, I spent a couple of months doing some classified stuff on ground radars with a unit that had no military designation; they were more of a civilian group. I was doing this for about two months. Then I went to H&HS-18, at Danang.

Jimmy Smith: After graduating from high school I realized the draft would get me soon. I did not want to be in the Army, so I tried for the Air Force, but I only weighed 107 pounds. My recruiter had me eating bananas all the way to the induction center but that didn't put any weight on me. The doctor told me I must want into the Air Force very badly and I told him I didn't want to be in the Army very badly! But I got into the Air Force and three days after I left for basic training my draft notice arrived.

I flew into Danang on a commercial airliner in January, 1968, and from there down to Qui Nhon. My orders were changed to Operating Location Army Airfield (OLAA), Qui Nhon; I was assigned to the Army! When we landed at Qui Nhon we started taxiing to the terminal. While we were moving the Loadmaster dropped the back cargo door and heaved our bags out. He pointed to a bunker and told us to run for it. Then mortar rounds started landing. This reception made me wonder what I had gotten myself into.

I worked 12/7 on the air strip at Qui Nhon. The Qui Nhon airfield was right on the edge of a residential area. My job was loading and unloading airplanes, rigging chutes with pallets of supplies and ammo and, of course, hauling body bags off and things like that. The planes that were assigned to OLAA were Army planes except the "bird dogs," the light observation planes which were Air Force aircraft.

A hard landing on Monkey Mountain -- Danang
Courtesy: Tim Smith

In addition to our full-time day job we also had some responsibility for the security of the base. There were other security people there but we pulled guard duty in some of the perimeter towers and bunkers and we were to supplement the regular security guys in the event of an attack, which happened fairly often.

We did have Vietnamese civilians that worked on the airfield at the In Cargo Freight Section. We used them mainly to untangle cargo nets. I thought the Vietnamese were appreciative of what we were doing; they wanted their independence and they appreciated that we were there to help them achieve it. I don't think they wanted to be part of the communist regime of North Vietnam.

There were also civilians working at Qui Nhon. We had a Korean trucking firm; they delivered supplies that came in to Qui Nhon out to some of the other smaller LZ's and bases. I sometimes rode shotgun with them as they made their deliveries. If we got caught outside our base when darkness fell we spent the night at the Korean compound.

I witnessed one of our people shoot a South Vietnamese civilian that was working on the base. He pointed his .38 at the lady and accused her of being a VC. The shooting was accidental. I was five feet away and I saw the bullet snap the lady's head back. They had that guy on a plane and out of the country that night.

Bruce Quinlan: I was trained as an instrument repairman. I flew into Cam Ranh Bay in August, 1968. It was very hot and I was very scared because I had no combat training and only fired the M-16 one time. When I saw all the veteran Army and Marine grunts with their weapons and backpacks I thought I was out of my element. My first duty at Phan Rang was sandbag detail. The irony of all our technological weaponry being protected by sandbags was not lost on me.

We had F100's at our base and I helped build the Quonset-type revetments for them. I did that for a couple of weeks and then I finally went to my outfit. The 315th was on the remote (east) side of the Phan Rang base, about nine miles from the Phan Rang Harbor on the South China Sea. We were surrounded by high hills. Our planes, about thirty, were housed in the revetments we built and we had about eight repair shops. I was assigned to the ComNav (Communications/Navigation) Instrument Shop where I worked exclusively on C123's.

We all worked twelve-hour shifts. I worked nights, 4:00 am to 4:00 pm. We were responsible for evaluating and fixing all the navigation, engine, hydraulic and electrical equipment in the C123. We also did the routine preventative maintenance; every sixty operational hours or so we'd pull the planes in for this. We'd actually go through the operating systems for the whole plane before they were given the green light. A lot of my stuff was in-shop repair, evaluating the computers and control boxes and things like that. There were eight of us on nights and about twelve on day shift in the Instrument shop. There were more guys on the radio and other shops.

In all we had eight maintenance buildings. Engines, sheet metal, hydraulics; there were a lot of different functions going on. If we ever had a problem getting a spare part we would cannibalize a damaged or shot-up plane. Parts were not a problem for us. We had about thirty C123's and probably four or five of them were out of service on a given day.

Due to the electronic equipment we were the only air-conditioned maintenance shop. We had to have a hermetically-controlled environment. We also had radios which put us in direct contact with Base Security. We were also the Disaster Control Center so we had all the M16's, flak vests, etc., for the unit. Any time there was an alert we had assigned posts that we were to man. My post was in a crow's nest in the dock area, about fifty yards from the perimeter.

Patrick Ryan: I arrived by plane on September 23, 1968. I worked on the Trim Pad where I tuned the engines on jet fighters to prepare them for missions. I had the night shift, working from 7 pm to 7 am, seven days on then one day off. I lived in a barracks with approximately fifty airmen. Because I worked at night I had to sleep (or try to) during the day and it was very HOT and difficult. During the monsoon I actually enjoyed the cooling off of the temperature and the work stoppage due to the fact we couldn't tune the engines during the rain.

Noah Dillion: I enlisted in January, 1968, on the new "Green Army Contract" for an aviation mechanics school. I completed the school third in my class, was promoted to PFC and sent to school for Single Engine Observation Aircraft Crewman, receiving my wings in June 1968 along with a promotion to Spc-4. I applied for OCS Engineering at Fort Belvoir, Virginia and went through the first eight weeks before the Narcolepsy whacked me and I dropped from sheer exhaustion.

Noah's story is found in his book: Surviving Vietnam: Tales of a Narcoleptic Hangar Rat

Narcolepsy is a sleeping disorder which affects over 250,000 Americans and for which there is no known cure. It is an uncontrollable desire to sleep. I can fall asleep very quickly – I have had many forty-five second naps at traffic lights – but I've had one major and three minor traffic accidents due to sleep attacks. Obviously a combat zone is not the ideal place for a narcoleptic but the Army didn't screen for Narcolepsy so I had to deal with it. It is a neurological disorder, not a mental illness, and recent medications can improve the quality of life for its victims. I have had this sleeping monster with me all my life.

I received orders for Vietnam and arrived via a Braniff 727, flying via Hawaii and Okinawa on Nov. 6, 1968. I was assigned to the 221st Recon Airplane Co. (0-1. My sleep was always an adventure but my first night at Long Binh was the scariest night of my tour. A disgruntled soldier popped a tear gas grenade in an NCO's hooch to register his discontent about how things were being handled.

When I arrived at Soc Trang Army Airfield I took a day time PE maintenance crew slot as a mechanic, declining to crew an aircraft. Later I chose to work on a night crew because the maintenance load required an additional PE crew. I felt safer working in the hangar at night when the worst of things might happen; Charlie was busy working his rice paddy's during the day time. My work schedule was from 1800 to 0600 but I usually went in early and there were no days off unless you pulled guard duty. The 9th Infantry was our airfield security and when they stood down and shipped back to Hawaii the aviation units had to take over the airfield security.

Courtesy: Noah Dillion

On July 29th, 1969 I was promoted to Spc-5 and reassigned to the 114th Assault Helicopter Company located at Vinh Long Army Airfield as an OJT Aviation Electrician. Vinh Long is a large town located in the middle of the Mekong River in an area of the Delta known as the Plain of Reeds. The Army airfield there was taken by the VC during Tet (February 1968). Support troops were gathered and used to retake it. I outranked the Spc-4 running the PE electrical crew so I was made NCOIC of electrical PE maintenance covering twenty-four slicks and eight gunships. Replacing someone who was doing a good job with a new guy who didn't know the ropes but had an extra stripe made no sense of course, and I worked up a compromise with this other guy; I handled most of the office and bookkeeping chores and he stayed a productive crew member.

My Vinh Long work day was from 1800 to 0600 but on many days I went in early to have a pass down from the day crew and stayed late that next morning to give the day crew their work assignments and a pass down. Lacking other diversions, I spent most of my days at Vinh Long sleeping and waiting to go to work. Part of my job was retrieval of downed helicopters. When we couldn't repair it in place, a Chinook would be called to lift it out. If Charlie arrived before the Chinook we sometimes had to burn the ship to keep it from falling into their hands.

Bill McGonigal: I received a degree in mineral economics from Penn State. My draft number was 44; I graduated on Sunday and the notice to report for my physical came on Monday. I enlisted to get the MOS I wanted. The nearest thing I could find to my college background was fuel handling specialist. As it worked out, I think my mechanical ability was of more help than my degree.

I landed at Tan Son Nhut airbase in September of 1970, and was choppered to Binh Long. I was sitting in the door gunner's seat and when we arrived, the pilot turned the chopper on its' side, and there was nothing between me and the ground. It was awesome. I think he did that to scare me but it didn't. I enjoyed it. After that I went up every chance I could get.

My duties included supplying fuel **to and from** helicopters. When I left Vietnam I was the ncoic of refueling helicopters. They occasionally had to work on a helicopter and this required taking the fuel out of it also.

Our living conditions were pretty good. We lived in a single floor hooch. No a/c or fans. We had spiders and mosquitoes. Spiders were out best friends because they provided the cobwebs to catch the mosquitoes. When you first get in country the first thing you do is tear down all the cobwebs. And you found out that that was a big mistake. You learned to live with the spiders.

<u>Guard Duty</u>

Stan Clingerman: The one month I did guard duty at Cam Ranh Bay was the scariest time I experienced over there. It got so dark. One of my posts was near the water and the sloshing of the water could really put you to sleep. I realized that I wasn't going to be able to hear anything. And you sure couldn't see anything. If you thought you saw or heard something you had to call one of the guard towers and they would shine their fog lights for you. There were some nights you weren't allowed to shoot over the berm because there would be friendlies in front of you.

One night we were walking guard duty at Bien Hoa and one of us would walk in one direction, and the other guy would walk in the other direction, and then we'd come back to where we started. We finally decided this wasn't working for us; we were afraid we'd shoot each other. Another time we saw several guys running. I turned my flashlight on them and I fired in the air. They stopped. It was some bandsmen from the 101st. They were coming back from guard duty but we could see they had no bullets. They told us that one of their guys had shot himself in the foot so they weren't allowed to have ammunition.

Noah Dillion: On one of my guard details I called the officer of the day to ask about a large clump of elephant grass I had seen between two rows of concertina on the perimeter. He told me there was no elephant grass on the perimeter. Then one of our gunships came by and fired mini-guns into the mysterious grass. When they went out to reset the claymores and trip flares the next morning they found a dead VC mortar crew in the elephant grass.

Courtesy: Noah Dillion

I was on guard duty one night, and I heard a boy yelling out *Choi Hoi.* He had his hands on top of his head. I told him to lie down in the road in my beam of light. I called the OD and several guys came down the road in a jeep and stopped. One of the interrogators found a live mortar round on the side of the road. I was later told the kid had been recruited by the VC against his will; they were holding his older brother as leverage.

When I made E-5, I was Sergeant of the Guard when I pulled guard duty. One night a guard complained about a pain in his hand. The hand was quickly swollen to the size of a football. This man was medevaced. A week later another guard on the same bunker called to tell me that a snake was crawling toward his position. I went out and identified the sand cobra with the STARLIGHT mounted on my M-14. I told the guard to keep an eye on it; seconds later he stood up and shot the snake with his rifle. He made his shot from the hip without taking aim. Naturally the OD pulled up in his jeep with three other men. Vinh Long airfield was a no fire zone. One of the men found the snake and verified that it was a cobra. I concluded that the bunker was a snake pit and requested that we be allowed to abandon it. My request was refused but they allowed the guards to stay up top on the tower. In the morning, engineers lifted the top of the bunker off and revealed the floor of the bunker was crawling with baby cobras.

Tom Gase: We were expecting a heavy attack coming out of Dogpatch one night. I guess we had some intelligence on this. To prepare for that we went out to the sand piles and we had Vietnamese civilians fill the sandbags. We walked around to make sure that they didn't steal any of the sandbags for themselves. They were known to bury some of the sandbags for their own use later on. In fact we caught a couple of them doing this. They lost their work permits. Our Gunnery Sergeant caught them and threw them off the detail. Anyway we were on 24-hour alert, sitting there waiting for trouble, hoping that it wouldn't happen, and hoping that it would, but it didn't.

Rockets/Mortars/Sappers

Tom Gase: We got hit with rockets three or four times during my time with H&HS-18. One of those attacks hit a fuel storage dump and that was a really loud explosion. The Gunny came over and said "Well, they just hit the command bunker," or so he thought. I was the only one that had my weapon with me so he designated me as his runner. But the command bunker was okay and I didn't have to do any running. That fuel bunker burned for about four days; big black smoke coming out of it. When I was doing that experimental ground radar thing with the civilian unit we did take some small arms fire.

Patrick Ryan: We were attacked by 122mm rockets on a regular basis, probably an average of 3-4 nights a week. Their targets were mainly the airplanes so I was always in harm's way. However I liked working at night so that I would be alert when the attacks happened. When they sounded the siren indicating rockets on the way I was able to get to a bunker quickly. But sometimes the rockets hit without warning so I just hit the ground. They were the loudest things I've ever heard.

One time I was in the cockpit of an F-100 tuning it up and we came under a rocket attack. They were hitting all around the plane and I jumped from the cockpit which was about fifteen to twenty feet high. I broke my hand when I hit the ground and the attack was so intense I just stayed on the ground to avoid any shrapnel.

When the Press talks about Tet, they always refer to 1968, which indeed was a big offensive. But Tet took place every year and 1969 was no exception. It was by far the most intense barrage of rockets and mortars we received at Bien Hoa AFB during the whole year. It was also the only time they attacked us on the ground and there were a few Cong killed inside our perimeter.

Bruce Quinlan: I was in the mess hall for midnight chow and the sirens went off. We all ran out of the mess hall and jumped into the nearby bunker. This was more of a trench than a covered bunker. Just after we reached the trench mortar rounds blew up the mess hall. We just missed real injury by a few seconds.

One night I was working in the shop checking an air-speed indicator when the radio announced a Red Option. I grabbed my weapon and I could hear mortar rounds hitting. They started getting louder and louder. The enemy sappers were trying to get inside the base to destroy our repair shops and the C123's. As I was running for the crow's nest the mortar rounds were landing behind me and one of them actually knocked me down. I took a quick assessment of my body and realized that I was not hit. I jumped up and climbed the thirty feet into the crow's nest. When I got to the top all hell broke loose. There were flares all around the perimeter; illumination flares, and red flares. I knew there was imminent danger for an invasion. The Army, the Air Police, the Koreans and Australians; we had a lot of people running around. We heard small arms fire going out but nothing coming in. There were a lot of explosions all around the perimeter. I was told later the explosions were the VC sappers being hit by our small arms fire. All this excitement was very new to me. I was just out of my mind seeing and hearing all these explosions. Once the All Clear was sounded I came down from my crow's nest and I saw that a mortar round had actually landed on my shop. There was shrapnel all through the shop; nobody was hit but some equipment was damaged.

Stan Clingerman: At Bien Hoa a Russian-made rocket round landed about 100 yards away. It made a small crater. The VC did shoot over our heads a lot, aiming for better targets at the air base.

Jimmy Smith: We were mortared at least four or five times a week. Our base was overrun nine times. When an attack started me and my buddies would be holding off the attackers as best we could with our M16's, and they would send the Chinook helicopters down a short distance to the South Korean compound and bring their troops up to repel the attack. It seems that as soon as the enemy saw the ROK's they stopped the attack! Having seen some of the ROK prisoner interrogations I know why they feared the Koreans. One of their techniques was to tie a prisoner upside down to two poles in town, and sometimes they would cut off the VC's ears, nose, and tongue, as a demonstration. They would put signs up telling the VC what would happen to them.

Bill McGonigal: One night we had nine mortar rounds come in. Three of them went off. The second night three more came in; one of them went off. They were one for three. Maybe their ammo was getting wet. I was on my way out to our fuel station when I spotted an unexploded mortar round on the airstrip. I asked somebody about it and he said it came from the nine-round attack from the previous night. I had slept through that attack! The second night I slept through the next three. That just proved how sound a sleeper I am. Or was.

Other Adventures

Tom Gase: We had to have a radio with us when we were working with the pilots. During our shift we had one person that would monitor a radio and listen for any calls that might be unusual or of an emergency nature. One time I heard a Vietnamese voice and I turned it in to the people in charge. Later I learned that it was a South Vietnamese pilot; their frequency had slid over onto ours.

We had what was called a Duty Cloud. It would come up every night, starting down low in the valley and then climbing up the mountain. When it reached us up on the mountain it was so thick you could hold your hand in front of your face and not see it. If you wanted to go to the Club you had to follow the noise to get there. A plane was coming into the Danang runway during a heavy fog. This was during daytime. We had handed this plane over to Danang Approach Control. It hit the side of Monkey

Mountain. Most of the plane was buried in the mountain from the wing on back.

George Burk: Due to extensive battle damage and pilot injuries, I saw and knew of many aircraft that crashed short of the runway; there were pilots that ejected after landing but their chutes didn't open in time to save them or they ran off the departure end of the runway and crashed in the ditch that was off the south airfield boundary. In one case the plane inverted after it stopped and the pilot drowned before rescue could get to him and cut him out of the cockpit. He was upside down and he drowned from three feet of water in the ditch that filled the cockpit. There were many other pilots and crews we knew and worked with closely, such as 366th TAC Fighter Wing, the AF Rescue, and Jolly Green Giants -- "Pedro" was their call sign -- and many other pilots and crew members who departed north or west on a rescue mission and never returned. It was an incredibly busy job; we had planes landing on both ends of the runway at the same time every day!

In July or August of 1968 I walked into Base Ops to deliver an OPS message to the NCO's on duty for transmission. I took a few steps into the open bay area and my peripheral vision caught a person who was lying on the small, three-cushion sofa that was against the west wall. I stopped, looked down at the person on the couch, took a double, then triple take. There, fast asleep in her Army Green Berets uniform, was Honorary Green Berets Colonel Martha Raye. We'd heard she was in country for quite some time and made many visits. Rumors were that she'd literally jump into a Foxhole and talk with the guys in the hole, then move to another Foxhole. I delivered the message and on my way out of Base Ops, stopped a second time just to make sure it was Martha Raye. That I saw her there, fast asleep, was a memory that still lingers with me today.

Bruce Quinlan: We had radio contact with everything going on around the base. One night the *USS New Jersey* was in Phan Rang Harbor, about nine miles east of us. We could hear them fire their 16 inchers and we ran outside; a few seconds later we could hear the rounds go over our heads and land on the hills west of the base. The shells traveled about eleven miles as I recall. It was pretty awesome and to have radio contact with the *New Jersey* made it that much more incredible.

Jimmy Smith: The big Tet Offensive started exactly four weeks after my arrival. We were kind of shocked by Tet. In relation to my landing at Qui Nhon it was actually kind of mild. There was activity all around us but the VC never actually got onto our airfield. Every helicopter we had was constantly in the air. We had an Air Evac Hospital at Qui Nhon so we had lots of casualties and body bags coming in. We were often pulled off our jobs to help them carry stretchers to the hospital. The body bags were eventually transported down to Cam Ranh Bay.

We had one medevac patient come in and he had an M79 grenade round lodged in his head! The round came from his own weapon; obviously an accident. When an M79 round is fired it goes through a certain number of revolutions before it is activated, but extreme caution was used with this man. He was carried to an isolated tent and they were able to get the round out of his head, but they ruptured so many blood vessels getting it out he only lasted a couple more days.

One major frustration hit me after I came back; it was thinking about all the body bags that were coming in. Another frustration was the 55-gallon drums of Agent Orange coming through often leaked. Of course we didn't realize it was deadly at that time.

George Burk: I also was assigned Temporary Duty as a Summary Courts Officer about 10 days after the TET Offensive. I flew to Dong Ha, just south of the DMZ. I was there for a week to identify a young AF Sergeant who was KIA by a fragment of a 122mm rocket and arrange for his personal effects to be shipped home. A small fragment from a rocket cut through the two by fours above and around him in the bunker like a hot knife through a stick of hot butter. The damage to his upper torso and head was significant. Despite having his military ID card I couldn't identify him at the temporary Morgue. I sorted his personal effects and boxed them for shipment to his home of record and wrote a letter for our squadron commander's signature. That night I had more than a 'few' warm beers with some Marines I'd met earlier.

The seventy or so Air Force Air Traffic Controllers in the RAPCON and Control Tower were the best! Every NCO was outstanding and performed their duties in a truly outstanding manner. I was privileged to work with men where the extraordinary was simply a routine event. I was honored to work with and for them and to represent them. They accumulated hundreds of "saves" -- lives and aircraft saved from potential loss as a result if their decisive actions and absolute professionalism.

In July, 1968, on the tarmac in front of Base Ops, Danang AB, Major General Paul R. Stoney, Commander of the Air Force Communications Service (AFCS), presented the AFCS Southeast Asia ATC Award to the Danang RAPCON squadron commander, LtCol Dick Bottom. It was the first award of its type to be awarded to any ATC Facility in SE Asia. That award epitomizes the professionalism and selfless duty demonstrated by every man assigned to the RAPCON.

Stan Clingerman: We were frustrated sometimes when the Air Force guys didn't like the way we rigged the chutes. The riggers that took them down to the planes had to re-rig them according to what the Air Force guys wanted.

Like Forrest Gump said: "When it rained in Vietnam, it rained vertically." It was cold and wet and we had really sticky mud. Cam Ranh Bay was nothing but a sand pile. They had to lay metal runway plating in the roads just to let jeeps go down the road.

Noah Dillion: A damaged helicopter was making a final approach. Our fire and rescue trucks raced with the chopper as it moved from the end of the runway to the hangar. The wounded pilot landed near the front of the hangar, which was against regulations, and shut the engine off. The main rotor and tail rotor were still spinning. A crowd of men raced to help remove the wounded. One of my friends went around the back of the chopper to get to a buddy; he realized his mistake too late and he raised his arm to deflect the blade heading for his head. He was struck on the forearm, and as he fell the trailing blade hit him again, which broke his arm and caused a serious cut on his forehead. He was put in the ambulance with the man he was trying to help, but he was still a lucky man that day.

Bill McGonigal: Somehow the commanding officer's helicopter had some bad fuel, some contaminated fuel and they came and got me out of bed because I was the only one that knew how to take the fuel **out** of a helicopter.

We were headed west (towards Cambodia), with a load of aviation fuel in drums. I was riding shotgun on a deuce and a half, and I had been given some directions as to which way to turn on the roads. There were three guys in the back and two of us in the front. We really didn't know where we were other than we were heading towards Cambodia. Three rounds went over our heads and we're sitting on a load of aviation fuel. One of the guys in the back had his M-16 on full automatic instead of safety. He had sent the three rounds over our heads. It was an interesting moment.

Towards the end of my tour they came in and put stationary pumps in. At the time we had little rubber-tired 350 gpm pumps that we operated the fuel station with, and they installed 500 gpm which were great if you were fueling fourteen choppers at the same time, they really put out the fuel, but if you were fueling just one the pressure was enormous. I had tried everything I could think of to reduce the pressure on those pumps. The way they were designed I couldn't do a thing with them.

About 43% of the helicopters used in Vietnam were destroyed. In total over 8,500 aircraft and 4,300 pilots/crew were lost in Vietnam. [xcviii] *Half of the hundreds of billions of dollars spent in Vietnam went in support of air operations. Over 8 million tons of bombs were dropped. The missions were completed, sometimes at great sacrifice. The war strategy was and is open to question.*

Over the three years that I've been on this project I had a few guys tell me they had an interesting job in Vietnam and then, for one reason or *another, they never participated in an interview. The guy I miss having more than any told me he **operated drone aircraft** in Vietnam! I was unaware that we had drones during Vietnam. He said he could talk about his job, but never did. My speculation is that they were used strictly for reconnaissance purposes and not the offensive capabilities now being demonstrated in the Gulf wars.*

AIR SUPPORT – AIR CREW

Don "Tip" O'Neill

Eric Dauphinee

Tom Emmons

Bob Janecek

Norris Woodruff

Bud Might

David Greene

John Lawrence

Dallas Johnson

AIR SUPPORT – GROUND CREW

Stan Clingerman

Jimmy Smith

Daniel Kreynest

Noah Dillion

Bruce Quinlan

George Burk

CHAPTER EIGHT

COMMUNICATIONS SUPPORT

Before the beginning, in 1951, there was a single half-duplex radio teletype circuit between Saigon and the Philippines. [xcix] *Communications were still inadequate in 1965 with a particular negative impact on the supply/logistics systems. In fact, the logistics needs mandated the development of the communications systems.*

The 1st Signal Brigade was activated in April, 1966 and reached 20,000 men within a year. [c] *Satellite communications were handled via the Satellite Communications Agency located in Fort Monmouth, New Jersey.* [ci]

TOWER TEAM

*Spc4 **Jack Stroud**, Teletype Operator, JUSMAG (Joint U.S. Military Advisory Group, Ubon, Thailand, USA*

*Sgt. **Allen Thomas Jr.**, Radio Relay Crew Chief, 507th Radio Research Battalion, Udorn AFB, Thailand, USA*

*Spc4 **Dave Fuchs**, Radio/Teletype Operator, Strat Com, Pleiku, USA*

*Spc5 **Tom Petersen**, Radio Repairman Tower Team, 459th Signal Bn, 21st Signal Corps, Nha Trang, USA*

*Spc5 **Bob Olson,** Microwave Radio Repairman/Operator, 459th Signal Battalion, Nha Trang/Cam Ranh Bay, USA*

Arrival/Duties

Jack Stroud: Wearing civilian clothes, I flew into Bangkok, Thailand, in February, 1964. We had been instructed not to wear uniforms. My qualifications sent me up to Detachment 2B in Ubon, which is near the Laotian border. I spent my tour at Ubon Ratchathani, which means Lawyer Town in Thai. I was a Signal Corps man but I always spent a lot of time assigned to artillery units. In Thailand I was an overseer for the 105mm howitzer training for the Thai Army. There was quite a bit of live firing always pointed toward Cambodia. The 105's had already been given to the Thais and we were there to train them on how to use them.

Allen Thomas Jr: In May, 1965 I landed at Don Muang Royal Thai Air Force Base, the main AFB in Thailand. I flew in there on a commercial airliner in civilian clothes, with a civilian passport; we were "advisors." We were supposed to have enough money to take care of ourselves for three days until someone came to take care of us. After just a few days at Korat I went to Udorn AFB where I spent four months.

I ended up at a site on some high ground between Udorn AFB and Vientiane, Laos. My job was to build the camp and keep the radio relay system running. I was crew chief of the thirteen guys maintaining the site. We were all technically "advisors".

As a radio relay station we weren't actually sending messages, we just provided a tower to help transmit the messages from one location to another. We were in the jungle in the middle of nowhere; if you went away for two days and came back there might be a tree growing in the middle of your tower. In the first days we used portable equipment. Later, we built a 150' tower.

I also had to go to Saigon once a month, mainly for paperwork issues. For example our codes would change every month and we had to pick up the new codebooks. On these Vietnam trips we also did some radio relay work in Vietnam where I helped some units set up their new radio equipment which was usually sitting around in unopened boxes. I also had to go to Bangkok to pick up food. We were paid with military certificates and we had to feed ourselves.

Naturally we were on call 24/7. We didn't have a regular work day; we just had to make sure the equipment was running. We could listen to the radio traffic going on around us so we had a good idea of what was going on in the world and in the war.

Jack Stroud: I served in Arizona and Fort Benning, Georgia upon return, but I was in Nha Trang, Vietnam, for my second Asian tour by June of 1966, circuit chasing VHF sites. This work was mainly night duty. After the first couple of months I got involved in profiling. This involved being dropped off in certain spots to determine the viability of using it as a communications site. This was always as a prelude to an upcoming operation. I worked with Captain Thomas and a couple of other men. We tried to pick areas of high elevation where we also determined we would be able to get vehicles in there. When we finished our field work we had to make our way to the pick-up point. When we returned the captain would write up the After Action Report and I would do the profiling on the map to see if our "shots" (line of sight) would work. I was to be at this work until July, 1967.

Dave Fuchs: I was working as a cable splicer for the phone company in June of 1965, and in November I received my draft notice. I enlisted to get into the Signal Corps. This meant an extra year of commitment but I did it. After basic at Fort Knox I went to Fort Ord, which was wire school. From there I went to pole school, which was Fort Gordon, GA. At this point, I figured the longer I stayed in these schools the longer I stayed out of Vietnam. The next school was antenna school, and they explained the qualifications: You had to climb a seventy-five foot pole on hooks. That would be your first test. There were about four hundred of us there and only seven of us stepped forward to try antenna school. The seven candidates were shipped to Woodbridge, VA, an Army antenna site near Ft. Belvoir. The Army tested various types of antennas presented by various manufacturers at this location. During this training I erected an antenna at a prison in Kansas, and I put one up at the Pentagon. Then I got orders for Vietnam. I guess I had run out of schools.

I went over as a replacement, not with a unit. We landed, or tried to land at Tan Son Nhut, but the field was under attack so we circled for a while. Our jets were strafing the area near the airfield. When we landed there were bodies all over the place.

This was November of 1966. After processing I went to Pleiku, in the central highlands. I was at Pleiku five or six weeks, long enough to see the

Bob Hope Show on December 18, when a call came through for someone at Nha Trang, on the coast midway between Cam Ranh Bay and Tuy Hoa.

When I arrived at Nha Trang the Army had facilities for most of their guys, but the antenna site was out on the Air Force side, about two hundred yards off the end of the runway. They had three broad antennas at this location. I had not seen this type of antenna before. They were in the process of building facilities for us to stay there. So the first part of my time there was pouring cement and building places for us to stay and sleep.

After working on our buildings at Nha Trang for a short period I began to do the job I was trained for. My hours were midnight to noon seven days a week, doing cable splicing and repair work on the antennas. We also patched overseas calls together for people. Nha Trang, Pleiku and Phan Rang were all big, electronic Comm Centers run by a civilian outfit called Page Communications. They were the folks that had built these antennas and there was a lot of electronic stuff involved; new things that were just now coming into play. They were testing a lot of stuff over there at this time.

Allen Thomas Jr.: After Thailand I spent the next year in Germany at a place called Goeppingen. We were way too busy since most of the battalion had been cleaned out to support Vietnam; all we had there was five sergeants trying to do all the work. There was no down time. That is where I was when my next orders to Vietnam arrived. I flew into Tan Son Nhut in May of 1967 and was choppered to Pleiku. After just a few days I was attached to the 173rd Airborne Brigade at Dak To, in the Central Highlands.

My small unit maintained seven radio sites at Dak To and in the neighboring countryside. This was a "line of sight" concept and the satellite sites were always on high ground, usually in a small clearing big enough to support several howitzers which were in turn supporting the infantry. My job was to maintain these vital communications and to take care of my people. Our antennas were usually crank-up types, about 75 to 90', but at Dak To 90' was not high enough to get above the trees so we built towers. At the fire support bases, small clearings at the top of a hill somewhere, we just had small vans that were air-lifted out to them. A hole was dug in the ground and the vans were plopped in there. As long as colonels and generals could talk to each other nobody bothered us.

We were just three or four guys there at Dak To working in support of the 173rd Airborne Brigade, parts of the 4th Infantry Division, the MP's; we were their communications link to the outside world. The biggest threat to our safety was our commanding general! General Stone insisted that all the NCO's should be leaders; regardless of your daytime job, you should be out leading patrols at night. I must have led about fifty of these patrols.

Tom Petersen: I flew into Cam Ranh Bay in July of 1968 with orders to report to the 518th Signal Company. Within a few hours of my arrival I was on a short hop over the mountain to Nha Trang.

Most of the guys in our company were radio repairmen. They were assigned to a specific signal site and they did rotating shifts keeping the radio sets tuned, replacing parts, and stuff like that. They also monitored the signal to ensure that it was clear. Each radio set had forty-seven voice channels. Channel #1 was always ours so we could call each other to monitor the signal strength. At least once a shift these guys would call around the network just to talk to each other and get a sense of how clear the signal was. Channel #1 was also kept open for what was called the command call; this would involve some important general needing to send a message or something from the Pentagon. Sites had three to five radio sets. So if a site had three radios they could handle up to 3X47 messages. This is primitive to what they could have today of course, but some towns in the U.S. still use that microwave technology.

It is my understanding that the U.S. Army handled the long distance communication for all of South Vietnam from I Corps down to IV Corps in the Delta. Some of the radio relay towers were on air bases or naval installations and some were on a mountaintop somewhere. This was a line-of-sight system with a tower every thirty kilometers or so from the next one. The maximum distance was around forty-five kilometers.

In my first year I was part of the Tower Team, which involved the erection and maintenance of the radio relay towers and antennas. When establishing a new radio relay site we looked for high ground. We also had to lease this ground from the South Vietnamese government. It was our job to go into this new site and make it habitable and defendable.

Courtesy: Tom Petersen

We were given our assignments each day by our Operations Officer. Of course some of these jobs lasted three or four weeks. The radio relay from one point to another was known as a "shot". An average day would be like the time they wanted to connect a shot from the Phan Rang Air Base to Nha Trang, Cam Ranh Bay and Da Lat. The latter three were already connected and Phan Rang was kind of outside the loop. We spent three weeks at Phan Rang, spread across two separate trips, trying to get this shot to work but it never did. But we were able to hit the "repeater" site which was Pr' Line Mountain. The land they leased for this repeater station was on a mountain owned by a Frenchman who used it for a tea plantation. By getting this shot to Pr' Line Mountain we were able to include Phan Rang. It was a funny, kind of triangular link, but it worked.

Bob Olson: I joined the 518th Signal Company, at Nha Trang, on April Fool's Day, 1969. I arrived just six hours after an attack. My work was building bunkers until I was assigned to the Tower Team. I had a Secret security clearance. There were only two tower teams in Vietnam; our sister unit, the 327th, was down at Long Binh. Our job was to erect and maintain the radio relay towers which provided the communications link to all our forces in Vietnam. The towers were line-of-sight across less than hospitable terrain.

We maintained the towers, antennas and wiring to the radios on old sites and were responsible for erecting new sites as needed. The towers were 48' to 186' high, and they came in 6' sections, which we assembled. The towers came in kits that included the tools needed for assembly. We usually had to go down to Saigon to pick them up. The antennas were 8' parabolic microwave antennas, something like chicken wire, with wires that went down to the radios. Signal Maintenance was responsible for the radios. If we put in a new site, we would run it alongside Signal Maintenance for the first two weeks to make sure that it was operating correctly. We had fourteen tower sites in II Corps, and we also supported other Signal units.

We put in new sites or took down old ones. In 1970, during the pullout, we took down three sites and erected just one, at Da Lat. For example, we closed down two sites at Pleiku when the 4th Infantry Division departed. When we finished that job there were only six or eight of us Signal guys there, guarded by hundreds of ARVN; we might have been the last Americans to leave Pleiku South.

A lot of our work was done on mountain tops, perhaps 7,000 or higher. And after the 100+ heat of most of Vietnam, it was actually cold up there. I wrote to my mother for some clothing that would help keep me warm in those conditions. I remember shivering under three Army blankets in a Quonset hut; it was so cold the ground was contracting, and the shifting ground was causing the protective shield of land mines to explode!

Allen Thomas Jr.: After my second Southeast Asia tour I went to the 3rd Armored Division in Germany. After that tour in Germany I flew into Danang in May of 1970. From Danang we were on a truck convoy to An Khe. I reported to the 124th Signal Battalion, my old unit, part of the 4th Infantry Division.

On this tour I didn't have a job! When I arrived they were supposed to have five staff sergeants in my MOS; they had fifty or sixty. I kept looking for something to do and I finally became an assistant to the battalion sergeant major. He called me his technical assistant and he used me to talk to people he didn't want to talk to. After a while I morphed into being a career counselor trying to talk to people about staying in the army. That work lasted until I took the seven top E-6's in the battalion out of their jobs. I guess I was too good at this work! These guys weren't ineffective but they wanted out of our unit; they wanted to go to a better place. They wanted a place where they had beds, lights and hot food; no mud.

Jack Stroud: For my final tour I flew into Bien Hoa in June of 1970 and was stationed at Ban Me Thuot. I was the Commo Chief for the 2/17th. This was the HQ Battery for the 17th Artillery Regiment. My job was sending SitReps every night! I would get the SitRep set up on the teletype and ready to go and my operators would send it. These things were usually ten or more pages long. Being in charge, I had a 24/7 responsibility. When I arrived there was no Commo officer, no commo anything. They threw me to the wolves. They gave me a bunch of potheads, a big bunker with a lot of radios, a repair position in the bunker; that's all we had down there was repair and supply. Just after I arrived they came in and wanted to swap out the old CRC46's, which they replaced with GRC106's. These new radios were better – better range and clarity -- but they were also harder to operate. But the guys caught on pretty quick.

I started my first tour in Thailand, living in a hotel. On my second tour we lived in hooches, although our work space was a hotel. On my final tour, home was a bunker surrounded by sandbags.

Around March of 1971 I was sent over to Charlie Battery. My job was to get them shut down and ready to move back to Cam Ranh Bay. I knew when I got over there in June of 1970 and they didn't have a Commo officer that there was something going on. Anyway my job was to get the equipment ready to go and get the radios mounted back on their ¾ ton trucks. I also prepared equipment and paperwork for destruction with thermite grenades. In April we convoyed down to Cam Ranh Bay with our guns and everything else. As soon as we left the gates the Vietnamese raced in to get at anything left behind. It was like a land rush in the old west. Once we got everything back to Cam Ranh Bay we horsed around for a week or so, then they loaded us on a plane and we were gone.

Vietnamese

Allen Thomas Jr.: On my first Asian tour our tiny camp site was supported by the Thai army. I was very proud that we developed a good relationship with the Thais in the village's right by us. Back in 1965 we didn't receive any fire but we did get a few mortar rounds at the air base in 1966. By late 1966, rebels were beginning to slip across the border into Thailand in an attempt to incite the Thais into converting to their side. It really was an Indochina war – a Second Indochina War -- not just a Vietnam War. Why don't they call it that?

Dave Fuchs: Not long after I arrived at Pleiku, a sergeant asked me to go with him into the town. It sounded like an adventure so I agreed. He pulled up to a Montagnard compound and told me to do exactly as he did. They opened the gate and we had to be led into the village. The sergeant looked at me and said, "Whatever I do, you do it. Don't refuse anything." We went into this one Montagnard's hooch and they had a custom that if you were a new person entering the village, they gathered around the table and in the middle was a bottle of rice wine. Everyone had to take a sip of the wine, for good luck or something. I had never had a drink in my life before this. I took just a small sip, which met the requirement, but my mouth burned for the rest of the day.

I met a Vietnamese guy in town. He was working on a phone and he spoke English, so I struck up a conversation with him. He was a phone company person in Nha Trang. To make a long distance phone call in Nha Trang you had to go to the post office. You had to set up an appointment to make your call, and you probably had to know somebody to get this done.

On some of our occasional runs to the beach during the day, we would pick up the seven-year old son of our housemaid, the lady that was in charge of all the housemaids. She invited a few of us to her place for dinner one Sunday night. She lived right near the base. I knew they had a dog from my many times picking her son up. She set a really nice table with the potatoes and the rice and this and that, but I didn't see the dog. Then I saw the main course and I figured out what was going on. The dog tasted like beef, I guess.

Bob Olson: When we finished our work on a site we had to find our way home. We usually headed for the nearest helicopter pad, and this usually required walking through some Vietnamese villages. Naturally we didn't do this at night. I remember going through Da Lat, and there were just three of us, and there were thousands of Vietnamese. We would buy coconuts, pineapples and other things from the villagers as we passed through. We went to their restaurants a lot, even if they were off limits. Their food was good. I didn't like the nucnaum sauce. We ate monkey once. The montagnards sat us down with their family one time; that might have been the time we ate the monkey.

For some reason the Vietnamese guarding us when we built our sites were always Rangers.

Courtesy: Tom Petersen

Tom Petersen: I was fluent in what I call "marketplace" Vietnamese. I could count to ten and I could haggle a bit over prices. I could also talk to the girls. There was an orphanage in downtown Nha Trang operated by Catholic nuns, and I spent a lot of time there. All the kids seemed happy, the facility was very clean and I never saw prolonged crying, angry outbursts or conflict of any kind. What I did see was devotion, contentment and a lot of laughter. The older girls took care of the younger kids and babies under the watchful eye of the nuns. The kids had great fun when they did laundry and if anyone, including the nuns got too close, they were splashed with lots of giggles and I dare-you-to-get-closer! One thing I never asked was where the boy orphans were; I never saw one over five or six while the girls were there well into their teenage years.

Jack Stroud: My contact with Vietnamese on my last tour was solely with the Montagnards. I found that the Montagnards were very strict with themselves. I thought they were a very nice people. They worked to make sure that everything was right. They would take anything you'd give them but they were happy with what they had.

Allen Thomas Jr.: On my second tour our Vietnamese interpreter had fought the Japanese in the Second World War. He was helpful when we took donations to the orphanage in Kontum.

We had an ARVN Battalion assigned to us at An Khe. This was during the Vietnamization period and we were supposed to be showing them the ropes. Every section chief, first sergeant, and supervisor had an ARVN counterpart with him all the time. Most of our work with the Vietnamese concerned technical stuff and they were bright. They were also cordial and we would share pictures of our families and things like that. Most of them spoke English very well.

The Vietnamese we were dealing with were pretty educated and pretty well trained. They had been around a while. Some of them had trained in France or the United States. Most of those people wound up here.

Adventures

Jack Stroud: On the tour in Thailand we did a lot of recon river trips and we worked with Air America (CIA). On the recons we experienced a lot of small arms fire. I carried an M14 and the first time I got shot at I pissed my pants. I was in charge of making sure the boats we took up the Mekong River had all the supplies they needed. We would follow the Thai patrols into Laos and wait for the Thai patrols to come back to debrief them. I wasn't supposed to be in Vietnam on this tour, but I was, reconning near Buon Ma Thuot. Strictly speaking we were only following the Thais; we didn't do anything! I ran into both South Vietnamese civilians and the guys in black pajamas on my treks into South Vietnam. Since this was a recon we tried not to get involved in any firefights or prisoner taking.

On my next tour we did our last profile in the Pleiku area. There was some intelligence about expected action by the enemy in this area and Captain Thomas and I went in there to do some recon. We worked on that job a long time and chased down some bad VHF sites that we couldn't use. We finally found a suitable site. Trees usually weren't so tall that our antennas wouldn't work so most of our profiling was successful.

The guys were all strung out. The only thing is I got them to where they respected me. They didn't do their drugs while they were on duty. They did that stuff on their own. I respected them for that. I asked them "What would you do if we were overrun like Delta Battery?" We had lost D Battery while I was there. They were located on the other side of the airfield. That was not a fun thing to clean up; I went over to see what was going on and it was a real mess.

Allen Thomas Jr.: On one of my trips over to Vietnam from Thailand (early 1966) I hit a land mine while driving a deuce-and-a-half from Dak To to Kontum; no one was injured but all of us had some blast damage from that mine. Sore necks, black eyes; I looked like a raccoon around my eyes. I had a couple of tiny holes in me from hot shrapnel and I thought "I'm dead," but the medic calmed me down and told me it wasn't bad. No Purple Heart; I had seen too many guys with no legs and stuff and I told him I didn't want it. I should have taken it but I didn't know I was going to have health problems later on.

During my second tour our bunker was blown up the second day I was there. We got mortared, we got rocketed, and we got shot at up and down the road. I hit another land mine while driving from Dak To to

Kontum; this was the same stretch of road where I had hit a land mine on my first Southeast Asia tour. In fact this mine was only three hundred yards away from where I hit the first one. Although lightning had struck a second time, no one was injured.

At Dak To, we were close enough to the Ho Chi Minh Trail and the NVA infiltration route that we could hear and feel the concussion from B-52 raids over there in Laos. We also had battleships firing support missions. That is amazing. You could actually see those huge rounds going over.

When Tet began we were in the village a few blocks outside our wire. When the shooting started we ran back to the base under fire, but when we arrived they had locked down the gate. We had to climb the wire which cut us up pretty good. When we got inside we ran to our bunkers. There was a *Chieu Hoi* Center building across the street from our perimeter wire where they processed enemy soldiers that surrendered. These "surrendered" guys were shooting at us from the roof of the building. We returned fire for a while and then leveled the building with fire from two of our supporting tanks.

On my third tour the 4th Infantry Division shut down; they were on their way home and I was sent to the American Division at Chu Lai where they had replaced the Marines. I would have preferred to chopper to Chu Lai but we drove. After hitting two land mines I was not anxious to be behind the wheel again, but we were short on drivers. That was a very long drive. We were shot at and they hit the front of our long column; I wasn't even aware of it at the back of the column. Unlike my first two tours of Southeast Asia I didn't drive over a land mine!

We got there right after a typhoon so they needed us; communications were out. So for a month I was doing what I was trained to do. After things were up and running I was out of work again. This time there were over one hundred E-6's so we just sat around with a lot of food and a lot of booze. I worked in the NCO club when I was off duty although I was never really "on" duty. I finally went out and **found** a job. I went to S-3 (Operations), The Operations group had a lot of communications issues and no one to resolve them, and so I fit right in. I ran S-3 commo. Both at the 4th Infantry Division and the American Division I was putting in time because they had too many people. The war was winding down. I just went out and found myself something to do to keep me occupied.

They had guard towers around the side of the mountain at our Chu Lai camp. That mountain was covered with monkeys. The Americal had harassed these monkeys so much that periodically the monkeys would come down and retaliate. The first time I experienced this we had an alert and I heard all this screaming, and everybody's locking and loading and it turned out a monkey had attacked one of these guard posts. When we found out what had happened we were all rolling with laughter.

Dave Fuchs: I was only at Nha Trang four or five days when a major called me in to his office and asked me if my MOS was towers and stuff like that. I told him it was. He took me outside and pointed in the air, and one light on one of the towers was out. This antenna was about 135 feet in the air, and 200 yards off the runway. The light was important! I asked him if he had a body belt and he did not. I told him I wouldn't go up there without a body belt so he got us one from the Air Force and we found a light bulb.

There were rules in place for climbing these antennas. The rule was the person climbing the tower would turn off the electricity, which required a key, and then pocket the key to prevent someone else from accidentally turning the juice back on. The staff sergeant in the Comm Center room with the antenna switch told me we couldn't turn the power off. I advised the major of this snag and he came over to the Comm Center but the staff sergeant continued to debate with him. The major was becoming irritated and he finally told the E-6 he would bust him down a rank every time he opened his mouth. The E-6 gave me the key and I locked the antenna down. The E-6 reached for the key but I pocketed it. He protested and the major looked at him and said you just lost a rank. The major never did bust the guy but he had him pretty well scared.

Anyway, I walked out of that place with the key in my pocket and I climbed the tower and changed the light bulb out, and it was really pretty uneventful. When I climbed down and took the body belt off the major says to me "You know, that was a pretty stupid thing?" "What?" I asked. "Well," he said, "If there was a sniper on that mountain over there it would be easy for him to pick you off that tower." I told him that climbing that tower was my job. That's what I did. Really, I could not refuse to climb that tower. It was not too long after that that I was promoted to Spc5. I think it was because I climbed that tower.

There was a group of Special Forces guys that had a small compound behind us, at the fringe of our camp. They had a helipad, with about fifteen helicopters out there at all times. One morning a sapper had come into the Special Forces area and placed satchel charges on seven or eight of those choppers. Somehow they got past the guard dogs to do this. I was awakened by the huge explosion of all those satchel charges going off. That is the only time our base was hit while I was there. Nha Trang was hit during the big Tet offensive of 1968, but I had left two months earlier.

I accidentally ran into the general at the PX. He asked how I was doing and where I worked. I asked him if he knew where the antennas were at the end of the runway, and he said he did. I told him if he had a telephone somewhere on the planet I could reach it. He was surprised. I picked up on his enthusiasm real fast; I saw a barter system coming in to play. I explained that I would put a call into an air base near his home, and from there they would patch the call to his wife. I didn't go to work until midnight, but that was daytime back home and I called his wife. Then I called him and he spoke with his wife. When he finished he called me back to break down the call.

The general talked to his wife for over half an hour that night, and he began calling her at least once a week after that. And of course if we had a hard time finding something I'd kind of let him know, and all of a sudden it would show up at the base. One time our major needed some cement and I asked him how much he needed. He figured it was at least a truck full. This was a Monday. I told him that there would be two trucks of cement here for him on Wednesday. Wednesday arrived, as did the cement! The major asked me how I did it. I asked him if he really wanted to know. He asked me if I was doing something illegal. I told him I didn't think so. I explained to him how I did it. It was a good deal for everybody.

Bob Olson: Just a couple of weeks after my arrival I heard the sirens going off. I ran to get my M-14 rifle and the rack holding them was locked and the key lost! Someone broke the lock and I ran outside and found cover by the sandbagged side of the barracks and a row of 55-gallon drums. I saw a mortar round land to the northwest, about 300 feet away, blowing a tower of sand into the air. Other rounds hit the roof of our church. The air conditioning unit and an icebox and part of a fence were destroyed. Later, ten of us lifted a replacement air conditioning unit with poles and carried it on our shoulders like ancient people must have carried things

We were hit again by mortars in May and June of 1969 but we took no casualties. The worst attack came on August 7, 1969, my dad's birthday. We had one man killed and twenty wounded. This was a late night attack. A lot of our guys were caught spilling out of the barracks when the shelling started. Two of my friends were among the seriously wounded; one lost a leg and the other a middle finger and arm injuries, and they were both sent home. One mortar round went through the roof of our barracks and destroyed an empty room. Some rounds also landed in our basketball court about 100 feet from our barracks.

I was on a mission to the Central Highlands during this attack; I returned about six hours after it was over. I visited my friends at the 8th Field Hospital a couple of days later and the guy with the missing finger and arm damage told me how it happened. Apparently, the VC dropped a couple of rounds in and then waited fifteen seconds to catch the guys running out of the barracks. When I reported to the Company Commander on our Central Highlands mission, he showed me the back half (fins) of an 81mm mortar round by the entrance to our bunker. For the next three days many of us worked to replace the wrecked sandbags. We sandbagged both entrances to our barracks where most of our casualties had occurred; we built 55-gallon drum walls, two drums high filled with sand, along both the north and south sides of our barracks.

Our next attack was the last week of September, 1969. We heard the sirens going off in the distance, and by now none of us wasted time getting dressed. We threw on our pants and pulled on our boots without tying them (the guy killed in August was tying his boots) and ran to the perimeter behind our microwave signal site. The next day, just before 0600, we were running to the perimeter again. On the third morning this was repeated and, right on time just before 0600, we were hit again. Three days in a row. The rounds were landing right where we would have been standing if we were doing our normal morning battalion formation. One of our Spc5's brought this up at a leadership meeting and all formations were stopped.

During the first week of October, 1969, we heard the sirens and we heard rounds hitting the airfield next to the Army's Camp McDermott. This was around noon, which we thought was funny because our planes were very quickly blowing up a small hill close to the nearby mountain range. We figured the VC mortar crews must have been high on drugs because it was suicidal attacking in broad daylight.

I was shot at (small arms) personally four times. In 1970, we worked on and off for three months at a site that had burned. When we were up on the towers, maybe eighty feet in the air, there were rice paddies all around us. Or we would be on the coast and be up that high or higher. I'm sure that snipers shot at us because when we were working on two 120' towers that had been damaged, we took one down and put up a 48'. Tom and I were up at the 80' level to take the antennas off, and I went back down for a wrench and saw a bullet hole in the support beam. Then I saw another hole and I could see the shots came from the direction of the city. I realized the holes hadn't been there before.

The next time I was shot at was in Lang Bin Mountain. I was driving up to it from Da Lat. This was in April, 1970. I took the wrong turn and we got on a high plateau. As I was turning around I heard a shot ring out. I thought about telling my shotgun to start shooting, but then thought better of it and we just raced away. I told someone in charge about where we had been shot at, and that night mortar fire came from that direction to a nearby camp, and they had a Green Beret KIA.

We put up a small, 48' tower near where we worked on the big 120' towers. There was a small piper cub runway there. There was a helicopter assault company located nearby. They were close to the perimeter fence. We were sitting there drinking one night and I mentioned that I heard gunfire. They thought I was drunk. I went outside and I saw a VC or NVA firing clip after clip into the parked helicopters. This was about four hundred feet away from where I was standing. I went back to the club and told the guys but they still thought I was drunk. We went outside, five of us, and we could see the guy, and he saw us at the same time; we dove for cover just as the sirens went off. Somebody suggested we illuminate a flare so we could see better. I set off a flare, illuminating our position perfectly!

The VC tunneling was getting too close for comfort at a 105mm artillery firebase (Landing Zone Betty), in July, 1969 so we were asked to install a tower for their anti-personnel radar. Their existing anti-personnel radar couldn't detect enemy when they were down in the trenches. This equipment required an anti-personnel dome on top of the tower. We thought we were going to an air base so we didn't take our weapons along. I should have known something was different when they assigned us a Caribou aircraft to get us there instead of a chopper or a truck. We landed on a flat area with mountains to the west. They told us to deplane because the war was going on there. It was supposed to take us two weeks to build the tower, but with danger as an added incentive and the obvious importance of the mission, it took us three days. I picked up a weapon from one of the wounded on the hill; this guy had been hit during a mortar attack before we arrived, but I never had to use it. This was the most dangerous tower job we had while I was there.

After the work was completed on the third day our chopper landed to take us out but the pilot said they had an oil problem and he didn't know if they were going to make it. He gave us a choice to go or stay. Just then we heard firing off to the right, perhaps a hundred yards away. I saw an NVA, with helmet and all and a weapon in his hand. He was firing at some others, but when he saw us he shifted his fire in our direction. The bullets landed maybe twenty or thirty yards away. We dove into the back of the chopper and away we went.

In December of 1969, we went out help the 362nd. This site had burned down and we could never figure out why it was so high priority, but it was near Cambodia and that was the reason. We were on a chopper flying to the site and we were near An Khe Pass, and the chopper pilot turned around and went back. He asked us if we could see the elephants. We did. He told us they were carrying VC supplies, and we went back to machine gun them.

When we went up to Pleiku North in April, 1970, our antenna was on top of this giant dish. Tom and I went up to dismantle the antenna. One of the lieutenants was underneath us, although we didn't really need any kibitzers. Anyway, one of us dropped a wrench, which landed near him. He moved away.

Often the wind would blow the tower back and forth four or five feet. We were used to it but guys would watch us in amazement from down below. We would swing the tower back and forth to freak them out sometimes.

Courtesy: Bob Olson

We were sitting having a beer in a club at the bottom of Hill 182 and a baboon came down out of the tree. We gave him a beer and he knew what to do with it. In fact, if you reached for his beer he would growl like a dog. His two inch teeth were formidable.

Allen Thomas Jr.: On my first tour in the mid 60's, we were dealing with a lot of professionals. The younger kids were still draftees but you had a core of trained officers and NCO's. By the time the early 70's came around we were dealing with six-month warriors. They were sent to leadership school after basic and they'd come out of there sergeants or staff sergeants with barely six months in the army; same with the officers; thirty months after leaving OCS the guy would be a company commander -- a captain.

By mid-1968 dial telephone exchanges, secure voice terminals and message and data transmission facilities were in all major logistical installations.[cii]

Radio Teletype Operators (RTO'S)

Radioman 3rd Class **Bob Goodall**, *USS George Clymer, USN*

LCpl **Don Campbell**, *RTO, 2nd Bn., 4th Marines, Chu Lai, USMC*

Spc4 **Ron Kappeler**, *RTO, 198th Infantry Brigade, Americal Division, LZ Bayonet, USA*

LCpl **Doug Garrett**, *Communications Center Man, HQ Co., 9th Marines, Danang, USMC*

Pfc **Bernie Wright**, *Wireman/Switchboard Repair, 79th Maint. Bn., Long Binh, USA*

Spc4 **Sam Hall**, *RTO, 4th Infantry Division, Pleiku, USA*

Spc4 **James Higgins,** *Comm Section Chief, C Company, 46th Engineer Battalion, Xuan Loc, USA*

Airman 2nd Class **John Ploof**, *RTO, 35th Tactical Fighter Wing, 7th Air Force, Phan Rang, USAF*

Arrival/Duties

Bob Goodall: On my first trip to Vietnam (1963), I was on the Attack Transport *USS George Clymer* APA-27. We sailed up the Saigon River with bullets pinging off the metal on the ship. Welcome to Vietnam.

On my second tour (1964), I landed at Tan Son Nhut but nothing exciting happened on arrival. When I departed a year later however, the counter at the airport blew up just after I was handed my ticket. I hadn't walked ten steps from the counter when it happened.

Both on the ship and on shore at Saigon my job was to receive and pass communications to various personnel. The job required a Top Secret security clearance. The job included radio and teletype repair and maintenance, code usage and work with transmitters and receivers. My day was spent establishing and maintaining communications. My average work day was twelve to thirteen hours.

Don Campbell: I crossed the ocean on the *USS George Clymer APA-27* and was stationed on Okinawa. We left there for Vietnam at the beginning of May, 1965 on the *USS Magoffin APA-199*, and landed in mike boats off the coast of Chu Lai, about 55 miles south of Danang.

The beach at Chu Lai was named by Marine Lt.Gen. Krulak -- an old China Marine -- for the phonetics of his name in Chinese. They planned to have an airstrip with a catapult, which was ultimately built by the Seabees (Mobile Construction Battalion 10, with help from marine engineers), but it was not built yet. We moved inland on Amtrak's.

At night my job was to maintain a foxhole and M-60 machine-gun bunker around the perimeter of the Command Post. The day job was supplying field wire communication through the switchboard from the Command Post to forward outposts. I also maintained direct field phone-to-phone situations as required. I supplied wire communications from the switchboard to Supply, Sickbay, Transportation, Message Center and the radio relay site within the compound by land line, overhead construction and helicopter.

Switchboard duty was the main part of the day and it included maintaining equipment (clean and service) and run or trouble shoot communications wire. We also ran wire out of a helicopter to the furthest outpost from the CP. This position was located on a hill with a mountain and rice paddy in front. We made the connection by splicing donuts of wire together into a canvas bag and feeding it out the gunner door while flying to the outpost. We knew this process before we deployed to Vietnam but had never practiced it. When the work was completed we radioed for the chopper to return to the CP. This was the older H34 chopper. In our haste to get on the chopper we had all gone to the rear, and we had to move forward quickly to balance the load so the chopper didn't fly back over itself. This line remained in service but we still had to troubleshoot it via foot patrol.

Doug Garrett: I flew from California to Okinawa and did some training at the northern training area, then sailed to Danang in February, 1966, along with some RAT (radio & teletype) Comm equipment. Radio wave was replacing land lines. The new radios were the PRC-6 and PRC-8's and a larger one called the PRC-25. That radio was kept in a large hole in the ground in the Comm Center bunker. I went to HQ Company, 9th Marines, upon arrival. The HQ was on Hill 327 overlooking the Danang airstrip. I was low man on the totem pole and pulled perimeter guard duty at night. By day I worked in the Comm Center -- almost an office setting; we handled SitReps (situation reports), Casualty Reports, Troop movements; things like that. We did this by teletype and by radio. We were using the new RAT technology. We passed the messages from our units on to the 3rd Marine Division by teletype. There would be about six of us working in the Comm Center. The security equipment was called a Cryptographic Decoder. You needed an 8x6" perforated card that went into a slot that would encode and decode the message. I used to jeep out to the battalions to distribute each mornings Crypt sheets to them. I carried an old .45 grease gun with me and I also had my M-14 modified with a selector switch, for automatic fire. In the Fall I went to 1/9 (1st Bn., 9th Marines), at Hill 55.

Ron Kappeler: We reached Danang by ship in October of 1967 and were transferred to an LST. Before the transfer took place we noticed a lot of men with carbines looking over the side of the ship for sappers or air bubbles signifying someone was in the water near the side of the ship. Once on the LST we sailed down the coast that night and went ashore around midnight at Chu Lai. My unit, the 198th HQ unit, ended up just west of Chu Lai at Landing Zone Bayonet.

When I worked with the infantry I would get dropped on a hilltop somewhere to set up the radio equipment. We were sometimes dropped by Chinook helicopters. Sometimes we had a jeep that had three different types of radio capabilities; radio, radio teletype and voice communication, Morse code etc. We were trained on Morse code but we didn't use it much. The Special Forces guys communicated a lot with code and they were so fast I couldn't keep up with it. I also pulled a lot of perimeter guard duty and shit burning details.

John Ploof: My Air Force recruiter kept stalling on accepting me and I was finally drafted, but he showed up at my induction and pulled me out of the line heading for the Marines and put me into the Air Force. Many Thanks!

On the way to Vietnam we stopped on Okinawa and saw a lot of SR-71 spy planes sitting around. This (1967) is about the time China detonated its' first nuclear device. Anyway, I took a slot for Phan Rang, since I had heard it was a very quiet base. I flew in during Tet, 1968; we were hit the night I arrived and every night thereafter during my tour.

We operated a repair truck with six guys and lots of radio equipment in it. We called it the Red Ball, and we would run it out to the end of the runway for planes that were experiencing radio or intercom trouble just prior to takeoff. We'd try to fix their problem so they could get on with their mission. If we couldn't we'd swap their radio for one we had in the truck. I also worked in the radio repair shop at the base. We also took occasional flights on C-47's going to Singapore, Hong Kong, the Philippines, and places like that, since the C-47 radio had an international frequency band. We weren't on those flights so much to repair the radio as to just give us a break from our work routine

We worked at least twelve hours a day, seven days a week. We worked longer hours if things were very hot. We usually walked to work each morning, about two miles, or we hitched a ride. We carried M-16's at times, especially during Tet.

James Higgins: I arrived in Vietnam by plane on June 19, 1969, and I served initially with the 25th Infantry Division. I was wounded and after I recuperated I was assigned to the 46th Engineer Battalion.   I had no engineer training so they assigned me to the commo bunker, first as a field wireman, and later as the commo section chief. Our average work day in the commo bunker was eight hours, monitoring the radios on twelve hour shifts if/when we were shorthanded which was most of the time.

Bernie Wright: I had no training for switchboard repair, either in the States or in Vietnam. They pointed me at one and they were very surprised when I was able to figure it out. I was always good at tinkering. We worked a six day week, 0730 to 1630 day but sometimes you had to work more. I was sometimes choppered to remote locations to repair their switchboards. I went to a number of bases in the general vicinity of Long Binh and I went down to the piers at Saigon a time or two. We lived in screened-in hooches. We had no problems with rats, maybe because our chow was so bad.

Vietnamese

Bob Goodall: The Vietnamese maids cleaned our rooms. I walked among the Vietnamese people every day. They were nice people but I don't think you could trust them. They wore white clothes during day time and black clothes at night!

Don Campbell: As a mighty mite (jeep) driver, I drove for a sergeant on village patrol to ensure that no marines were there since it was off limits day and night. I was able to interact with the villagers and take some pictures. Of course we didn't understand them or them us. However, they did know what a dollar was. They wanted to sell hats, wash clothes, sell soap, pop, etc. It was strange to see they kept these drinks cold from ice packed in sawdust. The young boys (8 – 10 years old) were curious. Since they don't have a bridge in their nose they were fascinated by mine. The young girls were shy and kept away. The people were friendly during the day, but this was the same village where our wire was cut and abandoned by us.

Doug Garrett: We did receive occasional mortar fire at Hill 55. We put sandbags on the roof of our Comm Center. We also started getting probed quite a bit at night. A decision was made to bring in a guy to teach us some of the tricks about being a sniper. I had the crash course and there were nights where I was out in the brush with a spotter and a starlight scope. I had good night vision, which helped. I did have occasion to do some shooting out there.

They also gave us claymore mines and listening devices. The listening stuff was worthless; you'd put on the earphones and all you would hear would be static. The engineers had done a nice job of clearing fields of fire around our perimeter. By sitting out there at night we were able to persuade Charley to leave us alone.

John Ploof: I did my own laundry but we did have Vietnamese working at the mess hall. One of our AP's noticed that one of the Viet's at the mess hall had larger breasts than usual. Upon inspection explosives were found on the girl.

Ron Kappeler: The Vietnamese men were small but highly competitive. In their minds they were strong. They always used to play games with me. They would throw sandbags at me, like a half-filled sandbag. They would throw it in the air and catch it on their forearm and they would look at me and say you do that. No matter what it was I had to equal them.

The Vietnamese would fill up cans from our garbage each night. They would tell us they were going to feed their pig but we were never sure.

Sam Hall: My biggest contact with the Montagnards was at the garbage dump. Those people would swarm all over the dump, and we had to post guards just to protect them from being crushed by the garbage trucks.

In my final days over there I was put on a detail relocating Vietnamese civilians from a free fire zone to safety. Naturally we also relocated their animals. We piled everything and everybody into deuce-and-a-halves and moved them to their new homes. This job went on for a week or two. They were very appreciative. I felt like we were really helping them.

Bernie Wright: We'd go out periodically to check our wires on the perimeter and the people would come up and try to bug you. Sometimes our wire got snipped and once we found a tunnel. We had to call the tunnel rats to go down there. The ones that did our laundry were nice enough but I really didn't like being near these people.

Adventures

Bob Goodall: We sailed up the Saigon River on my first tour. Everybody on shore wanted to shoot us and small arms fire was pinging all over the ship.

Every time there was a coup, and that was pretty often, we had to go around to all the hotels to keep the communications going. When we received communications during the night we sometimes had to wake a sleeping officer. We were not allowed to physically touch an officer. I was shaking the bed and moving everything in the room, and I finally shook the guy. I was reprimanded for touching an officer!

The enemy seemed to have no appreciation for life. They would load up their bicycles with plastique and pull them up in front of you, and BOOM. I was sitting in a restaurant eating once and saw this happen.

Don Campbell: We had run a land line (wire) out to an outpost just outside a village bordering Route 1. Some of the wire ran down the inside of an abandoned railroad track. On troubleshooting the line the next morning (the line went dead the night before) we found the wire had been cut in too many places to count and removed. We abandoned the line.

I was assigned to the furthest outpost on weekly rotation duty. I was informed on arrival that the week prior they had killed some VC sappers and buried them in the latrine dug on the hill. Fortunately, nothing of this nature occurred during my duty.

One night I was assigned to a night patrol beyond the outer perimeter through an area of rice paddies and small huts. We made no contact but it was spooky looking at my shadow reflected in the water of the rice paddy as I walked on the earth bank. This was how it was during the first part of the patrol; later, the moon would rise and set which led to darker conditions where you thought every bush was moving. Our Fourth of July was watching the parachute flares at night.

One time after repairing a cut in the wire on a foot patrol, we continued walking to the outpost. We entered the outpost area through a break in the barbed wire, passing two marines in a foxhole. Fifteen minutes after returning to our area via chopper, we learned that a short 105 mm round had landed in that foxhole. Both marines were killed by concussion but their bodies were intact. This was during a fire-for-effect coordinate for night patrol beyond the outpost.

Doug Garrett: In the act of distributing Crypt Sheets we came under fire one time. My jeep driver ("Weasel" Preston) was wounded in the head by our exploding windshield; I got some shrapnel in my hand. He received a Purple Heart but I declined mine. I've cut myself worse opening cans than with that wound and I didn't want to worry my parents. I got some antiseptic and a band aid and went back to work. Preston wasn't hurt too badly but future daily distribution was done by chopper. I enjoyed the chopper rides; you got to see a lot of the countryside. We were in constant need of Crypto repair parts. They didn't want to store parts in the field so when needed they were not right at hand.

Ron Kappeler: There were occasions when people would try to come in through the wire at night. And we would fire back; an exchange of fire. Sometimes we were exposed to sniper fire. We underwent mortar fire one time while we were at LZ Baldy and in a number of other places. A lot of times you could see the mortar fin sticking out of the ground. A lieutenant was pulling on one of fins one time and we suggested he get away from there.

Some guys would amuse themselves by shooting at the feet of Vietnamese civilians. I had some infantry guys shooting at the feet of my work party one time. I did my best to persuade them to stop.

I was always amazed by the number of accidents among the servicemen. We did some stupid things. I remember unscrewing a hand grenade and removing the charge. I would pull the pin and throw the charge minus the casing which constituted the shrapnel.

John Ploof: During an attack one night a guy jumped into a hole and was bitten by a viper. We also had plenty of noise, what with planes taking off at all hours, and we had a 105mm battery nearby firing their artillery a lot at night, and the battleships at sea would fire their big guns over our heads. We were shot at in one form or another seemingly every night. One attack blew up three or four aircraft.

On one of our flights our plane was apparently hit and the landing gear light came on, indicating we might have a problem when we hit the ground. So we diverted to Cam Ranh Bay, where they foamed the runway for us. The landing gear held.

My bunkmate was a big guy named Greenleaf, who I nicknamed "Moose." He used to claim that he swallowed goldfish back in high school. We had these large bugs, we called them rice bugs; they were copperish-brown in color, about three inches long, over an inch thick, and could fly. We challenged "Moose" to eat one, and passed around a helmet to sweeten the pot. We collected $75, and he went for it. "Moose" actually had to chew this thing to get it down, but, amid cheers of "Go Greenie go", and his eyes watering up, he got it down. That's one way to get rid of the bugs!

Sam Hall: I was originally a radio operator for a forward artillery base, at Fire Base Oasis. I spent my whole tour there. It was in an ammo dump, helipad; we had a lot of stuff there. Our unit had four batteries of six guns each -- 105mm howitzers. Each gun was supplied with several beehive rounds in case we were in danger of being overrun, but we never had to use those while I was there. Then I was reassigned as an RTO for an artillery observer.

I was on call 24/7 for fire missions and plotting defensive concentrations in the evenings. Most of our harassment fire was done in the evening.

We fired a lot at FB Oasis. We might fire several hundred rounds to a coordinate because someone thought they spotted a sniper. One person!

James Higgins: Apart from my wound while with the 25th Infantry Division I saw a steady diet of rockets at the 46th Engineer firebase. The rocket attacks always seemed to occur when I was in the mess hall, and I was forced to go through the side wall (screen wire) to get to my bunker.

In my first days with the 25th Infantry Division, no one would talk to me because I was a FNG (fucking new guy). We were on a little firebase and I decided to clean my M-16. It was a bit dark in the tent so I pulled the bolt back to make sure the chamber was empty. I didn't notice that there was a full clip in there, and when I let the bolt go forward it chambered a round. I held it up in the air and pulled the trigger, and it made a big hole in the top of that tent. I'm just glad that it was just one shot and not on fully automatic (rock and roll).

Someone who wasn't there would not believe that you could sleep in water on wet ground with water rushing between the crack of your butt, but if you hump a ninety pound pack all day, cutting through triple canopy jungle, I promise you that you'll sleep like a baby. To this day sometimes when it rains I'll go sit in it on the deck and get soaked and my family looks at me like I am crazy; things like that in war is enough to make you crazy.

I guess Tet had an impact on me. It was a worrisome time, not knowing what was going to happen. I still think about it every February.

I was one of the few guys who paid my way back to the war. After extending for six months, they gave me a thirty day leave. Back home, my sister was having her first baby and my mother said I had to stay a few more days and see it. The baby was seven days late which made me AWOL going back, but my mother would not take no for an answer. I did not get in trouble for this, but since I was late and missed my flight they flew me from Fort Dix (New Jersey) to Oakland for just $137. They handled things the same when I got to Oakland; they gave me another voucher from Oakland to Saigon, for $258.30. They never claimed the money until I was processing out of the Army. They said you owe us some money.

Bernie Wright: In my second year – this would be late 1971 or early 1972 – we had fewer people to do the work. They sent us a warrant officer to run things and he really didn't want the responsibility, so he pretty much let me run things. For about six weeks I was the company commander of our unit.

We were out on the perimeter one day inspecting the phone lines and I was taking a break and napping on a bunker. I woke up to the sound of my fellow troops laughing at me. They knew I was afraid of snakes and there was a cobra a few feet away from me. I killed the snake; I was going to be at that bunker that night on guard duty.

When I was due to rotate home they told me they wanted to send me to Fort Gordon, GA to train Vietnamese on switchboard repair. I told them I didn't like the Vietnamese in Vietnam and I sure didn't want to work with them in the United States.

INTELLIGENCE

*Spc5 **Mike Stockton**, 3rd Radio Relay Unit, Army Security Agency, Saigon, USA*

*Technician **Dick Trimbur**, Communications, 7th Fleet, USN*

*Spc4 **Don Helton**, Communications Center Operator, 509th Radio Research Group, ASA, Saigon, USA*

Arrival/Duties

Mike Stockton: I was trained for radio direction finding and fixing the targets. I landed at Tan Son Nhut on January 4, 1964, a week after a coup. ASA worked for the National Security Agency (NSA). It was pretty significant work tracking the NVA, the VC and the VC government. We had an operations building in Saigon and we had eight radio direction finding sites around the country. We had a Direction Finder location at Kon Ton Island where they had the infamous tiger cages for prisoners, both political and VC. I flew down there to do something with codebooks. I worked both day and night shifts. We also had an aviation section that did direction finding by air. I'd get the reports from these sites and my job was to plot these locations on the big map we had. Now this is all done by computers, which is infinitely easier. I'd compile a monthly Bearing Report for the NSA. These things could be pretty inaccurate due to atmospherics, terrain, and things, but with aircraft you could plot the site to within twenty feet! We had other people that determined **what** was being said; it was our job to pinpoint the location of the transmission. All messages were in code and were sent on to the NSA.

Dick Trimbur: After my tour in Turkey I arrived at Danang by plane in October of 1967. The monsoon had just started and it was a real joy to walk into that. The duties included message traffic interception from enemy planes (Migs) and North Vietnamese land batteries. We worked twelve-hour shifts on the *Coral Sea* carrier and four to eight-hour shifts at Danang or up to a couple of days when we were in the field.

Don Helton: I flew into Tan Son Nhut in January, 1968. We worked shifts 12 on, 12 off in the Primary Criticom (Critical Communications) relay communication center for Vietnam. Our center passed signal/electronic intelligence and other high security traffic (Arc light B-52 "flashes").

A typical day ("trick") included thirty to forty men who worked in sections in a "torn tape" Comm Center relaying messages: Incoming, Outgoing, Service, Read Off (there were other sections of the Comm Center, such as Maintenance, Quality Control, Crypto, etc.). Messages would arrive with one or more addressees and have to be resent based upon the precedence routine: Routine, Priority Operational Immediate, Flash, Critic. Routine/Priority were not normally separated; flashes would immediately be resent, even interrupting other messages; Critics would automatically pass through the Comm Center and were expected to be in the hands of the President/Head of the NSA within five minutes from original transmission. Besides direct circuits to the NSA we also had circuits to organizations within Vietnam, outside of Vietnam (Thailand, Japan, the Philippines, Okinawa, Hawaii, Washington and Europe). Since there was a lot of interconnectivity (such as a spider web) we had to know alternative routing options.

Vietnamese

Mike Stockton: When I first got there I was guarding the Saigon PX, and there was an American school behind the PX. This is one huge PX in a walled compound. This place sold 600,000 bottles of hair spray one year, which the guys were trading with in town. I saw a disturbance half a block away; a group of Vietnamese rolling around. I walked down there and found a big rectangular package wrapped up and a guy getting ready to poke it with a stick. I stopped him and called the bomb squad. Sure enough, there was enough plastique in there to blow up the whole block.

I did see Buddhist/Catholic riots with school children. They were fighting in the street. And I witnessed a twelve-year old girl stab an eight-year old boy to death with a long knife. I was frustrated by the lack of leadership from the Vietnamese politicians and the incredible corruption.

Dick Trimbur: We also had ARVN assigned to our unit. They were happy for the food and cigs. Everything we took for granted was a luxury to them. We depended on each other. No women cleaned our hooches due to the classified stuff. Some thought to be disloyal were executed at various camps.

Adventures

Mike Stockton: They blew up the Brink's Bachelor Officer's Quarters on the eve of the Bob Hope arrival in December, 1964, in downtown Saigon. Hope's line was "I passed the hotel on the way in here!" Three of us had just received our first drink in a bar behind the Brink's BOQ when it happened. The VC had put a 750lb bomb in a ¾ ton truck and drove it into the underground parking lot of the BOQ. The explosion knocked me off my bar stool, although I didn't spill my whiskey. On the way across the square to investigate the damage, a gas tank from a nearby truck blew up. We were very close to this and it knocked us off our feet. The hood of the truck flew past my head, missing me by just a few feet.

One side of Camp Davis faced directly at the Tan Son Nhut runway. We lived in barracks made of mahogany, which was hard as steel. We had a helicopter land on the runway once and it had an arrow from a crossbow sticking out of the undercarriage. Talk about a culture clash.

I witnessed some of the first B-52 strikes from the air; this was around Tay Ninh. We were flying at around 6,000 feet and all of a sudden we saw this eruption on the ground. I also had a chance one time to ride as a door gunner on a chopper. We flew to Can Tho, about ninety miles south of Saigon. We were flying about ten feet above the palm trees at 120 miles an hour. That was pretty cool. I fired at a few VC sampans going up the canals. We probably got shot at but we never knew.

We were on our way to a remote location south of Nha Trang. There was my boss, Sgt. Brown, and the direction finder driving the jeep, each of whom carried .45's, and me with an M-14. This road was full of mud and holes and we're going about five mph when about a hundred black-clad guys stood up in front of us. They were carrying machine guns and had red scarves around their necks. That is as scared as I ever got over there. We rode by them at five mph and they just grinned at us.

Dick Trimbur: We had an aviation guy on the flight deck of the *Coral Sea* who pushed an F-16 off the deck into the Tonkin Gulf. Turns out he was under the influence; they used to melt aspirin into Listerine and drink it. They'd get aspirins from the px and dissolve it into Listerine and get goofy that way. He was dishonorably discharged in a hurry.

We had four or five different supervising stations on the radio intercepts and you would get their attention when you thought you had something hot. And he would make a determination. There were more dummy communications than live ones. When we intercepted stuff it was usually a radio transmission in Morse code. Of course it was encrypted; we taped it and the intelligence people were responsible for breaking the encryptions. With so many dummy communications it was tough to discern. My boss disagreed with me on one and told me to ignore it. I thought it was hot and I went over his head. I got a commendation and he lost a stripe.

One time we intercepted a communication that discussed a proposed new North Vietnamese tunnel system. This communication was between the VC and the NVA. We got some fighters in there and bombed that out before they could get it underway and we got a Captains Commendation for that. Another time we intercepted stuff on enemy ground-to-air defenses around Haiphong. We diverted some fighters to take that out which prevented a possible catastrophe.

During Tet we had a lot more radio traffic to analyze; a lot more classification. We had to be more cautious on the job. They were hitting everywhere. We were quite busy. If you could pick up some classification that was in the works, naturally that was helpful.

Don Helton: Our flare ships would fly around the perimeter at night. The enemy came to realize that all they had to do was shoot for the outside of the circle of flares to hit the flight line or the center of the circle to hit the helipad. The flare method was changed.

During Tet we had a number of 122mm rocket attacks including one with over one hundred rounds dropped on us. I witnessed the first shots fired in the attack on Tan Son Nhut; I happened to be watching a Boeing 707 taking off and I saw tracers going up toward the plane. The pilots must have shoved their feet through the floor pulling the nose of the plane upward; they were not hit.

After the attack began a bunch of us were put up on the Comm Center roof with our M-14's (we had been trained on the M-16 but didn't receive them until later). We saw the base defenders backed up to our fence but we'd been ordered not to shoot (probably to avoid hitting our own guys). The sound I will never forget is the bull whip sound of rounds cracking by me. We were ordered to stay out of sight but we were still exposed and we had a panoramic view of the battle. Someone stood up on the other side of the building and was shot (I think in the buttocks). It was not a major wound.

At one point I was assigned as the LAW (light anti-tank weapon) man. This is a small, disposable bazooka-like weapon. I was shown how to work it but that was the only time I ever touched it. The guys in the Comm Center continued working during the attack and reported that some stray rounds came through the roof while they were working.

By 1969 there were about 14,000 communications circuits in South Vietnam. The colonels and generals could not only talk to each other, they could call home![ciii]

COMMUNICATIONS SUPPORT

Allen Thomas, Jr.

Jack Stroud

Tom Pedersen

Bob Olson

Don Campbell

Doug Garrett

Ron Kappeler

Bernie Wright

Dave Fuchs

CHAPTER NINE

SECURITY SUPPORT

PERIMETER SECURITY

There were no "secure" roads or bases in Vietnam. Security was everybody's job, or at least one of their jobs. Pilferage, sabotage or outright attacks were a daily concern. Defense of our many bases fell to infantry units, security units, or even the clerks, cooks, mechanics and other support troops that had been performing their primary duties all day long. This chapter provides a distinction between Perimeter Security and Convoy Security. Each of our installations was ringed by barbed wire and festooned with sandbagged bunkers, some of which were always manned and some populated only in the event of attack.

*Airman 1st Class **Ed Cranford**, Air Police, 23rd Air Base Group, Danang, USAF*
*Airman 1st Class **Mike Tillman**, Air Police, 366th Security Police Squadron, Phan Rang, USAF*
*Airman 2nd Class **John Mobley**, Air Police, 3rd Combat Support Group, Bien Hoa, USAF*
*Captain **Paul Kaser**, Admin Officer, 3rd Security Police Squadron, Bien Hoa, USAF*

*Spc4 **Barry Willever**, machine-gunner, G Battery, 65th Artillery, Dong Ha/Phu Bai, USA*
*Spc4 **Don Classen**, Psych Tech, 67th Evacuation Hospital, Qui Nhon, USA*

*Spc4 **Gary Nunn**, Military Police, 716th MP Battalion, Tan Son Nhut AB, USA*
*Sentry Dog **Turk**, Camp Granite, USA*
*Sentry Dog **Kato**, Camp Granite/Camp Humper, USA*
*Spc4 **Steve Newsom**, Light Direction Control Operator, 2nd Bn., 29th Artillery SLT, Pleiku, USA*
*Pfc **Rich "Saw" Negich**, MP, 101st MP Company, 101st Airborne Division, Phu Bai, USA*

*LCpl **Alan Webster**, Military Police, 23rd Military Police, Chu Lai, USMC*
*LCpl **Gordy Lane**, General Security, III Marine Amphibious Force, Danang, USMC*

Arrival/Duties

Ed Cranford: When I arrived (early in 1964) the runway at Danang was made of dirt! Shortly thereafter, construction began on a new and longer runway which was completed before I left in February of 1965.
I was responsible for the flight line, our radar site, and the security of the base itself. When I first arrived there were not that many planes to guard. There were some Hueys and some Argosys (Army planes), and the C123's and C124's. By the time I left the runway was completed and we had a lot of jets in there.

Mike Tillman: When I got there in early 1966 I had never seen the M-16. When they handed me one I asked what it was and they told me to talk to some of the newer guys; they might know. The added pressure was, in the Air Force only the AP's had weapons. So you knew you had to stop any enemy penetration because if they got past you there was no one behind you to stop them.

Gary Nunn: When we guarded a facility they would use an oval unit, called a kiat, which was a small concrete structure, with a roof. We'd then place sandbags around it and the guard would have an M-60.

Gordy Lane: I was at the Danang beach house -- an old French compound with a small helipad – in 1967. The front half of the compound belonged to the general and only had a chain link fence around it. The back part of the compound was for a group of SEALS. Later, they kicked the SEALS out and put the Vietnamese Language School and 2nd CAG (Combined Action Group) HQ in there.

General Nickerson took a big interest in his personal guard. We had special uniforms, special helmets, belts, etc. We also had plenty of ammo and plenty of grub. I was standing at the gate one time when the general came in and passed me; a bit later I got called in to his office to see his aide, a gunnery sergeant (recon) who had won a battlefield commission and the Navy Cross. They wanted to know where my rifle was when I saluted the general. I told them it was in the guard shack, several feet away. I was told (for the first time) that the rules here were that the guards be locked and loaded at ALL times!

John Mobley: An Air Force cop is not like a temporary duty job. In my first month I guarded the bomb dump. The next month I was in the perimeter tower, an old French concrete octagon- shaped thing. We could see most of the perimeter with our infrared starlite scopes. You could see most intrusions, or if mortar fire came in you could call in their position.

Barry Willever: I arrived by plane at Bien Hoa, in November of 1968, spent two days there, and then flew by C-130 to Danang. We spent a day there and then we reached our final destination at Dong Ha, which is pretty far north in I Corps. I spent most of my year there and at Phu Bai. My unit was G Battery of the 65th Artillery and we were Air Defense Artillery, although we were used solely as ground defense.

I was classified as a machine gunner on the Quad 50's, and then I became a squad leader. I don't understand why they didn't classify us as combat troops since we were with combat troops all the time, but they didn't. We provided perimeter security support and gunfire support on convoys.

There was a second Quad 50 working with us most of the time. We each had a four-man crew and we were responsible for our truck, our weapon, the ammunition and each other. We all knew each other's job so the first guy to the gun during trouble was the gunner. The four .50 caliber guns were wired electrically so that when the fired all four fired at once. Every fifth round was a tracer. This was a devastating weapon and the only place to hide from this gun was underground.

We had to clean the weapon in the morning and clean it at night. We might fire 1,000 rounds during an average night and it didn't take long to burn up one of the barrels. We worked more during the day than the night; convoys, for example, didn't run at night.

Alan Webster: In February of 1969 the colonel assigned me and two other MP's to oversee security at the second gate at Chu Lai, the entrance for most of the supply trucks. We ensured that they were only carrying what they were supposed to have. There was pilferage coming out that gate so I made sure the load on the truck matched what was on the chit the driver carried. I'd tear those trucks apart to make sure everything was correct.

Turk: John was my handler. He volunteered for dogs, which meant he volunteered for Vietnam. He liked dogs but he never had one until the Army assigned him to me. Our job was to detect and warn. Our responsibility was the ammo dump.

Steve Newsom: We did quite a bit of illumination of our perimeter. We already had the bunker grids so we could respond very quickly. We could also illuminated a few of the neighboring bases.

Rich "Saw" Negich: In August of 1971 we flew from Danang on a Chinook helicopter to Phu Bai. Camp Eagle. This section of I Corps was once the domain of the Marines but by the time I arrived there all the Marines were gone. The war was winding down.

MP's worked the three gates at Camp Eagle. The two secondary gates (Jollee and Rear Gate) were in a Free Fire Zone; you didn't have to ask permission to return fire. But the Main Gate was not a Free Fire Zone; that is why the mortar attacks always came from that direction. Being required to call for permission to return fire was immensely frustrating and damned dangerous. Our attackers at the main gate knew they were safe and that's where they would plunk their mortars from.

We also conducted patrols, both inside and outside the camp, we manned certain bunkers, later I did convoy escort, and we also escorted prisoners, both enemy and American.

Adventures

Turk: There was a tank farm (fuel) on the other side of the ammo dump. One night as our shift was ending the tank farm was attacked. Our casualties were heavy; seven guys killed and seventeen wounded. The two dog handlers working over there were wounded and their dogs were loose. John and I went over there to help out. When we arrived one tank was burning and it was really hot. Some of the guys were firing into the rice paddies. They told us we weren't needed so we went to the Qui Nhon hospital to check on the handlers. Two of the new handlers were told to round up the two loose dogs and finish walking post until relieved. When they were relieved a sergeant told them to tie their dogs to a chain link fence and go to breakfast. It was before 10:00 am when they came back but the dogs had died of the heat. One of them had tried digging a hole to get out of the sun. They had plenty of water but no shade. A dog's normal body temperature is around 102 but these dogs were at 126.

After this attack John and I returned to our routine at the ammo dump. Most nights the sentries would sit in the ammo dump and smoke dope. John would take me off my leash and we'd walk our post. He did that to give me a bit of freedom. A sergeant told him to leash me and he said something back using a word I'd not heard before. This got John some kind of reprimand.

We were walking our ammo dump post another night and the sergeant called us on the radio and asked us where we were. He had seen a pair of eyes when he pointed his flashlight into the darkness and he assumed John had unleashed me again. But John and I were not in that area. The sergeant had found the panther that used to hang around the ammo dump. About this time I got sick and was sent back to the states. Getting sick was the only way dog's came home; other than that they were there for the duration.

Mike Tillman: I pulled guard duty one day at the bomb dump. A guy with a fork lift was picking up empty pallets and moving them around. As he picks up a pallet, a cobra comes up with it. This snake is about fifty feet away from me. It was standing up, like they do, and it was taller than me. I always carried a round in the chamber, which the lieutenant told me I shouldn't do, and I emptied a clip into the cobra. Remember now, I'm doing all this shooting at the bomb dump! The shooting scared the hell out of the guy on the fork lift; he thought he was under attack. He jumped off his machine and took off. The sergeant calls me on the radio and wants to know what I am shooting at.

Kato: I had been in Vietnam about five years when Turk went home and John was assigned to me. All the dogs came into the military via Lackland AFB in Texas. I was small – about sixty-five pounds – part Shepard and part Collie. John and I went over to the air base for a party with Air Force dog handlers one time. Their dogs were all German Shepherds; good looking dogs. They looked like they were pure German Shepherds, not mutts like me. Dogs were dipped in something every month to deal with ticks. All dogs had a tattoo in their left ear that identified them. Seals and Green Beret dogs had no tattoo in case they got caught somewhere they weren't supposed to be.

We were walking our post one night and John stopped to chat with the guards in the tower. I could tell he was planning to sit awhile but the guards mentioned that they had killed a cobra near the tower earlier that day. We started walking again.

Courtesy: Paul Kaser

Paul Kaser: During the Vietnamization we were turning over all kinds of equipment to the ARVN. The worst thing is they wanted to turn over the dogs. Our K9 guys got really emotional about this. One guy told me, when he was notified that he had to turn his dog over to the Vietnamese, that he took it down to the Vet and asked him to put the dog down. He didn't want to turn it over to the Vietnamese.

In 1965 there were 350 sentry dogs in Vietnam. By 1968 there were 1,200. A total of over 3,000 dogs served, saving many lives, but when we withdrew all but about 200 were euthanized.

Gordy Lane: We picked up random mortar and rocket fire at the beach house, and we were always shot at in the villages during the CAG. I would have been in big trouble during a mortar attack at the beach house if there wasn't a ditch for me to get to; one of our guys did get hit during that attack. I guess this was the enemy version of our H&I fire; we were harassing them and they were harassing back.

As part of my security duties, I made the first arrest of a civilian (an American merchant marine) for a capital offense -- murder. This man was to be tried under martial law. This man allegedly killed one of his fellow sailors. These guys were hanging out, drinking, and they got into an argument. One guy stabbed the other one. I was standing on the front gate at my beach house security post, and a mamasan pointed the victim out to me down on the beach. I took one look at him and I'd been in Vietnam and seen enough to know that the stabbed guy was dead. So I went after the other guy. He didn't try to run, although he wasn't going to outrun my rifle anyway, and he had nowhere to go.

We often went into the field with the general as his personal escort. This was usually in a jeep, although I did take one chopper ride with him. And when there were visiting VIP's we had to be spit shined.

Ed Cranford: I was out on the flight line one night after we started getting our fighters, and there wasn't any electricity so they had the flight line lit with generator-power. These lights would draw insects and things to them, as they seem to do. Among the things attracted to the lights were rice beetles. These rice beetles were about six inches long. Anyway, I hear something approaching me and it is two ARVN soldiers with a shoe box full of rice beetles; they were collecting them for the next day's stew!

We stood guard in a short radar tower. This was a ground radar unit set up outside our barbed wire perimeter, kind of in the middle of nowhere. There was just this one ground radar unit at Danang. For some reason we manned it with only one man. They told you to be observant but you also had to watch the radar scope. If the radar scope stayed pointed at you for a bit you were to adjust it so it didn't get damaged.

We used to walk the cantonment area inside the wire. We walked behind the barracks, behind the clubs. There were some big rats around there. I always put my bayonet on my rifle, mainly thinking about the rats.

Paul Kaser: In the Security role my office was down in the squadron area; since most of the rocket activity occurred at night we'd be up most of the night. I would check the perimeter to ensure that our troops were at their posts and make sure our mortars were ready. When we received rocket fire our mortar crews, with the aid of radar, would determine the location of the rocket site and provide counter battery fire. The problem with the rockets was they'd move to another site very quickly after the first few rounds. There were 33 attacks in the eighteen months I was there. This would include rocket or mortar attacks or infiltrating sappers.

Don Classen: I drove for the new 1st Sergeant until reassigned to drive for the Base Chief of Security, a lieutenant. In my remaining time there I lived in the same place but worked on the air base side less than a mile away. I would report in the morning and sit until needed. Once they caught a lady coming through the gate with plans of the air base; drawings of the buildings and planes. She said she was going to use the paper for sandwich wrappers. She was not believed. She was arrested and taken away and I don't know what happened to her.

Kato: One of the other dog handlers put his M16 into John's belly one time and threatened to shoot him. John told him if he did I would "get him." John was right. John was my friend. He passed up his R&R on my birthday and fed me a steak. When John rotated home he looked at some records and found that I had been donated by a family in Chicago. He called and talked to them on the way home. They told him they didn't want to donate me, but I was very possessive and they feared I might attack other kids if they pushed their children. I would have!

Mike Tillman: We didn't take much mortar fire -- they probably sent it to the 101st down the road -- but we did have sappers inside the wire a few times. Bunker location was well known to them so I always slipped out and moved fifteen yards away after dark. One night there was a couple of guys out there; one of them had a gun. They popped one of our trip flares outside the wire. When they did that the guy with the gun emptied a magazine into the bunker that I had vacated. Then he took off. I put my M-16 on full automatic and led him like a bunny in eastern Kentucky. One round fired and the rifle jammed. I pulled the magazine and jammed round out. The flare was still going but the rifle jammed again. When the reaction force arrived, responding to my radio calls and the shooting, they could follow the trail of my magazines from the bunker to my current position about a hundred yards away. If I could have found a tree I would have wrapped that rifle around it. When my first round went off it obviously expanded in the chamber and the extractor wouldn't extract it. Normally we would have had two men in each bunker but we were short of people so we could only use one guy.

Air Force Security – Phan Rang Air Base
Courtesy: Mike Tillman

Mike Tillman: We had one period where we were up for about three days. I think we were preparing for a visit from somebody. Anyway, they gave us Benzedrine to keep us functioning. That kept us awake but I sat out there on guard at night and watched an entire circus train go by me; elephants, tigers, lions, clowns, acrobats; it was just as real as it could be. I got on the radio and asked them what the circus was doing out there. They came out and relieved me so I could get some sleep. Of course by this time I was so hopped up, how could I sleep?

Barry Willever: I was on guard duty in the A-Shau Valley and the bunker next to us sent up a flare indicating trouble. This bunker was firing a lot and I had my men up, but nothing ever came our way. It turned out that their bunker had been overrun by monkeys! At night you can't see what is out there!

Most of our time at Phu Bai we were traveling to LZ's, and we spent a lot of time in bunkers. We had a hooch at Dong Ha. We had plenty of company with rats but I only had one encounter with a snake. This was at a village off Route 1 near Lico Valley, near Marble Mountain, or Monkey Mountain. I was trying to get an ammo can from the area by the bunker where the truck was parked. There was a pit viper there, about four feet long. One of the Chieu Hois from the 101st came down, and he grabbed the snake with his bare hands and killed it. He said it was very deadly.

Alan Webster: I was sitting in front of the perimeter bunker as dawn was approaching, and it was very foggy. I'm just sitting there, no weapon or anything, and the fog is lifting, and I see this pair of black pajamas walking toward the base. Charlie is coming in through the fog! I couldn't yell. I couldn't speak. I couldn't move. I could see him and the fog kept lifting. And then it started to lift faster and he booked it out of there.

Rich "Saw" Negich: Another time at Camp Eagle they called our entire MP Company out. The commanding general had received a death threat. So the mp's surrounded his hooch. We figured the guy who threatened the general wouldn't do anything under these circumstances. But what he did was drive a deuce-and-a-half into the water tower that was near the general's quarters in hopes that it would fall into the general's place. I don't know if the general was even there at the time. The guy was crazy; he may have been on drugs, I don't know. Anyway, the water tower plan didn't work and the guy was hauled away.

The Easter (March 1972) offensive was going on and the NVA were overrunning some of the bases. They moved us down to Saigon. There simply weren't enough of our troops there to do anything. We never reclaimed much of that ground but our pilots really did a job on the NVA. That's the only reason they stopped them.

Perimeter security improved each year but the attacks also increased. The Danang air base, as an example, received two mortar attacks between

August 1965 and September, 1966; several years later mortars and rockets rained on the base almost daily. Barbed wire is not much of a defense against mortars and rockets.

Protecting your supply lines is one of the most basic requirements for a military organization. General Westmoreland insisted his subordinates were too reliant on the helicopter for re-supply. [civ] *He urged them to use the roads. Transporting supplies from one location to another was sometimes done by air, but usually by convoy. Some of these convoys were miles long and, as time went on, stiffened with heavy firepower.* [cv] *Trucks received some armor plating and sandbags and tanks and armored cars were used when available. Aerial cover was often provided by helicopter gunships.*

CONVOY SECURITY

Airman 1st Class **Mike Tillman**, *Air Police, 366th Security Police Squadron, Phan Rang, USAF*
Airman 2nd Class **John Mobley**, *Air Police, 3rd Combat Support Group, Bien Hoa, USAF*
Captain **Paul Kaser**, *Admin Officer, 3rd Security Police Squadron, Bien Hoa, USAF*

Spc4 **Barry Willever**, *machine-gunner, G Battery, 65th Artillery, USA*
Spc4 **Gary Nunn**, *Military Police, 716th MP Battalion, Tan Son Nhut AB, USA*
Spc4 **Steve Newsom**, *Light Direction Control Operator, 2nd Bn., 29th Artillery SLT, Pleiku, USA*
Pfc **Rich "Saw" Negich**, *MP, 101st MP Company, 101st Airborne Division, Phu Bai, USA*
Spc4 **Don Classen**, *Psych Tech, 67th Evacuation Hospital, Qui Nhon, USA*

LCpl **Alan Webster**, *Military Police, 23rd Military Police, Chu Lai, USMC*

Adventures

John Mobley: As a cop, I did a lot of escort duty with POW's. They would fly the POW's into Bien Hoa, which was a huge base, and we would have to take them by truck to Long Binh, a fifteen or twenty mile trip. We also used to take a flatbed truck out and have the POW's fill sandbags for us.

On February 23, 1968, which was during the "big" Tet offensive, our APC got bogged down. It was during daytime and the relief crew was out training in this vehicle. So we went out there to help them and we came under fire. I stood up to see where the fire was coming from and maybe return fire, and bullets were snapping by my face, and I saw the ground kicking up; it about scared me to death.

Mike Tillman: In my first days, since we were such a small base, we ran convoys from Phan Rang into Cam Ranh Bay for supplies. This was about a forty-mile trip, and we had a jeep with an M-60 machine gun and three guys. The jeeps without a machine gun had four guys. The convoy might be twenty or thirty trucks. When our convoys approached the rubber plantations – the mid-point of the trip to Cam Ranh Bay -- it was always tense. The rubber trees were right up near the road, and we were getting sniped at every time we went through there. No one was killed but we had a couple of people grazed. So we finally started bunching up about a mile before the rubber plantation and we'd take off and try to get past the trees at about 45 miles an hour. We would be blasting away as we flew through there. We shot down a lot of rubber trees but we quit taking fire. After a few months they started unloading supplies on the beach at Phan Rang, so the convoys stopped.

Paul Kaser: We would send out medical units from nearby Long Binh Hospital. These were called CAP's (Civic Action Patrols). My security guys would go out acting as guards for the medical people. I also went with Army guys on some of these missions. Also, some of our NCO's would go to the villages; one time our guys went to a village to build a well. Another time they built a barracks for an orphanage.

One of the CAP's was by helicopter to a leper colony in the area. I also made a lot of those trips to orphanages. I used to go there once a week. It was run by Catholic nuns. This place was actually quite isolated; I think it was near a village named Khe Sat. I flew in there on a Huey, along with our chaplain and some medical guys. A crippled kid from the colony ran up to me with a big can, which had a snake in it. The kid had this snake on a string. I looked at the padre as if to ask "what am I going to do with this?" In the first place, I was a little afraid of the lepers (I got over that), and now there is this snake. The colony people told me this kid was their best snake catcher and he was giving me this snake as a gift. This was right around Christmas so the snake was my first Christmas gift that year.

We made the rounds of the leper colony, visiting the sick. The strange thing was a lot of people were trying to get in there, even though they didn't have leprosy, because it was such a safe place. The VC left them alone. The VC did come in there occasionally to take their medical supplies. They made Ho Chi Minh sandals from old tires at the colony, which they would sell outside the colony; the VC would take those too.

Steve Newsom: We had four or five jeeps with the 23" light. Two men would take these jeeps around to the various fire bases. Of course we did all our driving during the day.

Rich "Saw" Negich: We were about twelve miles from the A-Shau Valley. The Pol bridge was always blown up and we had to cross the river on a ferry built by the engineers. The ferry would hold two tanks and a jeep at one time, or two deuce-and-a-halves and a jeep, or whatever. Anybody in that area was bad! There was always stuff going on. You were an easy target when you were in the middle of the river on that slow-moving ferry. There were always two mp's on each side of the river. We got shot at there. At this time the war was winding down, and as the firebases were being closed we would line up the traffic to cross the ferry. The engineers used to go fishing there with hand grenades.

Convoy Support
Courtesy: Rich "Saw" Negich

Don Classen: We occasionally sent a water truck up into the mountains for drinking water; about a fifteen or twenty mile drive. I rode with them more than once. It was kind of scary. We found a leper colony that the French had built for the Vietnamese. I had a camera and I took a lot of pictures of the architecture. The buildings were clean and neat and there was a lot of quality tile work and collages that made you think you were in heaven. A couple of lepers asked me to take their picture, which I did. I didn't notice until I had the slides developed that the one guy had only one finger on one of his hands, but it was an unusually long finger; almost like a hook. They were the only two people I saw that day.

I was put on a detail with some Vietnamese women picking up trash at the air base. I had this big dump truck they filled it and then we drove to a dump that was several miles outside Qui Nhon. Ho Chi Minh was born in Qui Nhon. This was during the week of his birthday, sometime in July. His birthday is somewhat of a holiday in those parts. Ho put out the news that he was going to capture his hometown during his birthday in 1966. The sergeant riding with me was handed a .45 for this trip but he insisted on a rifle, which they gave him. We had to drive through an area where a small convoy had been slaughtered a week or so before. I was pretty apprehensive and as we approached Qui Nhon we saw a number of machine gun emplacements manned by the ARVN. It was a little scary driving towards the barrel of the machine gun. I pushed that truck at top speed all the way out and all the way back on that trip.

Gary Nunn: When we escorted convoys we would have one jeep of MP's in the front, one in the middle and one in the back.

Protection for convoys soon went beyond jeeps with machine guns and sandbagged trucks. The Army used some very formidable weapons for both perimeter and convoy security, and sometimes for body retrieval missions, including dusters, Vulcans and quad-50's.

The duster is a crew-served weapon, firing 200 40mm shells a minute. They usually worked along with a second duster unit. A 40mm round is about 1.5 inches in diameter, and about 20 inches long. The rounds traveled at twice the speed of sound and had a pie-shaped killing field of about 100 feet when it exploded. The round would self-destruct at 3600 meters. It was designed to shoot down airplanes, but of course that is not how it was used. There **were** *no enemy planes.*

The M163 Vulcan is a 20mm Air Defense System, a 20mm electrically-operated six-tube Gatling gun on a M157A1 turret gun mount, fused to the chassis of an armored personnel carrier. It is a short-range, low-level, anti-aircraft defense system capable of 3,000 rounds per minute, or bursts of 10, 30, 60 or 100 rounds. This weapon used the same type Gatling gun, with six tubes, that Puff the Magic Dragon fired, except Puff fired the 7.62 round, and the Vulcan were firing the much more potent 20mm. There were only six Vulcans in South Vietnam.

By 1968 the V100 armored car was an effective convoy weapon.[cvi] Helicopter gunships were usually providing surveillance and fire support from the air. Engineer units also tried to clear jungle growth up to several hundred yards back from the roads.

Barry Willever: We had our quad 50's mounted on the back of deuce-and-a-halves so we could go with the convoys to provide support. We also took the weapon off the trucks and heli-lifted the guns into places like the A-Shau Valley. Out of Dong Ha, we ran a lot of convoys with the 3rd Marine Division. We'd start at Dong Ha and stop at all the fire bases around, like Camp Evans, the Rockpile and others, and we'd usually be back to Dong Ha in the late afternoon.

We were on a convoy with the 3rd Marine Division and I was in the gunner's seat on the Quad 50, and the convoy got mortar and sniper rounds as we were going through one of the villages. We couldn't fire back since we couldn't identify the origin of the rounds. When we returned from the trip, we ate at the mess hall and then I returned to the gun to check it out. My squad member Nate, was on the truck with me. He tells me we were hit that day. I told him I knew that. He said "No, I mean the truck was hit," and he pointed out a round that hit our gas tank. If the tank hadn't stopped that round it would have hit me in the right side.

Alan Webster: The Strike Force ran both day and night patrols in the Chu Lai area. If we were running a convoy, I was always in the first vehicle, a jeep, with an M-60 machine gun. Every time. I would say, "Why me?" So they let me drive one time and I hated it. I'd rather be behind the M-60.

We were ambushed while on a convoy south of Chu Lai. This occurred during the day. We were on QL1 with a mountain off to one side and rice paddy's on the other. The fire was coming from the rice paddy's. We took cover behind a log. Then I see a Vietnamese man walking towards me. He was wearing a white shirt and white shorts. He was looking at me and grinning. There was a line of VC behind him in the paddy's wearing black pajamas. Then, from back in our convoy, a captain pulled up and started blazing away with a quad .50. The VC took off. The two Army guys I had with me were new in-country and one of them jumped up and saluted the captain. I told him he shouldn't do that. I told him he just targeted that captain and, by right, the captain could have shot him. Then the captain came up and got on him. I looked for the guy in white clothes and he was gone too. I don't know who he was. I don't know if he was with them, or was being made to go with them, or what. I don't know. Afterwards I thought maybe I should have shot him, but I didn't. Looking back, I guess I'm glad I didn't. But I'll never forget that grin.

We were out on the road and we headed west into a field and drove over something and I heard a click. I told them to stop. I radioed back that we were sitting on a mine. They said they would get somebody out there to deal with it. The guys they sent knew what they were doing and they defused the mine. But that upset me. They were supposed to clear the mines before the convoys went down the road each day.

American and South Vietnamese Security
Courtesy: Alan Webster

Among the lessons learned in Vietnam from a security standpoint is that wars with no front lines and insecure rear areas and roads will require additional protection for convoys and warehouse installations. Trained security personnel, sentry dogs, listening devices and increased lighting are among the requirements for future deployments.[cvii]

Paul Kaser

Mike Tillman

Alan Webster

Ed Cranford

Rich "Saw" Negich

CHAPTER TEN

BLUE WATER NAVY – MIDDLE/LATE YEARS

By the Middle and Late years many Navy personnel were on their second and third tours. By 1972, with U.S. forces below 100,000, North Vietnam unleashed their Easter Offensive. Capable defense by South Vietnamese ground units and heavy reliance on U.S. air and naval support stopped the assault and cost NVA General Giap, the hero of Dien Bien Phu, his job.

CRUISERS

In terms of size, cruisers fall somewhere between destroyers and battleships. A cruiser mounts 8" guns as compared to the 5" guns on destroyers or the 16" guns on battleships.

Electrician Mate Third Class **Bill Pitts,** *USS Oklahoma City CLG-5*

Arrival/Duties

Bill Pitts: On my third tour I picked up the light cruiser *Oklahoma City* in Coronado, California in October of 1968. We initially went to Yokosuka, Japan, our home port, and then on to Vietnam. We were also the Seventh Fleet Admiral's flagship. The *Oklahoma City* had 8" guns and guided missiles aft. And we had nuclear warheads, which meant we had a detachment of Marines. We did gunfire support of land activities. On the *Oklahoma City* I was on the lighting crew. I also did generator watch.

Adventures

Bill Pitts: We took a ground fire hit between the stacks. We were off the North Vietnamese coast. There were no casualties. The ship also ran

307

aground during the day while we were doing 18 knots. We were sitting in the water there for I don't know how long. We were supposed to abandon ship at nightfall. We could see the enemy setting up artillery to fire at us. We were also concerned that frogmen would come out and try to plant a satchel charge under the ship. I don't think the ship incurred much damage but when we got free, just before dark, we had to flush all the condensers out. Our generators went out and we were using an emergency generator burning sixty gallons of gasoline an hour. We had two jets circling our ship and they just pulverized those land batteries. It was neat! We saw the war! But all the pictures we took of the event were quickly confiscated.

The *Oklahoma City* was told to shoot down a Mig which was flying out of an airstrip in Hanoi. We went to general quarters at 0800 and rolled two missiles out on the launch pad, with conventional warheads, and we locked on to this plane, but before we got permission to shoot the plane completed its mission and returned to its base. We were very discouraged by that. We thought we were really going to do something.

CARRIERS

Boson Mate **Gary Skibo,** *USS Oriskany CVA-34*

Boson Mate **Cliff James,** *USS Constellation CVA-64*

Arrival/Duties

Gary Skibo: After my *Coral Sea* tour they put me on the *USS Oriskany*, a World War II-Essex-class carrier heading for Vietnam, in June of 1967. My duties included bringing bombs, fuel and other cargo aboard from supply ships. We took on these supplies about once a day. Another duty I had was standing watch on the bow and communicating with the bridge. I worked sixteen to twenty hours a day. A number of times I worked two straight days without any time off.

Cliff James: My second *Constellation* tour was in 1967. I was one of over fifty boson mates aboard the carrier. I ran the paint locker, the sail locker, and was responsible for supervising some of the daily UNREPS (underway replenishments) of food, ammunition, mail, etc.

Depending on when you had the watch you might work twenty hours a day, but sixteen was probably the average. I do not remember doing much laughing; what I remember is heat and work, work, work.

Conditions aboard ship were fine. I lived in a cubicle with six bunks. But we were right under the flight deck so it was very noisy. In fact, after I was discharged I had difficulty sleeping in the quiet and I had to turn on a radio or something to let me sleep.

Adventures

Gary Skibo: We would get lots of sampans and junks alongside our carrier but no one ever fired at us. We did have to fire at the junk boats occasionally.

On my first tour on the *USS Coral Sea*, we went through a typhoon and they asked for volunteers to tie stuff down. I was one of the nuts that went out there trying to tie down life rafts and other stuff. We lost a few rafts and later they sent Skyhawks up to sink them so the enemy couldn't use them. We also lost one of our screws (propellers). The *Coral Sea* had four screws and somehow one of them was broken off. On that first cruise we had fourteen pilots shot down, ten KIA's and four MIA's.

Also on the *Coral Sea* one time they sounded the collision alarm so everybody was to clear the deck, and one guy wasn't going to make it and I tackled him. He could have been cut in half by a cable that snapped.

On my second tour, on the *USS Oriskany*, I saw the carrier *USS* Forrestal blow up. This happened on October 29, 1967. I was down in the hanger bay looking at it when it blew. A rocket from one of the jets on the flight line went off and it killed something like 120 sailors. We sounded general quarters and went nearby to pull guys out of the water. One African-American guy had burns over 95% of his body. The *Oriskany* had lost twenty-some guys during a fire a year or so before I joined her.

On the second tour, the *Oriskany* had 17 pilots KIA and 12 MIA.

While I was hospitalized in the Oakland Naval Hospital, I was placed near a Marine who lost an arm and part of his stomach from falling (purposefully) on a grenade.

Cliff James: We had one occasion where some suicide PT boats tried to make a run against our carrier. Our planes sunk them before they ever got close.

I was in charge of the high line when we transferred the comedienne Martha Raye from our carrier to a submarine. She sat there bravely in the boson's chair, and showed more courage than many men might on that trip across the water.

We went through a typhoon leaving the Gulf of Tonkin during a shift change and the wind was so strong it bent a metal catwalk off the ship.

We had a U2 spy plane land on the carrier once.

On my first tour some of the pilots that went into the water during takeoffs or landings didn't survive. On the second tour, most were saved. I don't know if this traced to better equipment, better training or what.

LPD'S (Landing Port Dock)

Quartermaster First Class **George Holloway,** *USS Vancouver LPD-2/USS Cleveland LPD-7*

Bosun Mate Third Class **Cecil Cox,** *Gunner, USS Cleveland LPD-7*

Boson Mate Third Class **Gil Eaton,** *USS Cleveland LPD-7*

Petty Officer Second Class **Rick Dolinar,** *USS Cleveland LPD-7*

Engineman 2nd Class **Jack Greeson,** *USS Cleveland LPD-7*

Cook Third Class **Vic Griguoli,** *USS Cleveland LPD-7*

Aviation Boson **Ed Rodgers,** *USS Cleveland LPD-7*

Arrival/Duties

Vic Griguoli: My first tour in Southeast Asia was on the *USS Cleveland LPD-7*. I was one of the original twenty or so that were sent down to Pascagoula, MS, to bring the ship back to Norfolk. We sailed up past Cape Hatteras and boy were we seasick. In October, 1967 we sailed from Norfolk with a full crew through the Panama Canal to San Diego, prior to departing for Vietnam.

On the *Cleveland* we fed about 750 sailors and a battalion (about 1,000) of Marines each day. As soon as breakfast was completed, you had to start preparing lunch. The captain inspected the galley and told us if we kept it clean he wouldn't bother us. I was actually in charge of making out the menu for each day. Our food was requested from Palo Alto, California. The guys still talk about my lasagna. As cooks, we worked 24 on/24 off, or 48 on/48 off.

Rick Dolinar: On my **second** tour I was on the *USS Cleveland*, LPD-7. LPD stands for Landing Platform Dock. We left San Diego in November of 1967; this was the first cruise for the Cleveland. All of us on that first cruise became what is known as "plank owners." I was still doing my Fire Control Technician job but now we were primarily off the South Vietnamese coast. The LPD was primarily designed for the marines; it was amphibious but not a man-of-war type of ship. Although it was a newer ship it had older technology in terms of guns; it carried Mark 56 and 63 guns, which were smaller than the 5" 54's on the *Berkeley*. But the fire technology system was essentially the same and that was still my domain.

On the *Cleveland*, I worked eight hours a day but, as an E-4 and E-5 I didn't have to stand watches so the work day was a little less intense for me.

Jack Greeson: I was a boat engineer on the small boats (four LCVP's) that were carried by the *Cleveland*. I also worked on auxiliary equipment such as air conditioners and things like that. I had shoring party duty during battle stations; if we were holed the shoring party would attempt to patch the ship up with wood and braces. The training we had for this duty was held in Norfolk; we were dropped in a tank with near-freezing water and worked to stop the leaks. We never did figure out how to stop the leaks but at least we got introduced to what it would be like under combat conditions. All of us also went to fireman school. They would set real fires in real ship's compartments and we would have to go in and put them out.

George Holloway: I was a plank owner, having participated in the *Cleveland's* first tour. We arrived in Vietnamese waters in November of 1967. We carried a battalion of U.S. Marines and several assault craft which they could board in the hold of the ship, and then exit when we lowered the stern gate. We also had a helipad. I was over and back to Vietnam aboard the *Cleveland,* until December of 1969.

I was the ship's helmsman on the *USS Cleveland.* I was the assistant to the Quartermaster Chief and our navigator, Lt. Paul Gesswein. Part of my job was training the newer men in navigation. I also helped them advance in their jobs. I also volunteered as a gunner on the LCM's (assault craft).

My second trip to Vietnam was aboard another LPD, the *USS Vancouver* LPD-2. This was an older ship. My duties aboard the *Vancouver* were more administrative and only involved navigation and days were from 0400 to 2200, just like the *Cleveland.*

Ed Rodgers: On the *Cleveland*, as an Aviation Boson we had responsibility for a lot of things mostly related to aviation. We dealt with helicopters, seaplanes; we were actually trained to launch and recover dirigibles! I was in the Deck Department and I supervised many of the newer men. I was twenty and they were seventeen or eighteen. The *Cleveland* from the captain on down really knew nothing of aviation. When I arrived they didn't know what to do with me so they put me in the Deck Department. I became a boat coxswain.

We put in very long hours on the *Cleveland*; you napped when and where you could including on hammocks on the flight deck, under the stars. We worked until the job was done. I slept on the bottom rack of a 3-high setup. Some compartments had four high; it depended on where you were below decks. Up near the bow was really tight and that is where I slept, on the starboard side. I slept there on both tours. It wasn't bad there because it was somewhat dark and that made it easier to sleep.

Gil Eaton: My duties were varied. I scraped paint, painted decks, handled cargo and ammunition during UNREPS, stood watches, went out on the whale boat in case anyone went overboard, worked cranes to put boats in the water through the well deck of the ship, I went out on the boats; I did anything to do with maintenance of the ship. Reveille for the crew was at 0600. Bosons were out at 0500 polishing brass and other duties. We worked until 1600 if you were lucky.

Cecil Cox: I manned a .50 caliber machine gun on the boats running out of the *USS Cleveland;* we also did some PsyOps on these boats. We would travel two or three miles up the Cua Viet River.

Adventures

Vic Griguoli: On Sundays aboard the *Cleveland* we had brunch and the guys were allowed to sleep a bit longer. We had a Second Class Yeoman who demanded more food than we gave him. The Mess Cook told him to eat what he had then come back; we had a lot more guys coming through the line. But the guy kept pointing to his two stripes and demanding more eggs. I made a suggestion as to what he could do with his two stripes. He told me he'd get even with me and he did! I got my orders for the LST and that was a rough tour of duty.

Rick Dolinar: We carried a battalion of marines and their heavy equipment, such as tanks, for insertion on land as needed. We provided support for the war in-country in terms of helicopter landings and also putting troops ashore in the small boats that were part of our LPD. During the course of this tour we had over 1,000 helicopter missions from the

Cleveland and hundreds of landing boats went ashore. Sometimes the landing boats returned to the ship with damaged equipment, like trucks, and we had repair facilities aboard to deal with that. The boats also returned sometimes with wounded Marines, and we had medical facilities aboard as well. If the injuries were severe we choppered them to a larger facility.

About half the LPD is hollow, and we had a tailgate on the stern much like a station wagon, and if you put the tailgate down the water would rush in and fill the well deck. The seawater would be let in or pumped out to accommodate embark or debark of the landing craft.

Jack Greeson: Our radar picked up Migs a time or two and we were called to General Quarters, but we never were attacked.

On the first tour, I came back with the ship. On my second tour I flew off the Cleveland on a helicopter into Danang. When I looked at my travel orders they said "Class Four Travel Priority;" Unlimited Travel Time to get back to the United States. At Danang, the chopper pilot had dropped us about three or four miles from the air base. I had two sea bags and other stuff to lug to the air base. When I finally got there they told me I'm at the wrong one! I did manage to get a ride to the right location. I had anticipated flying back commercial but I sat there for two weeks, during assorted mortar and rocket attacks, waiting for a flight out of there. I found out what a bunker was!

When I first arrived at Danang, I sent my wife a telegram telling her I'd be home in a week. Now I'm already a week late. Finally, I got desperate. I feared that I wouldn't live through this trip home! I approached a master sergeant and told him I needed to get out of the country. Did he have anything? He told me he might have something leaving around midnight for Dakota, Japan. I returned to see him about 11:30. He gave me a lift across the runway to a C141; I was to walk up the ramp and they would tell me where I could sit. It was a Medevac flight; nine seats, and one of the doctors couldn't go, so they put me on it. The patients on that flight were moaning and groaning and I didn't sleep.

I finally arrived in Japan and I sat there a week. A guy there told me to meet him around midnight, and he got me a flight to Olympia,

Washington. I got on the plane, another C141, and sat on one of the metal boxes in the back. The pilot came back and said "Son, would you mind not sitting on the bodies."

George Holloway: During Psyops in November of 1967, we were at anchor off Hue to disembark Marines. Our ship took on small arms and mortar fire. I received the Combat Action Ribbon for that encounter. As volunteer gunner we embarked on LCM Assault Craft and took fire many times. I had many occasions to return fire. Vic Griguoli and I helped to deliver mail, ammo and supplies to Marines up the Cua Viet, Dong Ha and Perfume Rivers in the Hue and DMZ areas.

The *Vancouver* also picked up small arms fire while disembarking Marines.

Our ship picked up two shot down pilots near Haiphong, off the North Vietnamese coast.

Tet 68 still bothers me. I have nightmares and my health is extremely bad due to exposure to Agent Orange in Vietnam and also the atomic bomb testing in the western Pacific in 1958.

Ed Rodgers: A few of us went ashore to visit the Naval Support Activity, Danang, to buy a car. The reason is we would not pay taxes on the purchase. We rode in to the pier on one of the mike boats and then thumbed a short ride in a Seabee jeep and then another ride in the back of a Marine six-by. We were still shy of our destination and we had to walk through town to complete the journey. It was four or five blocks to the NSA gate. That walk was the one and only time I wish I had a sidearm. The kids were terrible. We had been advised to carry our wallets in our front pockets and we found out why. The kids used razor blades to cut your back pocket to get at your wallet. The kids were just kind of mobbish around you. Afterwards, we realized that was how they survived. It didn't make it alright -- the feeling of being assaulted -- but it made some sort of sense in the end.

On the *Cleveland*, if a helicopter from in-country was carrying wounded, the rule was they had to touch down somewhere before they went to the hospital ship. I was told that this was to be in compliance with the Geneva Convention. So they would touch down on our ship first. Our doctors might patch them up a bit and then they'd head for the hospital ship, which was usually fairly close.

My brother was in Hue during the Tet. I tried my damnedest to get in there to see him, but I couldn't find a way. We worked around the clock and we seldom went anywhere but right along the coast. My brother made it; he was one of only seven survivors in his company. He was hit three times; he did spend some time on the hospital ship and in the hospital at Danang. But we never did hook up.

We brought a lot of ammo in to shore from the supply ships farther out. When some of our guys went in to fight the fire at the Naval ammo dump I manned a .50 caliber machine gun on the fantail of the *Cleveland* as protection. We were able to see them; we were not very far off the coast. The concern was some VC would try to flank them by coming down the beach and that is what I was there to prevent.

Gil Eaton: A number of my shipmates were sent in to help the marines battle a fire at their ammo dump and their base. It was dangerous work of course, and one guy did get his hand blown off, but it was nice to see that we could go in there and help them out.

Often on Sundays, we would be on a holiday routine; they would let us sleep late, things like that. But one time, they rousted me and about 25 other guys from our bunks, took us down into the well deck and put us on an LCM, and took us to the Cua Viet River to fill sandbags on the beach. This was where the river spills into the South China Sea. They intended to use these sandbags as protection for the Mike boats as they made their forays up the river. One member of the boat crew had a .45, and there was a .50 caliber machine gun on the LCM, but none of the rest of us had weapons other than shovels.

We were all feeling a bit naked without weapons, but we're hard at work filling these sandbags. I look out to sea and I saw my ship, the *USS Cleveland*, but I also see a cruiser nearby. The cruiser may have been the *Boston* or the *St. Paul*. While we were working the cruiser opens fire, and the shells are lobbing over our heads. You couldn't see them but you could hear them going over. The twenty-five of us dove into the sand because we don't know what's going on. We get up spitting sand and I turn to my buddy Bill Dimino, from Brooklyn, and he says, "Coney Island was never like this!" That broke the tension.

Later on I noticed a Marine Amtrac drive onto the scene and I was interested to see where it was going, so I climbed the sand dune to look. I see a marine camp that we didn't know was there. I also see about a hundred cases of Budweiser beer. I start walking toward the beer and a marine walks toward me and says, "Sailor. Your next step will be your last." So we finished our work and went back to the ship, minus any beer. War is hell!

One of our boats came back from a mission around nine in the evening, and when it reached the *Cleveland* they noticed that they were missing a man. Someone had fallen overboard! They tried to retrace their route and they did find the guy; he had used the techniques he had learned in training by removing his pants and tied knots into them, made them into a life preserver, and it worked! He told us he was always within sight of the ship but his yelling was to no avail.

It was difficult to do our work on deck during heavy rains and the monsoon. The ship had heavy green foul weather gear that we could wear, but someone didn't want them to get dirty. "Doc" Phillips talked to someone after seeing a rise in the number of respiratory ailments and other problems resulting from exposure to the wet conditions.

We increased our security around Pearl Harbor day, anticipating some sort of incident, but nothing happened. We spent six hour watches on the gun mounts, day and night, for about a week. But when Tet exploded, we became very active. Our boats, filled with marines, were going up and down rivers constantly.

Cecil Cox: We made more river runs when I was on the *Cleveland's* boats. Coming into the mouth of the Cua Viet River from the sea during the heavy seas of the monsoon, the swells would be so high we could not attempt to get through it. I was on the *Cleveland* during Tet and the river was shut down for two weeks. When they finally re-opened the river we made a run to Dong Ha with about ten small boats, and we had three choppers overhead for security. That was a real hairy trip.

It always bothered me that we had to call for permission to return fire.

FRIGATES

Seaman Apprentice **Larry Burger,** *Radar man, USS King DLG-10*

Arrival/Duties

Larry Burger: After basic and two schools I was on my way to the Far East. I flew from California to Clark AFB, in the Philippines and boarded my ship over there for a six-month cruise off Vietnamese waters. The *King* was named after Admiral Ernest King, the Chief of Naval Operations during WW II.

The *King* was a guided missile frigate with a crew of 360. Her armament included a 5" gun forward, two twin 3" guns amidships, ASROC anti-submarine rocket (8 tubes), 3 torpedo tubes on each side, 24 anti-sub hedgehogs (from the WW II days) and the twin terrier missile system.

The King's first duty was as a plane guard for the *USS America*, an aircraft carrier. Our responsibility was to pick up any pilots that splashed during takeoffs or landings. During my tour we picked up no pilots. We also operated a PIRAZ (Positive Identification Radar Advisory Zone), a twofold thing where we picked up any unidentified incoming planes and could use our terrier missiles against them, if need be, and also an aircraft control supervisor who would guide incoming aircraft into their strike and then back to their carrier. We also did some NorthSAR, search and rescue activity in the northern part of the Gulf of Tonkin; we launched helicopters to retrieve downed pilots. This rescue helicopter was designated "Big Mother." Our final overall duty was shore bombardment on the Gun Line, usually four ships firing on enemy shore activity or in support of our ground operations.

Another duty we had was mine removal from Haiphong Harbor. This occurred as part of the January 1973 cease-fire; we had to pull out all the mines we had sown in the harbor. We used minesweepers and salvage ships for this work and we were there to screen the minesweepers. We were part of Task Force 78 for this sweep detail.

My day was spent in the Combat Information Center (CIC) with about forty other guys. We had the Naval Tactical Data Systems, a computer-assisted radar system, on the *King*. We were one of the first ships in the Navy to have this system. This system was the answer to tracking the fast-moving aircraft. We had lots of computers in the CDC. After I left the *King* I went another ten years or so before I went on another ship that had NTDS.

I didn't get into the air side of the radar, being a new guy. I worked on the surface contact radars. We plotted contacts from the surface radars on what were called maneuvering boards. We also used a DRT (Dead Reckoning Tracer), which gave us a better fix on the surface contacts when they were moving. The surface radar work alone would require at least six radar men. We might have twelve maneuver boards being updated at all times.

Adventures

Larry Burger: We were fairly close to shore on the Gun Line on one occasion and there was a tank or some sort of self-propelled gun that chose to take us under fire. He couldn't reach us but we reached him with our 5" gun. No more tank. This was on the South Vietnamese coast.

Another time on the Gun Line, we had to depart for an Unrep for a bit and the ship that replaced us, the *USS Goldsboro*, was hit. I think about this occasionally; it could have been us!

We had a chief reporting aboard for duty aboard the *King*. He was coming aboard via our helicopter. There were rough seas at the time so this was a bit of a tricky operation. It looked like the helicopter was right over the deck but the helicopter dropped suddenly, I don't know why. The chief went in the water. The helicopter came up real quick when they realized what was happening, and when they did this the chief was swung hard into the side of the ship. When they got him aboard he was deceased. His name is on the wall. He is the only guy that was killed during my time on the ship.

OTHER SHIPS

*Hull Technician Chief **Jim Sooy**, USS Samuel Gompers AD-37, USN*

*Boson Mate Third Class **Cecil Cox**, LCM-8*

Arrival/Duties

Cecil Cox: On my second and third tours I had my own boat, an LCM-8. LCM means Landing Craft Mechanized. We covered the same area with the LCM's that I did with the *Cleveland*; the Cua Viet River, the Perfume River, Dong Ha, etc. We carried supplies, ammo, anything that was needed to support the troops. We sometimes carried troops up the river for a landing; when we did that we supported them until we brought them back.

On the LCM's we had a crew of four. The LCM was a large barge capable of holding hundreds of people. It was 72' X 21'. The LCM took a draft of about 2'. The bottom of these boats was steel although we had two that had aluminum bottoms. At low tide we could go in very close to shore, particularly in the aluminum-bottomed boats. This was the kind of situation where each guy had to know the other guy's job but when the shooting started, everyone had one job! We only had two .50 caliber machine guns on the LCM but we each had a sidearm as well.

On the LCM's my work day started about 10:30 at night. We would make amphibious landings. I would pick up supplies from various ships and then run them into the beach. When we would stay overnight up river we would throw occasional concussion grenades into the water to deter sappers. Basically we couldn't run the rivers after sundown or before sunup. We would wait for the minesweeper to clear the river before we ventured out. I was the leading petty officer of my unit which included four LCM's. Some nights we went back out to sea and nested with bigger ships.

Jim Sooy: The *Gompers,* affectionately known to the crew as "Fat Sam," was a Destroyer Tender – a floating repair shop. The *Gompers* had a hospital on board and seven complete repair shops and could literally build a new ship. We had metal smiths, machine repair, electronics, radiation, weapons, etc. Up to seven vessels could nest alongside the *Gompers* while being repaired. We always had three or four ships tied alongside. March 13, 1970 *Gompers* deployed to South Pacific. The *Gompers* had its' 5" gun removed, and had only four .50 caliber mg's, and was never supposed to be put in harm's way, but everything around Vietnam was in harm's way. I had a ship fitter working for me that had been wounded on a previous tour. He was shot while welding on a PBR. No job was safe over there.

"Fat Sam"
Courtesy Jim Sooy

Adventures

Cecil Cox: When I got to the LCM's, we took occasional sniper fire as we moved up the rivers. Our most prolonged battle was the assault of some island off the coast of northern South Vietnam. We were over there for about three or four weeks -- every night.

Jim Sooy: We were steaming from Yokosuka to Subic Bay ending a seven-month deployment but en route we were diverted back to Danang. The emergency was the *USS Higbee* (DD-806) which had been bombed by a Mig. The armor piercing MIG bomb had started the ship listing by the stern. The *Gompers* sent an emergency crew to patch it so it could be towed to meet Fat Sam at Danang.

The *Higbee* may or may not have been carrying nuclear weapons, (only the captain, XO, and the weapons officer, and maybe the chief in charge of the weapons locker would know for sure) and they are not supposed to send a ship into a harbor under those conditions. Our ship DID carry nuclear weapons since we supplied destroyers that carried anti-submarine weapons. You are dealing with some Top Secret equipment here. No one can say because it's so damn classified.

The enemy had to be aware of the weaponry aboard the *Gompers*. Their intelligence was so superb. The VC wanted badly to hit ole Fat Sam as the value on our ship was in the billions of dollars. Fat Sam was not meant to go in harm's way.

Work commenced at Danang but the VC do have frogmen. They're not very good but they do blow themselves up! I don't recall what time of day it was (it was daytime), but I heard the explosion. We sent a diver and a corpsman to investigate. They determined that the frogman had carried at least a 40-pound satchel charge. They found part of his foot in his flip flop and part of a fin. They couldn't find his breathing apparatus. Their usual plan was to take a tree bush and float it down the river, and hide within the bush. Repair work finished, the *Gompers* got out in the Gulf of Tonkin and the engines went dead. One of the boilers died.   We maintained radio silence until repairs were made.

DESTROYERS

*Electrician's Mate 3rd Class **Bill Pitts**, USS Radford DD-446*

Machinist Mate 3rd Class **Ron Rock,** *USS Dennis J Buckley DD-808*

Petty Officer 2nd Class **Jim Hansen,** *Electronics Technician Radar, USS Joseph Strauss DDG-16*

Petty Officer 3rd Class **Charlie McDonald,** *Gunner's Mate, USS Joseph Strauss DDG-16*

Electricians Mate/Fireman **Bob Miller,** *USS George K. Mackenzie DD-836,*

Boson Mate Chief **Don McMurray,** *USS Lawrence DDG-4*

Arrival/Duties

Bill Pitts: I flew to Hawaii to board the *USS Radford* DD-446, a destroyer that had participated in WW II and Korea. We arrived off Vietnam in the beginning of 1967. The *Radford's* duties included escorting two carriers, including the *Coral Sea*. We would do plane guard for these carriers. We also fired in support of operations on land. My duties included working in the shop and standing generator watch like I did on the *Mogoffin*.

Ron Rock: We did gunnery practice in San Diego, and then our destroyer steamed to Vietnam. I was assigned to the engine room. Among other things I was responsible for fresh water distillation. The engine room was also my battle station. Our destroyer was mainly assigned to shore bombardment and escort duty for carriers. In her early (WW II) days the *Buckley* could make 35 knots, but during Vietnam 31 knots was about top speed. It was tough to keep up with nuclear-powered carriers like the *Nimitz* and the *Enterprise*.

We did shore bombardment in II Corps. We fired 2400 rounds while on the gun line. Someone may have shot back, but we were never hit.

Work was divided into four-hour shifts, but the ways things overlapped sometimes you could end up working 22 hours out of 24. The best shift was 4 am to 8 am. An average day involved fixing valves, washing deck plates and other housekeeping duties. We slept three high in hammocks.

I had the top bunk, and there was a beam six inches over my head. I found it the hard way a time or two.

Jim Hansen: I boarded the *Strauss* in 1969, and my first Vietnam cruise was in March of 1970. This was a six-month cruise. My second Vietnam cruise ran from January 1972 to August of that year. I worked in the Operations Center as a radar technician. I was responsible for the air and surface search radars.

Bob Miller: In early 1971 I flew over to join my ship at Subic Bay, in the Philippines. On the way we landed on Guam. We saw rows and rows of B-52's but were pointedly told there would be "no pictures taken." I was an electrician's mate/fireman aboard a WW II tin can. My battle station on this tour was the forward 5" gun mount.

As an electrician my main job was to replace lighting and wiring damaged from all the heavy firing. My battle station on the first tour was the twin forward 5" gun mount. Our ship operated on what they called the Gun Line, which meant we patrolled the Vietnamese coast providing gun support for our troops inland or targets identified north of the DMZ. Our captain volunteered us quite a bit for this duty since we had a dual propulsion system, like all WW II destroyers. If gunfire knocked out one of our propellers we could still operate. Newer destroyers had just one propulsion system. On my second tour in 1972 I was still an electrician's mate/fireman but my battle station was the After Steering compartment.

Charlie McDonald: My first tour began in January, 1972. I worked on, and my battle station was Mount 51, the forward 5" 54 gun mount. I did the maintenance on Mount 51. I also stood anti-sapper watch when we were in Danang Harbor, patrolling up and down the lifelines and watching for bubbles. In port your watch was four hours. At sea we stood port and starboard watches. During battle stations it was all hands on deck.

Don McMurray: I flew over for my third tour in August of 1972. The *Lawrence* was a guided-missile destroyer. My job was at the starboard port wing, at the Polaris (compass). As a support troop repairing river boats on my previous two tours I was always on the receiving end of enemy fire. Now I had a chance to be on the shooting end.

Adventures

Bill Pitts: The *Radford* carried a torpedo drone, a remote control device that looked like a helicopter, except that it was real small. We had a situation where they couldn't control the drone, for no apparent reason, and it flew away. It did not have a torpedo in the belly at the time; they were just taking it out for a test flight.

Ron Rock: One of our destroyers, the *USS Frank Evans*, was involved in a collision with the Australian carrier *HMAS Melbourne*, with the loss of 74 crewmen on the *Evans.* This occurred in June of 1969. The bow of the *Evans* sank immediately, but the stern was towed into Subic Bay.

During our SAR (Search and Rescue) missions in support of carrier takeoffs we rescued a helicopter that went into the water.

I never experienced the monsoon or even a typhoon, but we had lots of rough weather. Down in the engine room, you could really hear the screws (propellers) when the stern came out of the water. But rough seas never really bothered me. I could eat just fine.

Jim Hansen: Operating outside of Haiphong Harbor on June 4, 1972, the *Strauss* hit two floating mines which caused the ship to go dead in the water. I was at my General Quarters post, Radar 2, and in the prone position when the first mine exploded. I recall being blown off the deck by several inches, and I believed that Mount 51 had just exploded. As I stepped across the threshold from Radar 2 to Radar 1 a second mine exploded, which made me wonder how Mount 51 could explode twice. Although our battle lanterns were on I could not see across Radar 1 due to the thick dust. We were dead in the water for twenty minutes or two hours, depending on who you talk to. There were no sailors hurt in the explosions but the ship had some structural damage in the boiler and pump rooms which would ultimately require some repairs at Danang.

Charlie McDonald: I worked for a short, wiry gunner's mate on Mount 51. He was very high strung. You could see this when you fired the 5" gun. When you fire the gun there are some gasses that come out before the powder gets kicked out, and sometimes when the oxygen gets in there it can re-combust, and there is a small flame. This guy would always jump back and say "Whoa." Well, we were steaming along at general quarters waiting for our next fire mission and the first mine goes off. I reach down for the phones and I notice that the door to the mount is open. This guy is gone! I close the door, which we were required to do, and report that we've been hit on the starboard side forward of the gun mount. Seconds later, WHAM, we hit the second mine. The door slams open again, and there's the gunner's mate coming back in, soaked from head to foot. He had been soaked by the wave from the second explosion. After the first explosion he headed for the life raft station. He was on his way back to the gun mount when he got soaked from the second explosion.

Jim Hansen: The two mines the *Strauss* hit on June 4, 1972, were our own mines that the U.S. Navy had sown just outside of Haiphong Harbor. The North Vietnamese had surreptitiously towed them farther out to sea and we hit them because of this. The *Strauss* was operating under some space constraints, sailing within a "box," so to speak, rather than having complete freedom of movement. Some have speculated that if we had hit those mines in more shallow water the damage would have been much greater.

During our 1972 cruise we were doing our usual ammo unrep. I was stationed on the ladder to Mount 51, about halfway down. We were passing shells down the hatch to each person in line. All of us had a shell in our arms when someone topside dropped a shell into the hatch. The shell fell all the way down, hitting each of us on the way. Despite the fact that all of us had our hands full, the dropped shell came back up the ladder faster than it fell. As it passed me I noticed that the protective nose cone was indented about half, indicating that it fell right on the fuse.

When the shell reached topside it was quickly dispatched over the side. Instead of a "good job, men," the sailor that tossed it over was scolded for throwing it over the port side, between us and the ammo ship, instead of the wide open starboard side. But since the forward hatch was closer to the port side, it was only natural to toss the shell from that side.

Charlie McDonald: We were fired at many times from North Vietnamese shore batteries. We did a lot of cruising up and down the North Vietnamese coast shelling the SAM sites to protect the flyboys.

We went up north one time to try to rescue a couple of pilots that had gone down. A helicopter picked up one of the pilots but the other one was grabbed by the North Vietnamese. We could have moved on them by force, but they would have shot the pilot.

We were in Danang Harbor working on the gun mounts and the USS *Higbee* took our mission up to North Vietnam. Our missile guys were really upset after the *Higbee* was bombed by a North Vietnamese Mig because *Higbee* had no missiles and we did. The *Higbee* was a WW II tin can.

We had some white phosphorous shells that needed to be returned to the ammo ship, probably because their expiration date had been reached. These are potent shells and they have to be stocked vertically. The box we had these shells in caught on the lip of the rail on the way to the ammo ship. The shells fell down to the main deck, a distance of about ten feet. They're normally good for about six feet. We had to grab these shells and throw them over the side. Each shell weighs seventy-two pounds. Most of the guys scattered when this happened; only one or two guys were up to the task of throwing these live shells overboard.

We were there for the Easter Offensive launched by the communists, and it was our gunfire support in many cases that kept guys alive. We were considered one of the most reliable gunships there. When the Easter Offensive started, the *Buchanon* was there with us, but within a few weeks there were twenty destroyers there providing support.

There were a lot of frustrations. Being at sea for months at a time is difficult. Getting replacement parts was a serious problem for us. It was an exceedingly serious problem not only getting the parts, but getting the time to do the repairs. We were so busy firing there was no down time for maintenance.

Since we were not allowed to open the doors to the gun mounts at night our gas ejection air system eventually broke down. Depending on how the wind was blowing we might get a lot of smoke right back into the gun mount. We tried to rotate our positions to give each guy a chance to stick his head out of our vent, and we even tried wearing gas masks. What it took for them to finally acknowledge this need for maintenance and repair was the time we were busy firing and the smoke got so bad I started to have seizures. I could not control my muscles. I had to go outside the gun mount to get fresh air and someone else took over. They finally seemed to realize that this kind of situation could kill somebody. We also had two extra guys in the gun mount, and one of them would have to pry the round out of the cradle into the transfer tray because one of the mechanisms was not working right. The other extra guy was beating on the projectiles with a mallet to get them to seat correctly due to another mechanical problem.

Bob Miller: While we were escorting the cruiser *Chicago* we followed an enemy freighter from the Canary Islands. The *Chicago* received orders to sink it. I thought it was a routine bang-bang but we got caught in a cross fire between the *Chicago* and the beach. The loudspeaker barked "Tempest (our call sign). Tempest. You are expendable. Draw fire." I don't ever want to hear that again.

***USS Chicago* at Work**
Courtesy: Bob Miller

There was one time the Engineering Officer didn't tell the captain that he had shut down the after turret. So the *Mackenzie* started in on a gun run without the aft gun. They jury-rigged everything to bypass the electrical problem and pulled it off.

We were shot at all the time. A 5" gun shoots seven miles. We were near the shore and we would sit there for eight to ten hours lobbing shells. The spotter would say "there are tanks on the beach." We'd fire from the forward mount going in, then we'd turn, and the aft mount would kick in. And the boiler technicians would put in extra oil to create a smokescreen as we pulled away. And we'd zigzag. Their shells would walk up our wake. They were smart. I'm unsure whether this was North or South Vietnam. I was never told where we were; all we knew was that we were on the Gun Line.

Don McMurray: The *Lawrence* made 116 high speed attacks with our 5" guns on Haiphong Harbor. We'd go up there every night and hit it, and they'd rebuild it. Coming back we would give support to infantry units on land. We got this one call; they were surrounded but they had spotters to direct our fire and we got them enough relief that they got out of there.

In our early days on the *Lawrence* we were stationed in the waters off Danang. We had a lot of what we called rice paddy duty; the enemy floated one-man sampans full of rice into shore to supply their troops. Our job was to prevent this; it was boring duty. While on this rice paddy duty at night we would encounter high speed aircraft overhead. Procedures called for us to exchange recognition signals with this plane. Often each of us accused the other of not always following procedures, which was important since any boat or plane in this area could be ours or theirs. The next time we signaled a plane and received no reply our captain did what the captain of a guided missile destroyer should do. We prepared to launch a missile. When the plane, which was one of ours, saw that we had "locked on" him, he quickly squawked his recognition signal.

One time on the rice paddy patrol the CO was in the Combat Information Center and the XO was on the bridge. The XO is jerking the ship right to left. The captain storms up to the bridge wanting to know why we were swerving. "I was dodging all the sampans," the XO responded. "Just ram them" the captain ordered.

We were providing gunfire support to some action in-country in January of 1973, just prior to my return home. When we started to send in rounds I saw the flash of return fire and my job was to take a bearing. Just as I did that I heard bing, bing, bing, as shrapnel was hitting right behind me. A lookout was standing beside me. I told him to get inside. I felt like I was indestructible. They didn't hurt me in two other tours . . . . and they aren't going to get me now! The ship got a Purple Heart for that.

Charlie McDonald: When the *Strauss* was new, in the early 1960's, we could fire forty 5" rounds per minute. By 1972, we were firing about thirty rounds per minute. The constant firing took a toll. There were two trays in the lower part of the magazine, and each held twenty rounds, which were loaded electronically. Once those twenty were fired, the rate of fire was cut in half as the crew loaded each round into the tray. In 1972 we fired 12,753 rounds, 3,052 rounds on April 1 in support of Colonel Ripley at the Dong Ha Bridge. On my second tour we hardly fired at all. We played more cards than we did firing.

Congress found their voice and repealed the Gulf of Tonkin Resolution in 1970, and a cease fire went into effect on January 28, 1973. Financial support to the South Vietnamese was drastically reduced. In blatant disregard of the 1973 Paris Peace Accords North Vietnam sent its' entire army south. The stellar U.S. bombing and naval gunfire support response to the 1972 Easter Offensive was replaced by diplomatic notes and, ultimately, the evacuation. Our dreams may have been different but the footsteps still led to defeat.

In all history there is no evidence of a nation that has benefited from a prolonged war -- Sun Tzu -- 500 bc

THE BLUE WATER NAVY

Charlie McDonald

Vic Griguoli

Bob Miller

Ron Rock

Gil Eaton

Rick Dolinar

EPILOGUE

In a sense, the support troop story is universal. World War II and Korea also had cooks, clerks, drivers, medics, engineers and air and naval support. Of course technology added the helicopter and other upgrades to the Vietnam battlefield, but in most respects, the job titles were the same across all three wars. What was different in Vietnam was the lack of front lines. There was no plan to capture (and hold) terrain. The plan in World War II was to TAKE ROME, then TAKE BERLIN, then TAKE TOKYO. In simple terms, the plan in Vietnam was: BODY COUNT. Despite Douglas MacArthur's warning not to get involved in a land war in Asia, we did.

The absence of front lines in Vietnam complicated things for everybody. The combat troops had to use one third of their fighting strength protecting their base camp. Likewise support troops had to designate some of their force to security matters, usually men who had just finished working a twelve hour day. And despite the enormous expenditure of lives and money, there was never any progress. It got worse every year.

The need for Support Troops is and was always there. When combat troops were withdrawn from Iraq in August, 2010, thousands of support troops remained. We see a trend on today's battlefields of Iraq and Afghanistan to outsource some of the support troop functions. American civilians went to these combat zones to drive trucks and perform other non-combat duties while earning large salaries and ostensibly freeing some troops for other duties. Indications are the support troop ratio to combat forces did decline from Vietnam levels, although civilian contractors were also used in Vietnam.

Despite record levels of achievement by our engineers and medical personnel, great accomplishments by the logisticians and communications people and a solid effort by the brown and blue water navies and our air support and security troops, the ninety percent serving in a support capacity in Vietnam remained a Hidden Army forty years after we left Vietnam. The hidden army was a very silent majority of those who served. It is my hope that Hidden Army has provided an understanding of what really happens when our military goes to war.

About our experience in Vietnam, Bernard Fall said "Americans were dreaming different dreams than the French but walking in the same footsteps." Fall covered the French Indo-China War (Street Without Joy and Hell in a Very Small Place) and then stayed on for the American effort. He was killed walking some of those same footsteps with the Marines in 1967.

ACKNOWLEDGEMENTS

More than 150 veterans were interviewed for this project, which resulted in The Tooth and the Tail and Hidden Army. Most of the interviews were conducted by phone during 2010 and 2011 but some of this work took place in 2012 and 2013. First and foremost I thank the veterans who participated in this project. When I realized back in 2010 that the Support Troop story had not been told I was amazed. I'm not sure if the support troops from World War II or Korea have done anything either. I wish I had thought of this sooner – perhaps while my father was alive – and tackled those groups, but I think it is now too late for that, at least for me.

Along the way an agent said that The Tooth and the Tail would fill in a "missing piece" on the literature of the Vietnam War. I hope that Hidden Army, which focuses on the challenges and issues each support troop faced and how they resolved them will further that process.

I offer my continued thanks to Tom Emmons for his computer help and overall counsel and to my youngest daughter Caitlin for picture insertion and submission of both manuscripts to Create Space. The help from Tom and Caitlin was essential and allowed me to concentrate on the book itself. I also thank the veterans along the way who helped me with additional names, pictures and other encouragement.

It is my sincere wish that The Tooth and the Tail and Hidden Army do indeed fill in a "missing piece" on Vietnam. I hope that the support troop stories are read and appreciated by many, both veteran and non-veteran, for what they represent – a selfless dedication to perform some very difficult jobs under less than ideal conditions. With Hidden Army I render my final salute to the support troops of Vietnam.

GLOSSARY OF ACRONYMS AND ABBREVIATIONS

AFB	Air Force Base
AIT	Advanced Infantry Training
Amtrac	Amphibious Tractor used by USMC
APC	Armored Personnel Carrier
Arty	Artillery
ASROC	Anti-submarine Rocket
BOQ	Bachelor Officer's Quarters
C-4	Explosives in Play Do form
Chieu Hoi	Amnesty Program for VC
Chinook	Helicopter Used for Hauling Big Loads
CIC	Combat Information Center
HQ	Headquarters
LAM	Light Anti-aircraft Missile
LOGISTICS	Maintenance and transportation of supplies
LPH	Landing Platform Helicopter (ship)
LST	Landing Ship Tank; a supply ship
LZ	Landing Zone
MEDCAP	Medical Civic Action Program

Medevac	*Air rescue of wounded troops*
MGYSgt	*Master Gunnery Sergeant (E-8) USMC*
NCO	*Non-commissioned officer, i.e. Corporal, Sgt.*
P	*Piaster – Vietnamese currency*
ROTC	*Reserve Officer Training Corps*
RTO	*Radio Teletype Operator*
SAM	*Surface to Air Missiles*
SAR	*Search and Rescue*
Tender	*Repair Ship*

SELECTED BIBLIOGRAPHY

Books

Carrico, John M. Vietnam Ironclads. A Pictorial History of U.S. Navy River Assault Craft, 1966-1970

Dillion, Noah B. Surviving Vietnam: Tales of a Narcoleptic Hangar Rat. Lakewood, California: Avid Readers Publishing Group, 2011

Fall, Bernard B., *Hell in a Very Small Place*, Philadelphia, Lippincott, 1967.

Gibson, James William, *The Perfect War*, New York, The Atlantic Monthly Press, 1986.

Gray, John Edward. *Called to Honor*. Asheville, North Carolina, R. Brent & Co.

Halberstam, David, *The Best And The Brightest*, New York, Random House, 1969.

Heiser, Lt. Gen. Joseph M. Logistics Support. Washington, D.C., Dept. of the Army, 1974

Karnow, Stanley. *Vietnam: A History*. New York: The Viking Press, 1983

Maurer, Harry. *Strange Ground*, New York, Da Capo Press, 1998.

Moore, Harold G. and Galloway, Joseph L., *We Were Soldiers Once...And Young*, New York, Random House, 1992.

Nalty, Bernard C., *The Vietnam War*, New York, Barnes & Noble Books, 1998.

Neel, Major General Spurgeon, Medical Support of the U.S. Army in Vietnam, 1965 – 1970

Sheehan, Neil, *A Bright Shining Lie*, New York, Random House, 1988.

Summers, Harry G. Jr. Historical Atlas of the Vietnam War. New York: Houghton Mifflin Co., 1995

Westheider, James E. The Vietnam War. Westport, CT, The Greenwood Press, 2007

Other Sources

A Pocket Guide to Vietnam, Department of Defense

Military Sea Transportation Service Society History

[i] Lt. Gen. Joseph M. Heiser, Jr., Logistic Support (Washington, D.C. Dept. of the Army), p. 37.

[ii] Harry G. Summers, Jr., Atlas of the Vietnam War, (Boston/New York: Houghton Mifflin), p. 94.

[iii] Ibid.

[iv] Bernard C. Nalty, *The Vietnam War*, (New York: Barnes & Noble Books) p. 146.

[v] Maj. Gen. Spurgeon Neel, Medical Support of the U.S. Army in Vietnam 1965 – 1970, Department of the Army, Washington, D.C. p. xiii.

[vi] Summers, p. 70.

[vii] Heiser, p. 37.

[viii] Ibid. p. 22.

[ix] Ibid. p. 38.

[x] Ibid. p. 95.

[xi] Ibid. p. 110.

[xii] Ibid. p. 8.

[xiii] Ibid. p. 163-164.

[xiv] Ibid.

[xv] Ibid. p. 171.

[xvi] Ibid. p. 23.

[xvii] Ibid. p. 24.

[xviii] Ibid. p. 25.

[xix] Walter Geer, *Campaigns of the Civil War, (Old Saybrook, Connecticut: Konecky & Konecky), p. 13.*

[xx] Stanley Karnow, *Vietnam: A History*, (New York: Viking Press), p. 436.

[xxi] Heiser, p. 71.

[xxii] Ibid. p. 23.

[xxiii] Ibid. p. 255.

[xxiv] Maj. Gen. Robert R. Ploger, U.S. Army Engineers 1965 – 1970 (Washington D.C. Dept. of the Army), p. 3.

[xxv] Ibid. p. 5.

[xxvi] Ibid. p. 6.

[xxvii] Ibid. p. 70.

[xxviii] Ibid. p. 80.

[xxix] Ibid. p. 124.

[xxx] Ibid. p. 116.

[xxxi] Ibid. p. 26.

[xxxii] Ibid. p. 176.

[xxxiii] Heiser, p. 50.

[xxxiv] Neel, p. xiii.
[xxxv] Ibid. p. 3-4.
[xxxvi] Ibid. p. 170.
[xxxvii] Ibid. P. xiii.
[xxxviii] Ibid. p. 80-81.
[xxxix] Ibid. p. 32.
[xl] Ibid.
[xli] Ibid. p. 39.
[xlii] Ibid. p.34.
[xliii] Ibid. p. 38.
[xliv] Ibid. p. 109.
[xlv] Ibid. p. 41.
[xlvi] Ibid. p. 40.
[xlvii] Ibid. p. 41.
[xlviii] Ibid. p. 42.
[xlix] Ibid. p. 47.
[l] Ibid. p. 37.
[li] Ibid. p. 99.
[lii] Ibid. p. 100.
[liii] Ibid.
[liv] Ibid. p. 104.
[lv] Ibid. p. 51.
[lvi] Ibid.
[lvii] Ibid. p. 146.
[lviii] Ibid. p. 147.
[lix] Ibid. p. 149.
[lx] Ibid. p. 172.
[lxi] Ibid. P. 76.
[lxii] Ibid. p. 60.
[lxiii] Ibid. p. 59.
[lxiv] Ibid. p. 71.
[lxv] Ibid. p. 70.
[lxvi] Ibid. p. 75.
[lxvii] Ibid.
[lxviii] Ibid. p. 49.
[lxix] Ibid. p. 164.
[lxx] Ibid. p. 166.
[lxxi] Ibid.
[lxxii] Ibid. p. 167.
[lxxiii] Ibid. p. 53.
[lxxiv] Ibid. p. 54.
[lxxv] Ibid. p. 144.
[lxxvi] Ibid. p. 143.

[lxxvii] James E. Westheider, *The Vietnam War,* (Westport, CT: Greenwood Press) p. 72.
[lxxviii] Ibid. p. 114.
[lxxix] Ibid.
[lxxx] Ibid. p. 126.
[lxxxi] Lt.Gen. Joseph M. Heiser, Jr., Logistic Support (Washington, D.C., Dept. of the Army), p. 212.
[lxxxii] Neel. P. 168-178.
[lxxxiii] Heiser, p. 204.
[lxxxiv] Carrico, p. 10.
[lxxxv] Ibid. p. 11.
[lxxxvi] Ibid. p. 19.
[lxxxvii] Summers, p. 100.
[lxxxviii] Ibid.
[lxxxix] Nalty, p. 212.
[xc] Carrico, p. 120.
[xci] Heiser, p. 153.
[xcii] Ibid.
[xciii] John Edward Gray, *Called to Honor, (Asheville, North Carolina: R. Brent & Co.) p. 248.*
[xciv] Heiser, p. 141.
[xcv] Ibid. P. 145.
[xcvi] Ibid. p. 147.
[xcvii] Ibid. p. 148.
[xcviii] Encyclopedia.com.
[xcix] Heiser, p. 194.
[c] Ibid.
[ci] Ibid. p. 195.
[cii] Ibid. p. 197.
[ciii] Ibid. p. 194.
[civ] Ploger, p. 115.
[cv] Heiser, p. 35.
[cvi] Ibid. p. 36.
[cvii] Ibid. p. 260.

PERSONNEL INDEX

Gase, Tom, 228-229, 237, 239-240
Gesssein, Paul, 177-179, 191
Glazerman, Chuck, 159-162
Gombos, Larry, 164-165, 168
Goodall, Bob, 268-269, 272, 274
Gott, Dale, 82, 84, 91
Gray, George, 80, 85, 93
Greene, David, 196-197, 212-213, 219-220
Greeson, Jack, 311-312, 313-314
Griffin, Pat, 119-120, 122-125
Griguoli, Vic, 177, 182, 187-188, 311, 313

Hall, Sam, 273, 276-277
Hanke, Ed, 78-79, 84-85
Hansen, James, 324-327
Harkins, William, 143, 147-148
Harris, Ted, 13-15, 17
Helton, Don, 280, 283
Higgins, James, 271, 277
Holdrege, Larry, 162-168
Holloway, George, 312, 315
Holz, Mike, 150-153

Jackmauh, Frank, 74-77
James, Cliff, 22-23, 309-310
Janecek, Bob, 197, 210-211, 217-219
Janke, Fran, 128, 130, 134-135
Johnson, Dallas, 198, 219, 221-222
Johnson, Jimmie, 48-49, 53
Johnson, Philip, 82-84, 88-92
Jones, Floyd, 113-116

Kappeler, Ron, 270, 273, 275-276
Kapolka, Dennis, 142-143, 147
Kaser, Paul, 151-153, 157-158, 293-295, 299-300
Kato, 292, 295
Knuff, Robert, 101, 103-108
Kotrola, Al, 118, 123-124
Kreynest, Daniel, 203-205, 209, 218
Kuipers, James, 81-83, 87-90
Kutac, Louis, 63-64, 66

Rodgers, Ed, 207-208, 213-214, 221, 312-313, 315-316
Roy, Bill, 111-112, 115
Ryan, Patrick, 232, 237-238

Simmons, Bob, 59-61
Simons, Gary, 23-25
Skibo, Gary, 21-23, 308-309
Smith, Jimmy, 229-231, 239, 241
Smith, Tim, 143, 145-147
Sooy, Jim, 321-322
Spriggs, Rick, 33-34, 42-43, 148-150, 152-154
Squires, Scott, 120-122, 127-128
Stockton, Mike, 279-280, 282
Stroud, Jack, 249-251, 256-257, 259-260

Thomas, Allen, Jr., 250, 252-253, 255, 257, 259-262, 267
Tillman, Mike, 288, 292, 295-296, 299
Towns, Frank, 201-202, 214-215, 218-219, 221, 225
Trimbur, Dick, 279-282
Turk, 290-292

Vinson, Dan, 34, 41
Voytek, Frank H., 29-30, 37-38

Warman, Dave, 35-36, 43-46, 49
Webster, Alan, 290, 297, 303-304
Welty, John, 70-72
Wiebe, Rob, 144-145
Willard, Larry, 69, 73
Willever, Barry, 289-290, 296-297, 302-303
Wilson, Don, 36-37, 47-48
Woodruff, Norris, 210, 222-223
Wright, Bernie, 272, 274, 278
Wyrick, Bill, 63-67

Made in the USA
Lexington, KY
22 November 2013